ROOTS & OFFSHOOTS

SILICON VALLEY'S ARTS COMMUNITY

ROOTS & OFFSHOOTS

SILICON VALLEY'S ARTS COMMUNITY

JAN RINDFLEISCH

Articles by Maribel Alvarez and Raj Jayadev
Edited by Nancy Hom and Ann Sherman

Publisher's Cataloging-in-Publication Data:
Names: Rindfleisch, Jan, author. | Hom, Nancy, editor. | Sherman, Ann, editor.
Title: Roots and Offshoots: Silicon Valley's Arts Community /Jan Rindfleisch.
Description: First trade paperback original edition. | Santa Clara [California]: Ginger Press, 2017. | Includes bibliographical references.

Identifiers: ISBN: 978-0-9983084-0-1 (pbk: alk.paper)
Summary: "A behind-the-scenes look at the development of arts and culture in the South San Francisco Bay Area, with profiles of cultural activists and alternative institutions, and insights into the art of community building"—Provided by publisher.

Subjects: LCSH: 1. Art and history—Silicon Valley (Calif.). 2. Art and culture (Silicon Valley). 3. Art and community. 4. Title. | BISAC: ART/History/American/General. ART/Art & Politics.

Classification: LCC N5310.5.C2.S336 | DDC 709.79473

Cover painting: Ruth Tunstall Grant, *Protect the Child*, c. 2004. Acrylic and spray paint on canvas, 5'x8'. From the series entitled *Breaking the Chain of Abuse*. According to Tunstall Grant: "[The lines represent] life lines. ... The very small figure stands for the core conscience we all have."

An enlarged reproduction was used as part of the *Japantown Mural Project* (2012–2013), a community project by rasteroids design and the City of San José Public Art Program to celebrate an historic San José neighborhood. Art by 50 local artists on more than 60 large panels covered the chain-link fencing surrounding barren land that, 100 years ago, was one of San José's first Chinatown settlements known as "Heinlenville."

Cover art and design: Ruth Tunstall Grant, rasteroids design, and Samson Wong.

Title page painting, with details on section pages: Paul Pei-Jen Hau, *Fishing*, 2011. Ink and color on paper, 18"x21".

Design: Samson Wong

For information about the author and editors, see www.gingerpressbooks.com

Printed in the United States of America

Published by Ginger Press, Santa Clara, CA. www.gingerpressbooks.com

Contents

Carol Marschner Malone, *Grant Road Mountain View*. Marschner Malone has drawn/painted our evolving Silicon Valley; in the '80s, she chronicled old Cali & Bro. on Stevens Creek Boulevard, the Olson Orchard in Sunnyvale, St. Leo's Church in San José, guys playing Pac-Man.

Roots and Offshoots: The Blossoming of Silicon Valley's Arts Community

The death of Consuelo Santos-Killins in 2012 was a wake-up call for me and other arts activists to start telling the story of arts community building in Silicon Valley. During her long lifetime, she was a key figure in the effort. She brought an overarching vision integrating art, socioeconomic issues, and politics, with an understanding of basic human needs, important for leaders and activists of any age. The vivacious redhead served on the San José Fine Arts Commission, the Santa Clara County Arts Council, and the California Arts Council (CAC), among other arts organizations. She argued for substantive arts programs in the schools and community and for more diverse participation in arts governing boards.

Compassionate and generous to all in need, Santos-Killins—once a nurse—did not limit her activism to the arts, but the arts remained foremost for her.[1] A columnist remembers you could talk to her about "the need for corporate directors to ask more questions, and before your talk was over, she would have convinced you utterly of the need for ceramics and music and painting in the schools."[2]

Making an Arts Community

Building an arts environment requires energy, courage, and determination, but Santos-Killins wasn't the only one trying. Silicon Valley blossomed in the last quarter of the 20th century with the formation of innovative arts collaborations and organizational structures—offshoots, spin-offs, and startups—that tapped into the area's increasing ferment of ideas and involved myriad supporters across all walks of life.[3] But it was not easy. The valley's art history is filled with people who were often marginalized, who questioned and stood up to the establishment to build a community that nourished all and welcomed innovation. As a museum director, curator, community activist, artist, author and college educator for over 35 years, I have witnessed the growth of this community, collaborated with many exceptional people to find new ways to support arts and community in Silicon Valley, and co-initiated many groundbreaking projects that exemplify the principles discussed in the book.

The innovation and cultural disruption of Silicon Valley startups has a hidden parallel in arts and community building, and a long history. What follows combines my personal narrative with perspectives drawn from my work experiences in the art world plus additional viewpoints from Silicon Valley and neighboring artists and arts institutions that stood apart from, challenged, or broadened the mainstream perspective. Underlying our joint effort is a shared intent to provoke questions and draw answers that elucidate what it means to build a vibrant arts community. Among the key factors for success that will be revealed are recognizing the importance of small organizations in the cultural mix and experimenting with open and flexible organizational structures.

The Early Cultural Landscape

The road toward arts development in the South San Francisco Bay Area was paved by the San Jose Art League,[4] formed in 1938 by a group of San José artists, mostly San José State University (SJSU) teachers and students, to stimulate public interest in art. In Depression-era Santa Clara Valley, the agricultural economy still functioned because of the blossoming of trees, the stone fruit that followed, and the diverse labor pool available.

Post–WWII movements for civil rights in the 1950s and '60s laid the groundwork for change, opening doors in academia, community, and workplace. But change took longer to resonate in Santa Clara Valley, better known today as Silicon Valley. Conservatism accompanied Cold War fears and a local economy that increasingly stemmed from defense (Lockheed, FMC, Varian, later Fairchild Semiconductor, Intel).

There were valiant attempts to open up the valley to new ideas. When post–WWII migration to California brought urban sprawl, the Art League sought to improve San José's downtown image and bring culture to the city center. Pioneers like art professor John De Vincenzi and artist Mary Parks Washington guided the Art League in the 1960s and '70s, went on to influence further art developments like the San José Museum of Art (SJMA) and its Black on Black Film Festival, and provided counsel during tumultuous times. The community branched out to found new museums, such as the Triton Museum in Santa Clara. De Vincenzi and Washington racked up decades of teaching, honors, and community service in the arts via multiple tracks, from the San José Fine Arts Commission to the San José Chapter of The Links, Incorporated.

The de Saisset Museum at Santa Clara University featured a permanent California history exhibition, including Native American art and art from Mission Santa Clara, plus changing contemporary art exhibitions. The de Saisset, in keeping with the university's culture of service, had a social justice component from the start, reaching out to diverse communities, and hiring women directors[5] when that was not the norm.

Despite these efforts, a sustained cultural blossoming has been difficult. Maintenance of routine practices with exclusionary results checked the momentum built on the groundwork of the 1960s. The newborn San José Museum of Art sought instant status and funding in the 1970s by emphasizing art history exhibitions, a common tactic using conventional groupings—artists abroad, Impressionism, Post-Modernism—rather than the diverse talents available here and elsewhere.

Simultaneously, the SJSU art department, a white-male bastion closely aligned with the SJMA, banked on their 1960s legacy "School of San José," with its elegant objects, industrial techniques, and materials. Not surprisingly, for Stanford Museum of Art's 1974 *Ten West Coast Artists*, all ten artists selected were male. Even as late as 1986, when the SJSU galleries featured the *School of San José* exhibition for *The First San José Biennial*, of 23 participating artists, only one African American and one female were included.

To make matters worse, in the 1970s and long afterward, people of means in the South Bay often went north for culture as our lingering orchards gave way to tract homes[6] and de facto segregated communities.[7] Scantily funded and considered a frill, the arts—in education and the community—encountered rough times. Many artists left the South Bay

Mary Parks Washington, *Erik*, 1999. Mixed media, c 38"x30".
Image courtesy Mary Emma Harris, Black Mountain College.

A memorial tribute to her son, a screenwriter. Washington—artist, arts advocate, educator, historian—created "histcollages," embedding historic documents into her art. Her research shows artistry in the local African American community going back to the 1800s; a story of a janitor, a leading suffragist, and art stars from different centuries, three women of different racial/ethnic backgrounds; and the contemporary politics of art placement, substance, and importance in the Dr. Martin Luther King, Jr. Library and city spaces.

for San Francisco.[8] As a result of the enactment of Proposition 13 in 1978, funding for our fledgling Euphrat Museum of Art (then called Euphrat Gallery), founded in 1971 at De Anza College in Cupertino, was essentially cut to zero.

Large arts organizations,[9] often the backbone of an arts community, had their survival problems as they tried to cultivate basic support from individuals, local government and the business community.[10] The loss of funding from tax revenue was particularly devastating to public arts education, social services, and community cultural programs.

The 1970s: Pervasive Exclusion

The politics of inclusion in the arts was and continues to be contentious. Today, various kinds of discourse are taken for granted—how the arts might be used to advocate for human rights, social justice, and peaceful conflict resolution and promote cultural understanding and recognition; examinations of the function and place of art in the schools and our lives, or the relationship of art with government; the interaction of the arts with other academic disciplines. We had to fight to have those ideas taken seriously.

When I was a student in the 1970s, exclusion was pervasive—of women, people of color, people with disabilities, people considered "different" for whatever reason. There were essentially no women in art history survey texts used in universities. My first art history text was the 1973 version of H.W. Janson's *History of Art: A Survey of the Major Visual Arts from the Dawn of History to the Present Day,* the then prevailing college text in the United States. It was a man's art history; no women were included, not even Impressionist Berthe Morisot or the legendary Georgia O'Keeffe. Much of the non-Western world was passed over or lumped into a section on "primitive art" and a nine-page postscript, "The Meeting of East and West." Contemporary non-European art scarcely merited a mention, with the exception of a dismissively judgmental paragraph about Expressionism in Mexico.[11]

Visual Dialog, Vol. 2, No. 3, 1977, the second of two issues on "Women in the Arts." Roberta Loach published, edited, and wrote for *Visual Dialog,* 1975–1980, a scholarly California journal of the visual arts.

It was a long road from the woman as nude model or male fantasy object to a fully realized woman as professional artist, academic, and/or cultural leader. SJSU art department alumnae remember "fanny pinching in the elevator back in the '70s. Wine and cigarettes were the bill of fare for critiques." There were some discussions,[12] but the art world clearly

Getting into the Game

For the arts to function in support of community and democracy, one needs freedom of expression and an educated populace, not rebuked and marginalized citizens. Exclusion has been a deep-seated issue in art history, and Silicon Valley is no exception. Many artists and viewers experienced ongoing exclusion.

The marginalizing of women in art elicited strange behaviors from artists, viewers, and students in the 1970s and '80s. Some women ignored or laughed off demeaning male behaviors, sexual innuendo, trivializing of ideas. Some fought back.

In the mid-1970s, a local sculptor and university arts professor exhibited a college art gallery full of his nude female bronzes, shown bound and gagged, prostrate and laid out. The academic gallery context offered lofty, elaborate interpretations. Instead of accepting them, Silicon Valley cartoonist Gen Guracar created a cartoon panel that stood up to such demeaning content. In the first cell, the male artist is shown sculpting a bound woman. But in subsequent cells, the female sculpture comes to life, jumps up full of anger, throws off the bindings and mouth gag, grabs the hammer and chisel, and chases the sculptor out of the studio.

In 1985, as I was writing *The First San José Biennial* essay for SJMA, I noted the minimal ethnic representation overall. The biennial exhibitions did not give a sense of our ethnic mix nor in any way reflect the unique experiences of major portions of our population.

Exclusion in the early 1970s also extended to those who veered from the mainstream. Web designer Marte Thompson reminded me of Bill Martin, the legendary visionary artist who taught at SJSU in 1973–74, and Michael Whelan, a student there at the same time, who became a celebrated science fiction book cover illustrator. "In those years, representational painting was frowned upon by mainstream art. These artists, and any instructors ... were ostracized for their insistence on teaching what is now called 'classical realism.'"

Progress came with visionaries like the dynamic Helen Jones, who did not let her wheelchair limit her goals. In 1980, Jones, head of De Anza's Physically Limited Program, proposed the exhibition *To Deny the Right of Any Person is to Deny Our Own Humanity*, which highlighted the art and needs of differently abled people. To place this in context, Oakland's Creative Growth, the oldest and largest art studio in the world for people with disabilities, was established in 1974, just six years before her exhibition. It took a long time to get to that point. Likewise, Jones struggled in those years but she persevered.

The large organizations' advances in valuing diversity were often limited to Women's History Month or Black History Month, although there were occasional deeper forays. Topping the social/economic/academic hierarchies of collecting and validation, these institutions emphasized established artists and were often quite removed from basic life experiences of most artists. As a result, many arts professionals have succumbed to a tracked "careerist move" and climbed the requisite "career ladder."

Inclusion is not simply a matter of numbers or demographics or just working with the community around you. The crucial question is how organizations and individuals interact with the world and how we demonstrate day to day our understanding of underlying racism, sexism, and other forms of oppression. All of us—as individuals, as a people, as a country—have to constantly ask ourselves, "What are we doing? What are we saying? What are we teaching?"

needed a jolt and an overhaul. At SJSU, visiting professor Judith Bettelheim did shake things up. In my early years as the director of the Euphrat Museum of Art, she contributed to the museum's first major publication (1981) with an essay about "women's hobby art," citing barrier-breaking art historian Lucy Lippard.[13]

Pioneer artists Patricia Rodriguez and Marjorie Eaton with Rodriguez' heart sculpture, which was exhibited in the exhibition, *Staying Visible, The Importance of Archives*, in 1981. Rodriguez, from San Francisco, described prevalent art world responses in the '70s: "[they] turned up their noses," "they didn't know how to accept my art," "it was difficult because I was not in step." She chose to do hearts instead of the usual abstract "yellow canvas with a white dot." Her art was cultural, emotional, as was Eaton's, and both had a passion for evocative murals.

Eaton could have told Rodriguez about how it was painting with emotive artists Diego Rivera and Frida Kahlo in the 1930s, because she lived it. Eaton loved people. For many decades, Eaton nurtured a diverse avant-garde arts colony in the Palo Alto foothills on the historic ranch site of legendary Juana Briones and shared her legacy of caring. Contemporary academic research on Briones and Eaton is illuminating their times and their lasting meaning for California cultural development. Photo: Helen Carlisle Fleming.

In her magazine *Visual Dialog*,[14] satiric printmaker/educator Roberta Loach of Los Altos published statistics quantifying the appalling discrimination against female artists. Not only did that resonate with my scientific training in basing theory upon measurable information, it made the case to others who need to see the numbers.

In the 1970s more women, people of color, and those with diverse gifts and backgrounds were hired in teaching and administration, but the institutionalized culture then prevalent in academia, galleries, and museums did not truly value diversity of issues and ideas. Working within these organizations, one often paid a heavy price personally, politically, and economically for advocating openness and inclusion. Tokenism reigned. Hiring and promoting practices gave the appearance of equality in arts leadership positions, and programming exhibitions encapsulating artists by gender or ethnicity "demonstrated" the institution's commitment to diversity. The general climate in many university arts programs undercut initiatives for change. Art that had any sort of socially relevant content (different from the status quo) was disparaged as "political art," as opposed to "real art."

Breaking New Ground: Creative Strategies

The blossoming of Silicon Valley into a home for vibrant cultural startups was the result of three key growth factors: 1) The desire and courage to widen the vista and dialogue of new ideas and values begun by pioneering activists; 2) Formation of flexible, open structures that combine vision with a grounded understanding of real-world struggles that kept in touch with our basic humanity; and 3) Involvement of dedicated individuals, who counseled, advocated, and invested time and money. The combination of these attitudes and actions energized the breaking of new ground in addressing the issue of exclusion in the arts.

As a college instructor in studio art and art history, I was one of the change-seekers who rewrote studio and art history courses and books in the late 1970s, early '80s,[15] adding women and people of color, as well as unusual media and ideas. Some women altered their first names; others, including artist/activist/educator Ruth Tunstall Grant and me, occasionally used only our first initials to sidestep prejudice (for example, to get our work into an exhibition). Most exciting of all, we started to connect with others around the Bay.

For me, as a motivated educator/presenter/activist, that meant learning from acclaimed visionary artists/activists, including Ruth Asawa, who developed whole-person art programs in San Francisco public schools starting in 1968 and her renowned Ruth Asawa San Francisco School of the Arts in 1982; Patricia Rodriguez, founder of Las Mujeres Muralistas (women muralists), who created brightly colored murals in Balmy Alley and elsewhere in San Francisco's Mission District from 1970 to 1979; Carlos Villa, who directly challenged the entire academic/cultural establishment from within,[16] organizing diverse, thought-provoking programs at San Francisco Art Institute; and then-novice artist Mildred Howard, Berkeley, who curated a *Heartfelt Hearts* exhibition in 1977 that included her own mixed-media textile constructions, *Chocolate Hearts*.[17] Years later, Howard would be featured in top galleries, museums, and art history survey texts.

Building New Forms

We began to build new forms of arts startups from scratch in the cities of the Peninsula and South Bay, gathering together a unique blend of people from the arts and academia, along with forward-thinking government and business leaders. Without the decades-long dedication of a broad base of partners and leaders, all the good that was accomplished would have taken much longer and been far more difficult. Our new hybrids included old-timers, newcomers, people finding their way in satellite cities, special-needs populations, supportive nonprofits, people from other parts of the world. Building community with a group of insightful, innovative dynamos proved to be the real energizer.

Two such dynamos were cartoonist Gen Pilgrim Guracar and historian Connie Young Yu, an amazing duo on the Peninsula who moved past barriers as early as the 1970s. Using pen and paper, needle and thread, they combined living art and democracy. Guracar organized the dozens of women creating *The People's Bicentennial Quilt* (1974), and Yu wrote the book *The People's Bicentennial Quilt: A Patchwork History* (1976) that tells the story behind each square. At the Euphrat, we wrote about this early collaborative public art as part of our exhibition and publication *The Power of Cloth: Political Quilts, 1845–1986*.[18] In her foreword, Connie Young Yu writes: "We wanted to portray the people as making history: the nameless, countless members of movements and struggles that have affected the soul and character of America."

In the same time frame, Deanna Bartels (now Tisone), Betty Estersohn and Joan Valdes used video—then "cutting-edge" technology—to explore and document breadth in San Francisco Bay Area art making, including art and open space. The three Peninsula artists taped early social activists/environmentalists Frank and Josephine Duveneck, who purchased and used their land, Hidden Villa in Los Altos Hills, in order to protect an entire watershed, advance social justice, and promote environmental education. The trio's Marjorie Eaton video opened a world of hidden Silicon Valley cultural histories from Ohlone Indian and local pioneer struggles in post-Mission days to a modern family-like community of artists. It inspired me to collaborate with them on an exhibition, publication, and further programming. The NEA-funded First Generation videos included visual art stars like Ruth Asawa, dancers Jasmine and Xavier Nash in the early '70s in the Fillmore, and clay artist Bea Wax in Palo Alto. First Generation was one of Tisone's many collaborative, interdisciplinary art projects over the last decades. Today we are working on making more of this history accessible and available online.

Shoots and Offshoots

In the late 1970s in San José, a group of aspiring curators with a strong SJSU contingent began a series of attempts to create viable spaces where emerging artists could show their work. Art professor Tony May and I first wielded hammers for art in an old building on Santa Clara Street in downtown San José. May was, and continues to be, a key catalyst. We put our energies into Works Gallery (1977), an offshoot of Wordworks, which in mid-1980 reopened as the San Jose Institute of Contemporary Art (SJICA). Works Gallery, SJICA, and others could be termed alternative art spaces, art lingo for increased nontraditional exhibition opportunities for emerging artists. Because artists, poets, and other creative people need multiple venues to flourish, the creation of these alternative organizations sparked cultural growth in Silicon Valley and put the area on the arts map.[19]

The core groups I speak of here, however, might be called "alternative-alternative" organizations. These smaller organizations (and offshoots from large organizations that manage to grow independently from their parent group) often begin with altruistic goals and a commitment to community-building, and are free to exhibit more flexibility. Pioneers in this arena, like artist Ruth Tunstall Grant, led the way and overcame obstacles within and outside of the mainstream. Tunstall Grant gave SJMA and Silicon Valley new dimensions by drawing in community diversity, giving opportunities to creative people of color, and starting unusual studio art programs in city schools and the county youth shelter. The alternative-alternative groups have often served as reality checks, providing grounding for the large institutions. These shoots and offshoots find new doors to open, notice diversity of ideas in their own backyard, meet needs of diverse artists and the student in all of us, and understand the social dynamics and issues of their communities.[20]

Opening the Door

During the late 1960s and continuing into the '70s and early '80s, various small organizations—hybrids of business, education, and volunteer models, supported at times with government funding—opened doors to other cultures. I grew to know and value their work, and collaborated extensively with some of these innovators. In 1968, two visionaries, artist/educator Cozetta Gray Guinn and her physicist husband Isaac "Ike" Guinn, established Nbari Art, a museum-quality gallery in Los Altos, highlighting the work of students at Stanford and UC Berkeley. Their gracious and welcoming shop featured imported African art and African American art, and offered us an invaluable cultural resource for four decades.

In the early 1970s in an abandoned downtown San José storefront near First and San Carlos streets, artist Mary Jane Solis and activist Adrian Vargas (founder/director of San José's Teatro de la Gente, 1967–1977) co-founded El Centro Cultural de la Gente, the South Bay's first Chicano/Latino cultural center. El Centro's exhibitions, art programs, and luminaries had an impressive roster, including: Lorna Dee Cervantes and her Mango Press, Las Mujeres Muralistas, and Luis Valdez, the father of Chicano theater. Solis curated art exhibitions, managed arts programs, called attention to social justice related art, and spoke out for multicultural arts—for "a place to come together and feed the spirit."

Patchwork History, The People's Bicentennial Quilt, Connie Young Yu. The 1976 version was printed by UP PRESS, East Palo Alto, CA. The book was republished by the Saratoga Historical Foundation in 2010.

In 1973, renowned painter Paul Pei-Jen Hau (Hau Bei Ren) and Mary Hau opened their Chinese Fine Arts Gallery on State Street in downtown Los Altos. Their personal invitation to understand Chinese culture countered lingering anti-Chinese sentiment, and in 1979,

Paul Pei-Jen Hau, as a guiding spirit, founded the American Society for the Advancement of Chinese Arts with artists and friends.[21]

Artist Terese May remarkably opened the stubborn art world door to the culture of domesticity through her quilts and paintings. Periodically, she assisted the San José Museum of Quilts & Textiles, the first museum in the U.S. to focus exclusively on quilts and textiles as an art form. Started in Los Altos in 1977, the museum was a collaborative, volunteer organization for a decade before hiring its first paid director.

In the 1970s and early '80s, visual and performing artists and community members laid groundwork for a haven of cultural experimentation in Japantown, just north of downtown San José. With humor, political insight, and a love of sports, cartoonist Jack Matsuoka had bridged generations and cultures early on. Together with other enthusiastic novices, Roy and PJ Hirabayashi learned and built the drums and ever-more-creative performances of San Jose Taiko. PJ, along with Ellen Reiko Bepp and Linda Ito, began their Earthenwear shop, a forerunner of the art and design collectives to follow, featuring handmade items with ethnic roots and, as PJ put it, "made-in-America" art forms.

In 1981 in Palo Alto, Trudy Myrrh Reagan started YLEM: Artists Using Science and Technology. With our similar backgrounds in science and art, Reagan and I exchanged ideas and collaborated on exhibitions. In 1984 at SJSU, quiet-but-determined art professor Marcia Chamberlain took the initial lead of Computers in Art, Design, Research, and Education (CADRE) Laboratory for New Media, an interdisciplinary academic and research program dedicated to the experimental use of information technology and art.[22] We strategized frequently, and she invited me to write the essay for the *CADRE '84* catalog.

Expanding the Boundaries

While doors were opened, the struggle to change minds continued. Quilts, fiber arts, and "computer art" were saddled with countering prejudices about "women's work" or "right/ left brain" thinking, and had little acceptance in the academic and institutional art world. In fact, the worlds rarely communicated.[23]

In 1979, when I became director/curator at the Euphrat Museum of Art at De Anza College, I brainstormed with activists and potential staff and board members how we could build community, foster civic engagement, ensure equal opportunity—including featuring 50% women—and go beyond disciplines and narrow definitions to explore new ideas.[24] For us, the open-door policies of the community college system and the logic of partnerships were great avenues for experimentation. We realized the urgent need for new systems to open up opportunities, give visibility to contemporary artists and ideas from diverse sources, and promote thought and discussion. With this in mind, we initiated a unique campus/community partnership.

Working with incredible and legendary innovators, beginning with artists/activists Jo Hanson (*Art from Street Trash*) and Carlos Villa (performance art with dramatic installations of feathered capes) and poet George Barlow, we expanded the boundaries of what could be considered art and what merited attention or discourse, and began a stellar poetry series that would include Dennis Brutus and Quincy Troupe. Early exhibition examples were *The Workplace/The Refuge* (Janet Burdick and Scott Miller recreating their San José studio in the Euphrat—what an opportunity to interact daily, up close, with artists as they worked!) and *Men and Children* (views from six Bay Area male artists with diverse backgrounds) in 1980; an exhibition to celebrate the 1981 International Year of Disabled Persons, developed with De Anza's Physically Limited Program; followed by our seminal *Staying Visible, The Importance of Archives*, which directly addressed visibility issues. *CROSSOVER*, the first of many art and technology exhibitions, came in 1982, and *Commercial Illustrators*, 1981, and *Illustration/Design*, 1983, introduced processes and artwork from Bay Area commercial artists, another discipline not recognized at that time by the art world.[25] And that was just the beginning.[26] We responded to suggestions from the community. A student asked me why there never seemed to be any religious art in modern art galleries. So in 1982, we investigated the subject in *Art, Religion, Spirituality*.[27]

Paul Pei-Jen Hau (born in 1917) and Mary Hau in 2009, celebrating at the reception for *Looking Back, Looking Ahead.*

There were noticeable structural parallels between the growth of the alternative arts scene and that of Silicon Valley tech culture, although tech culture has had its own problems with insularity. From Hewlett Packard in its early days to Google, many companies saw the wisdom of loosening reins and regulations, and were more open to new values, different cultures, and varied schedules and ways of working. Dress codes relaxed from the stiff suits of previous eras. Size played a role in cultural development. Large companies gave rise to spin-offs, and startups were staffed by even smaller teams. Via these spin-offs and startups, innovative individuals could make direct connections with education, youth, music, and gamers, as well as counterculture, geek and activist cultures, and the global community. Steve Jobs started Apple Computer in Cupertino in 1976, just down the street from the Euphrat. Apple supported and participated in many early Euphrat Museum exhibitions, and the Euphrat created art exhibitions in numerous Apple buildings. We connected with Apple on many levels.[28]

The Late 1980s/1990s:
New Ventures, Ethnic Dimensions, Community Building

At Stanford, Cecilia and José Antonio Burciaga did something different. From 1985–1994, the couple lived at Casa Zapata as Resident Fellows—she as a top university administrator, he as resident artist—both working closely with student and community needs. José (a.k.a. Tony, Toño) created murals at Casa Zapata, used comedy to attack racism and narrow divisive thinking, and published poetry and writings, e.g. *Weedee Peepo* (1988). ("…Tony remembers his parents preparing for their citizenship tests and saying to each other: 'Have you learned el Weedee Peepo?' That was how the Burciagas pronounced the words that perhaps more than anything else make Americans, American: 'We the People,' the first three words of the preamble to the Constitution." Jose Cardenás, *Arizona Republic*, 2005.)

Signe Wilkinson, 6/23/82, *San Jose Mercury News*, reprinted in *Illustration, Design*. Commercial art was not recognized by the art world in the early '80s. To broaden the institutional mindset and see larger contexts to struggles, we worked with people in related fields, such as Wilkinson. A cartoonist extraordinaire who got her start sitting in on *San Jose Mercury News* editorial sessions, Wilkinson went on to Philadelphia and became the first woman to win a Pulitzer in cartooning. Feisty and funny, she could open anyone's mind.

In 1989, artists/activists Betty Kano of Berkeley and Flo Oy Wong of Sunnyvale founded the Asian American Women Artists Association (AAWAA) in the Bay Area to "promote the visibility of Asian American women artists" who lacked recognition in their own traditional culture and were again overlooked when national museums sought Asian art stars. Also in 1989, Maribel Alvarez, Rick Sajor, and Eva Terrazas founded Movimiento de Arte y Cultura Latino Americana (MACLA) in downtown San José. Core organizers, including Solis and another powerful arts couple, poets Juan Felipe Herrera and Margarita Luna

Robles, envisioned arts programming as a vehicle for civic dialogue and social equity. Alvarez recalls, "When we got involved, the way to ignite the sort of movement included in our name…was a literary movement." Herrera and Robles organized poetry readings downtown, in East San José, and at the Euphrat Museum in the 1980s, lifting us all in spirit, bringing poems by, from, and for the people, without shrinking from telling hard truths.

I marveled at the ongoing vibrancy of Ruth Tunstall Grant, who in the 1990s founded from scratch the nonprofit Genesis/A Sanctuary for the Arts in San José creating exhibitions, presentations, performing arts, and artist studios, bringing together different cultures and simultaneously establishing a visible presence for the black community. Somehow, in the same decade, she developed the art program for foster youth at the Santa Clara County Children's Shelter, after directing and building the outstanding children's art school at SJMA in the 1980s.

After she worked in San José, artist Jean La Marr introduced us to *Urban Indian Girls,* which became part of Euphrat's 1984 *FACES* exhibition; a decade later La Marr collaborated with the local Muwekma Ohlone Tribe to create *The Ohlone Journey* mural in Berkeley. Given the Native American Diaspora, my early knowledge of local Indian art often came through transient artists who connected both with far-flung traditional communities and part-time academic assignments around Northern California.[29] As artist Consuelo Jimenez Underwood, Cupertino, put in an artist statement: "With beauty, grace, and traditional form, my work expresses the quiet rage that has permeated indigenous peoples of the Americas for over five hundred years."[30] Underwood would develop and head the textiles/fiber program at SJSU for over 20 years.

The above is just part of the story. There has long been arts activity beyond nonprofits. In her 2005 book *There's Nothing Informal about It: Participatory Arts Within the Cultural Ecology of Silicon Valley*, published by Cultural Initiatives Silicon Valley, Maribel Alvarez chronicled amateur, folk, commercial, and avocational arts.[31]

In the new millennium, Silicon Valley's cultural ecology was changing rapidly with immigration: the white population became a minority, displaced by a massive population of emigrants from India, Taiwan, Vietnam, and Mexico.[32] At the same time, new systemic disparities in formal education and income levels would increasingly present both opportunities and challenges in social, economic, technological, and government realms. At a forward-looking event in 1995[33] at the Euphrat, the Arts Council under new director Bruce Davis applauded the "arts as an intervention for social ills,"[34] connecting arts with government, schools, youth, veterans, social services, and prisons. Presenters included a county supervisor, a judge, and arts/community leaders from Menlo Park and East Palo Alto to Gilroy. "We had to run two sessions!" Davis recalled.

Counsel, Advocacy, Support

What kept innovators going even in the face of personal attacks, political maneuverings, and endless barriers put in their paths by resistant administrators, colleagues, and institutions? This brings me back to Consuelo Santos-Killins. Ruth Tunstall Grant and I both sought seasoned perspectives from Santos-Killins. She possessed insight and understood the unique value of new ventures. As she battled cancer for five years, Santos-

Killins continued her wide-ranging activism, firing off letters to top policymakers. Tunstall Grant and I, like many other arts advocates, faced incredible struggles. Tunstall Grant: "One gets beat up. You think you know the answers; but after a while, you are not sure anymore." Even on our worst days and hers, Santos-Killins could be counted on. Good advice and support were gifts she brought to so many who struggled to build the arts and art education systems we have today.

Jean La Marr, *Urban Indian Girls*, 1981. Etching, 16"x18". In 1969, La Marr, a Paiute, Pit River from Susanville, drew indigenous youth in San José at the end of her workdays guiding a retraining program.

Advocacy was another gift of Santos-Killins. Advocacy, little heralded or discussed, is a well-worn term with levels of meaning. The advocacy I laud and refer to here includes speaking up for people, ideas, and/or organizations in a letter or at a public meeting.[35]

None of the blossoming could have happened without supporters, from a key trustee to a bold city councilmember or a few visionary county and state policymakers like Santos-Killins, to donors, board members, students, volunteers, brainstormers, barnstormers, activists, collectors, companies, and educators in other disciplines with fresh perspectives.[36]

The New Millennium: Business, Democracy, Change

Today, our traditional cultural, educational, and media institutions, so important to our democracy, are challenged by new technologies and a changing economy that demand new business models. Daily newspapers search for successful ways to develop and monetize their online product. Educational and cultural institutions participate in online and other technological changes, adapting through private funding and unusual collaborations. As we sort out what is gained or lost,[37] we have examples of new "alternative-alternative" organizations forging the trail, such as Silicon Valley De-Bug, with whom I worked often. This media, community-organizing, and entrepreneurial collective coordinated by Raj Jayadev has an expanded reading of art, information, and democracy as its basis.

An open door in the arts plays an ongoing role in democracy; this is even more important today as we see exclusion continue in many ways. In *News in a New America* (2005), Sally Lehrman of Santa Clara University describes the "invisibility" of people and ideas in journalism and new media, emphasizing how access to information about each other is essential for our democracy. It is this same communication that is at the core of the arts.

However, many people do not think of arts organizations and institutions as being essential for our democracy. "Invisibility" of people and ideas in the arts precludes exchange of information about each other. Jeanne Wakatsuki Houston reminded us of that in *The Manzanar Lesson: Telling our stories strengthens democracy*,[38] in which she urges people to tell their stories, experiences, and perspectives because "democracy depends on it." [39]

In 2004, Euphrat Museum spotlighted Titus Kaphar's *Visual Quotations* series,[40] drawn from classical paintings illustrating one version of the founding of our country. Kaphar only painted the African American(s); the rest of the scene is white, leaving a disjointed figure(s). Kaphar wanted viewers to consider the individual represented, to see "a people of dignity and strength, whose survival is nothing less than miraculous," bringing the visibility issue to light.

Abraham Menor, *The Art Of War*, 2009. Digital print. B-boys (breakdancers) presenting their skills at San José's largest b-boy/b-girl event. Menor has worked with Silicon Valley De-Bug and photographed a hidden Silicon Valley for years.

Have things changed in Silicon Valley's contemporary arts environment? Yes and no.[41] We can see a lasting breakthrough in MACLA, which has an inclusive community vision that has brought dimension to South First Street in San José. The San José Museum of Quilts and Textiles has become another crucial anchor for the South First Area (SoFA) District arts community. The annual SubZERO Festival, a DIY, artistically bent, high/low-tech mashup focuses on subcultures thriving in the region, where street meets geek.

Technology-oriented ZERO1 focuses on convening changemakers through American Arts Incubator, exhibitions, and events. San José Japantown has become increasingly visible as a cultural catalyst. Silicon Valley De-Bug boldly plows new ground.

More Work to be Done:
A Challenge to Extend and Document the Arts Forum

More than 50 years after the March on Washington for jobs and justice, so much community-building work remains. Does discussion about an "open arts community" really exist in our local academic world and cultural institutions? Much of Silicon Valley academia has dropped the ball in terms of providing a center for cohesive, open discussion, let alone a base for support, in part because funding cuts have exacerbated academic departments' territorial tendency to focus on their own bread-and-butter programs. Thus traditional arts departments have tended to be insular, with other fields—women's, gender, and cultural studies; humanities; other social and physical sciences; and campus-wide diversity initiatives—filling in where needed. Our local cultural institutions have suffered from similar problems and financial vulnerability.

Moreover, even institutions grown in opposition to exclusion can, by defining themselves narrowly or through unconscious prejudicial behaviors, become almost closed systems— clubby or clannish—and continue exclusion by class, educational level, discipline, or background.

It is so easy to separate ourselves. In terms of visibility and participation, clearly more work is needed—with arts at the table—across all sectors, including with at-risk youth populations, low-income neighborhoods, threatened environments, out-of-whack justice systems, and out-of-balance boardrooms focused only on a myopic bottom line.

It remains difficult to develop or discuss the region's integrated art history within its ongoing context. Recognition provided through random, selective awards and obituaries typically fails to provide a coherent, integrated appreciation or understanding. One local artist labels the drag on any art scene as "selfishness, contentment, lack of desire to do the hard work."

To further enhance Silicon Valley's cultural development would require:

- A central Silicon Valley historical online archive and a locus of discussion that extends and documents the arts forum across cultures, disciplines, and sectors and includes the role of arts roots, startups, and offshoots. Advancing previous initiatives without clear examination of past efforts is especially challenging.

- Ongoing attention to build on the contributions of our diverse forerunners. Too often websites are not archived and disappear. Cultural Initiatives Silicon Valley, Nbari Art, and Arts Council Silicon Valley (ACSV) sites no longer exist. Major institutions like ACSV (now Silicon Valley Creates, 2013) and SJMA have not given web attention and context to pioneers and change agents like Ruth Tunstall Grant.

- Increased receptivity to challenging interdisciplinary and cross-sector projects. One option could be a multi-year interdisciplinary campus and/or community project, with periodically published essays related to the meaning or practice of "the spectrum of the arts in Silicon Valley"—a way to open doors, collaborate across disciplines and sectors, and connect side history with mainstream history. An ongoing web presence would be an essential element, combined with the involvement of students doing related research, documentation, and projects on individuals, organizations, and/or concepts.

Gathering and Flourishing

Consuelo Santos-Killins stated, "The assumption is that quality exists only in highly visible cultural institutions—the truth is an abundance of artistic quality exists in Santa Clara Valley … As in San José, significant progress in the arts will occur when people speak up in order to change attitudes toward art—people who believe in the area they live in."

Juan Felipe Herrera, our United States Poet Laureate, expresses this sentiment beautifully in his poem *Let Us Gather in a Flourishing Way.* "Let us gather in a flourishing way … Let us gather in a flourishing way," he intones. We can learn from the various elders and all those who have worked "in a flourishing way." Their experiences will be our guide as we plant the seeds for the future.

A version of this essay was first published in Californian *magazine by the California History Center and Foundation.*

Nancy Hom, *Culture is the Seed,* 1996. Mixed media, 22"x 22".

Notes

[1] In addition to arts organizations, including San Jose Symphony, Pacific Peoples Theater, and Institute for Arts and Letters at San José State University, Santos-Killins served two antipoverty agencies, as well as the Santa Clara County Mental Health Association and Friends of Guadalupe River Park.

[2] Herhold, Scott. "Renaissance Woman Was A Dynamic Valley Fixture." *San Jose Mercury News*. February 21, 2012.

[3] The local contemporary art scene was then anchored by the academic/exhibiting centers of Santa Clara University, Stanford University, and San José State University (SJSU), augmented by the new community colleges, and by art associations, centers, leagues, guilds, societies, estates, and clubs usually of a regional nature, such as Los Gatos Art Association, or related to a specific arts medium.

[4] In 1875, The Art Association, as it was then named, was formed in San José, with their first exhibition in 1876 at the Normal School (now SJSU).

[5] First de Saisset Director Joseph J. Pociask, S.J. (1955–1967), in 1958 presented a prescient solo exhibition of Paul Hau, who had recently arrived from China and was teaching at the Pacific Art League in Palo Alto, then known as the Palo Alto Art Club. Directors Brigid Barton (1978–1984) and Georgiana Lagoria (1984–1986) gave early opportunities and critical exposure to women. Santa Clara University, a Jesuit institution, and the de Saisset Museum, which includes both art and history components, have been in a unique position to join arts, interdisciplinary and social justice programming, and discussion of values and ethics.

[6] For decades, Carol Marschner Malone's drawings have captured the valley's rapid changes: the orchard at Homestead Road and Lawrence Expressway, where a giant hospital now stands; the orchard growing on a former toxic waste site off Highway 237; and Maryknoll, a large monastery turned into a site for expensive homes and a recreational open-space area popular with runners and hikers.

[7] The ethnic distribution in Santa Clara Valley during the 1970s could be generalized as follows: an overwhelmingly white population (94% in 1970); a small black population (in contrast to 61% in neighboring East Palo Alto in 1970); a sizable Latino population in areas of Mountain View, Sunnyvale, Santa Clara, and San José; and a small, fast-growing Asian population scattered.

[8] Mountain View's Community School for Music and Arts began in 1968 with volunteer teachers; their first art education contracts with the Mountain View School District came in 1981. Support for the arts was so low in Cupertino that, in a budget crunch, high school art teachers told me administration wanted to let some of them go and have physical education teachers teach their art classes.

[9] The major arts organizations included Stanford Museum of Art (established 1891, reopened in 1999 as Iris and B. Gerald Cantor Center for the Visual Arts after completion of revival begun in 1963; commonly called Cantor Arts Center), Montalvo Center for the Arts (1939), de Saisset Museum (1955), Triton Museum of Art (1965), and San José Museum of Art (1969 in the former city library, 1991 new wing).

[10] During my term as Euphrat director, I crossed paths with two San José mayors who stood out as supporters of the SJMA and of the arts in general: Janet Gray Hayes (1975–1982) and Susan Hammer (1991–1999). While Hammer built a solid arts support record and inspired a 10-year cultural plan for Silicon Valley, she also personally connected with local artists and collected their work.

[11] The Janson text (1973 edition) said José Clemente Orozco and "a group of young painters" in Mexico in the 1920s and '30s, inspired by the Mexican Revolution, often overburdened their works with ideological significance. Orozco was identified as the artist "least subject to this imbalance." The text made no mention of iconic artists Frida Kahlo or Diego Rivera, who would have lasting international impact, he with provocative murals, she with piercing self-portraits.

[12] Most of us were aware of artist/activist Judy Chicago (*Through The Flower*, 1975; premiere of *Dinner Party*, 1979, at San Francisco Museum of Modern Art) and, to a lesser extent, of artist/activist Carlos Villa (*Other*

Sources, 1976, San Francisco Art Institute, symposium, events, publication, exhibitions of artists working on the "shadow side" and margins of the mainstream Bay Area art world).

13 Art historian Lucy R. Lippard inspired many of us, e.g. with *From the Center*, 1976. Bettelheim referenced Lippard's "Making Something from Nothing (Toward a Definition of Women's Hobby Art)," in *Heresies*, Winter 1978. Lippard described how women look at the objects in their physical environment and use them for their own creative goals. Bettelheim's dissertation on Caribbean street masquerades and her training in African art history also led her to greater understanding of the vast scope of art in our country.

14 Dickinson, Eleanor and Loach, Roberta. "Does Sex Discrimination Exist in the Visual Arts?" *Visual Dialog*. Vol. 1, No. 2, 1975–76. The U.S. box scores at the time for numbers of men (M) and women (F):

Group invitationals	M 1324, F 699
One-person shows	M 1421, F 38
Oakland Museum collection	M 413, F 119

Females made up 75 percent of students in U.S. art schools in 1971. Other statistics Dickinson and Loach researched and reported compared degrees, faculty, reviews, acquisitions, and gallery representation. *Artweek*, a major publication featuring West Coast artists founded by artist Cecile McCann, reflected the S.F. galleries and essentially ignored women—articles were few and far between, and only the most prominent women got coverage. ("The galleries saw it as a 'man's world,'" Loach states.) The Dickinson/Loach research showed only one or two women in most S.F. galleries and literally no, or at most, one woman in museum shows. Loach challenged McCann, who gradually came around: "She got nervous when I started saying things." Around 1973–74, Loach offered to write the articles herself. She became a contributing editor.

15 Not long after, books like Karen Peterson and J.J. Wilson's *Women Artists: Recognition and Reappraisal from the Early Middle Ages to the Twentieth Century* (Colophon Books 1976), were published. The descriptive title highlights a long-standing conundrum; we are not "women artists," but artists. The same issue is raised by Samella S. Lewis and Ruth Waddy's *Black Artists on Art*, Vol. 1 and 2 (Contemporary Crafts, 1969 and 1971). (Lewis founded the Museum of African American Art in Los Angeles in 1976.)

16 Villa (1936–2013) for decades developed diverse, thought-provoking programs at San Francisco Art Institute, nurtured students, connected with other artists and activists on a broad scale, and challenged the mainstream art world through exhibitions, conferences, and symposia.

17 *Chocolate Hearts* at Berkeley's Fiberworks (founded 1973) consisted of candy boxes where each "chocolate" was a portrait of a family member or ancestor, presenting black experience and history seldom seen in a "mainstream" art gallery. Howard and I reconnected in 2011 when she created a *Blue Bottle House* temporary public artwork in front of Palo Alto City Hall, almost a stone's throw from where three decades earlier we had visited the small international art colony of painter/actress Marjorie Eaton.

18 *The Power of Cloth: Political Quilts, 1845–1986* was based on the national research of two other Silicon Valley quilt enthusiasts, Jane Benson and Nancy Olsen. The exhibition included an unknown artist's *Underground Railroad* quilt, c. 1860, supporting the abolitionist cause, and contemporary artist Faith Ringgold's *The Purple Quilt*, inspired by author Alice Walker.

19 "Art Wars" T-shirts memorialized the late '70s conflicts and growing pains. Works/San José and some others have good basic organizational histories on their websites. metroactive.com/papers/metro/12.19.96/works-art-9651.html

20 On national and state levels, various government programs utilized artists and gave them a taste for public service. Those with local impact included the federal CETA program employing artists in hospitals, prisons, and other public service (1973–1982), and California Arts-in-Corrections in the state prisons (1982–2003). The latter began in the '70s as the vision of Eloise Smith, the first California Arts Council Director, and her spouse Page Smith, founding provost of Cowell College at University of California Santa Cruz and activist for the homeless in Santa Cruz.

21 In the coming decades, Hau would become very popular with an influx of Chinese into Silicon Valley who know and buy his work. But Hau's personal reach was always cross-cultural. Only two of the first ASACA

members were Chinese. Connie Young Yu highlighted Hau in her 1986 book *Profiles in Excellence: Peninsula Chinese Americans*, published by the Stanford Chinese Club (1965). She did not gloss over how unfriendly some Palo Alto residents who did not want to have a Chinese family as neighbors were to Hau.

22 SJSU Professor of Art Marcia Chamberlain initiated the CADRE Project and served as first Project Director for the CADRE 1984 conference, papers, and publication. Mary Sievert designed the logo adapted for the cover of the 144-page book, its opening and closing pages filled with hundreds of names, institutions, and businesses who "actively contributed time and thoughtful energy" to the multiyear project.
Joel A. Slayton became CADRE director in 1988, and we would work together again after he went on to direct ZERO1, the Art and Technology Network, founded in 2000.

23 For women, support would come from maverick female art historians, like Moira Roth at Mills College; from Stanford's Center for Research on Women (later name changes), which would also collaborate on the early Djerassi Resident Artists Program (1979) in Woodside; and cross-disciplinary campus groups that organized women's history months. Cultural support would come from campus departments, such as Intercultural Studies and a range of social sciences and language arts, along with historical societies, sororities like Links Incorporated, churches, and community organizations like Mid-Peninsula YWCA in Palo Alto. For over 30 years, artist Huellar Banks, an East Palo Alto resident, painted childhood remembrances in oil on canvas after spending her days cleaning houses. Her art was recognized by the Mid-Peninsula YWCA and Stanford's Institute for Research on Women and Gender. paloaltoonline.com/weekly/morgue/news/1994_Aug_3. PEOPLE03.html
Community activists were supportive in general. Science- and technology-related arts were often orphans, but had energetic core supporters in specific areas. Early computer graphics were highlighted in the '80s by Bay Area ACM/SIGGRAPH, a local chapter of the Association of Computing Machinery/Special Interest Group for Graphics. A former Stanford research scientist, Penny Nii spanned two worlds in her 1986 *Building Blocks* quilt to celebrate the 30th anniversary of the field of artificial intelligence; created the Penny Nii Art Quilt Gallery in Mountain View and curated an exhibition at NASA Ames in the 1990s; then delved into book art, some of which I chose for 2005 and 2010 exhibitions, one collaborating with Bay Area Book Arts. Nii's *Totality*, 2001, led to *Totality*, 2012, a Digital Over Analog (D/A) book Nii created with Mohammed Allababidi and Enrique Godivia, game animators and app developers. D/A books "straddle the world of the book (analog) and e-readers (digital)." http://digitaloveranalog.com/resources/totality_prospectus.pdf youtube.com/watch?v=7Z4w1KhNxZ0&feature=related

24 The idea was to exhibit and feature women and men 50:50, unless some good reason came up not to do so. It was rare for a reason to come up to reduce the percentage of women to less than half.

25 There were people who "got it," and could speak up. For our exhibition *FACES*, 1984, we connected with vocal LaDoris Cordell, Superior Court Judge, Santa Clara County, 1982–2001, at the forefront of social justice; she understood the connection with art. Mary Andrade created a vehicle for art in 1978 as co-founder, co-publisher of the bilingual *La Oferta*, the oldest continuous Latino publication in San José. Andrade, an artist/activist and expert on Day of the Dead altar traditions, and I would discuss the importance of art in building community. I was overjoyed to exhibit her tender 1985 photograph, *Juana Chavez*, of Cesar Chavez's mother crocheting. Andrade's early photography and interviews of local elders inspired *Ethnic Community Builders: Mexican Americans in Search of Justice and Power—The Struggle for Citizenship Rights in San Jose, California* (AltaMira Press, 2007) by Francisco Jiménez, Alma M. García, and Richard A. García.

26 For decades, much of the art world was still distancing itself from communication and content. To quote art historian Moira Roth: " … the Aesthetic of Indifference was a more potent and dangerous model for the 1960s. It advocated neutrality of feeling and commitment in a period that otherwise might have produced an art of passion and commitment." Euphrat Museum cited Roth's 1977 "Aesthetics of Indifference" essay in our publication *CONTENT: Contemporary Issues*, 1985.

27 For the book cover Peretz Wolf-Prusan, printmaker and calligrapher, created *Ancient Religious Symbols*—crescent, earth mother, pilgrimage of the soul, menorah, Vesta, and Russian-style cross. Calligraphy of various spiritual traditions was passed over by modern art institutions, although happening upon a Zen calligraphy class helped Steve Jobs develop a new way of seeing. We all lost when the art world distanced itself from spiritual or philosophical issues, from exploring a range of shared core values and the accompanying questions

and dialogue. Investigations of fundamental human concerns occur, say, in a good literature class. The arts have the potential to play an equally important role in these universal inquiries.

28 The Euphrat created art exhibitions in numerous Apple buildings: an extension of 1984's *FACES* with Luz Bueno, using Via Video System One; and 36 artists from our 1988 *Art of the Computer* exhibition, with works from a broad spectrum of research, artistic and commercial computer graphics. Euphrat placed exhibitions at Hewlett Packard and Tandem Computers, also. We organized an event with sculptor Bruce Beasley at the home of Hewlett Packard VP Joel Birnbaum.
Steve Jobs saw the art in all he built, so I add a few thoughts about local artists and designers—sometimes a small world. Regis McKenna, whose advertising firm marketed Apple computers, chose designer Rob Janoff to create the iconic Apple logo, originally drawn by artist Carlos Pérez, in 1977. McKenna credits artist Tom Kamifuji, Palo Alto, with inspiring the rainbow look. Kamifuji's bright-colored, bold kabuki silkscreen posters were hot items, and the Euphrat included him in our 1981 *Commercial Illustrators* show. Decades later, in 2007, we enjoyed working with McKenna when Steve Yamaguma Associates designed our lively new Euphrat logo and we prepared for our impressive new building facing Stevens Creek Boulevard, not long before Apple designed their own new circular headquarters. Carlos Pérez in 2015 had a retrospective exhibition of his many talents in Stockton; included was his portrait of UFW co-founder Dolores Huerta, who attended the opening.

29 Regarding traditional arts with a dispersed population, in our early efforts to connect and learn, we featured Pomo basketry and Mabel McKay in 1982, included Central Coast baskets from the collection of local historian Austen Warburton in our *CROSSOVER* technology exhibition in 1982, and presented *Art of the Bear Dance, A traditional Spring ceremony of the Maidu Indians* in 1984. La Marr recalls, "Bear Dance posters were produced for 10 years." In 1986 the Muwekma Ohlone Tribe, with a central San José location, constructed a tule house for the de Saisset Museum, and subsequently contributed to public art projects, such as the *Ohlone/Muwekma Tribute* along the Park Avenue Bridge in Guadalupe River Park & Gardens. La Marr has presented a larger picture of indigenous art in Peter Selz's *Art of Engagement, Visual Politics in California and Beyond*, University of California Press, co-published with the SJMA, 2006.

30 Underwood identifies as Latina, Chicana, and Amerindian. Many of her weavings honor the indigenous Yaqui, whose homelands were cut open by the U.S.–Mexico border. She was one of Euphrat Museum's "tell-it-like-it-is" board members.

31 For a larger context, artist/faculty member Carlos Villa was the organizer and producer of "Sources of a Distinct Majority," a series of four heated symposia at San Francisco Art Institute, 1989–1991, that upped the pace of moving past stale structures. The publication *Worlds In Collision*, drawn from the symposia series, includes "diverse concerns of artists, activists, academics and street scholars from both ethnically marginalized and mainstream communities throughout the country. These four symposia, organized around issues of multiculturalism, education, identity politics and the role of the arts in contemporary culture, became venues for intense dialogues with broad implications for rethinking the relationships around cultural theory and activist agendas. The nearly 90 participants collectively and collaboratively explore strategies for a progressive art agenda that reflect a more accurate American Art History." I participated. It was invigorating to explore new strategies collectively. The concurrent Global Cultures, the 1990 Congress of the Arts, Los Angeles, described California: "Its successes and failures at managing the issues posed by ethnic diversity and interdependency with the global economy are a proving ground for the rest of the world." While I didn't attend, the event, sponsored by California Confederation of the Arts, helps understanding of context. Subtitled "A Challenge for the 1990s," this pragmatic gathering centered on government, business, foundations, and the arts, and included a mini-conference on "Art and Disabilities."

32 To give an idea of demographic changes, in 2000 the ethnic makeup of the county was roughly 54% white, 2.7% black, .7% Native American, 28% Asian or Pacific Islander, 24% Latino. In 2010 the three largest population groupings changed to 35% white, 32% Asian or Pacific Islander, and 27% Latino.

33 Also in October 1995, a public meeting on multicultural exhibition collaborations was held in San José. As Joe Bastida Rodriguez (then of the San José Office of Cultural Affairs) put it, the purpose was "to identify issues relevant to collaborations between San José-based multicultural arts groups which lack exhibition spaces, and visual arts organizations with space to house exhibitions."

34 With a welcome by County Supervisor Dianne McKenna, the two panels included Santa Clara County Superior Court Judge Tito Gonzales, East Palo Alto City Councilwoman Myrtle Walker, and artist/educator Ruth Tunstall Grant. Arts Council director Davis worked with an arts/activist staff that understood grassroots: Diem Jones, Lissa Jones, and Audrey Wong.

35 Consuelo Santos Killins spoke up in multiple ways. She promoted Northern California on the CAC, which has been dominated by Southern California. At a CAC meeting in 1989, Killins wanted to serve "all the people of California," and stated, "This is the last time I'm going to vote to fund applications for large-budget organizations unless board of directors' makeup starts to change radically." Advocacy normally isn't "speaking to the choir;" there is an element of activism, standing up to power on behalf of individuals. One of our Euphrat board members, Judy Goddess, used to work on "Individual Advocacy" for parents and kids having problems with public schools. She relates the joy of "bringing a system around to give a service a kid deserves." Where would we be without such advocates for the arts, education, for the marginalized, for those in need? This advocacy can also arise with active participation in a commission, nonprofit, or startup group.

36 Countywide, Adobe supported graphics grants. Applied Materials supported "Excellence in the Arts." Under director Bruce Davis (1994–2011), Arts Council Silicon Valley made great strides in helping fund diversity, increasing seed funding to small and mid-sized organizations.

37 MACLA and ZERO1 with its biennial festival have hit the big leagues. Cultural Initiatives Silicon Valley (1996–2006) inspired by Mayor Susan Hammer, a leader in regional cultural planning, brought movement on cultural policy and art education. Then 1stACT (Arts, Creativity, Technology) Silicon Valley, 2007, a high-end, five-year hybrid, leveraged a "network of networks" for leadership, participation, and investment in art, creativity, and technology. Silicon Valley Creates, 2013, a merger of the Arts Council with 1stACT, has multiple programs. Enlightened government is a boon to cultural life when it's lucky to have someone like Barbara Goldstein, San José Public Art Director, 2004–2013. I worked in recent years with Goldstein on the City Hall Exhibitions Committee, with Ruth Tunstall Grant from the Arts Commission serving as chair. One of our first exhibitions in City Hall connected art, history, and research; early artist/activist Mary Parks Washington collaborated with others to spotlight ties to the local African American community going back to the 1800s.

38 *San Jose Mercury News*, May 12, 2012. Also Houston's memoir on the WWII internment of Japanese Americans (*Farewell to Manzanar*, Houghton Mifflin, 1973) was one of five books anchoring a 2012 yearlong initiative by Cal Humanities (formerly the California Council for the Humanities) to create opportunities for Californians to explore the nature and needs of our democracy.

39 Nationally, Americans for the Arts has a special program Animating Democracy aimed at cultivating a landscape for creative social change and fostering civic engagement through arts and culture.

40 Euphrat *Edges* exhibition. In referencing Emmanuel Leutze's *George Washington Crossing the Delaware* (1851), the African American appears disjointed—a head, part of an arm, half of a leg. Kaphar calls attention to the secondary roles African Americans played in a composition, that artists used formal devices, such as "light vs. dark, up vs. down, to visually reinforce institutionalized views of race and hierarchy." Kaphar, BFA from SJSU, MFA from Yale, focuses on alternative history. Priscilla Frank, "Titus Kaphar's Disrupted Histories," *Huffington Post*, July 2, 2012: "Kaphar cuts and shreds, he erases and whites out, he rumples, sews and paints in tar. … There is rebirth in the residue."

41 Nationally, there have been articles about the advances and alterations in curricula and strategies, e.g., in the women's movement, including the controversy that can surround change described by Susan Faludi in "American Electra" (Faludi, Susan. "American Electra, Feminism's Ritual Matricide." *Harper's Magazine*. October 2010). The National Museum of Women in the Arts reveals that even in 2013, with over half the visual artists today being women, a whopping 95% of art on display in U.S. museums is by male artists.
The field of arts-based community development has grown substantially, and William Cleveland states: "Many of the ideas that were considered radical fruitcake in 1977 can be found in the guidelines of many funders." Cleveland has produced arts programs in educational, community and social institutions, including leadership of California's Arts-In-Corrections Program and the California State Summer School for the Arts, and has written extensively on arts-based community development.

"Our study [1970s sex discrimination study in *Visual Dialog*] really blew the art world out of the water. I got requests from all over the U.S. and Canada for copies of our article. We made a dent as other publications picked up on what we did, and soon in the late '70s and '80s, women in the arts were treated much better, but a certain amount of prejudice still remains." Loach notes the worst offenders can be other women—artists, curators, gallery, and museum directors. The struggle has been amplified because to be successful, not just many men, but many women have bought in, put blinders on, closed the door, and looked no further. Once on a Los Angeles panel, other panelists were alarmed that she did not call her publication a "feminist magazine;" Loach countered, "I was just making up for lost time!" In the 1980s a younger artist spoke confidentially to a young-looking Loach, "We would have made more progress if the old ladies had stayed out of the graduate program." Loach tells me, "My hair caught on fire!" as she recalls all the obstacles [as Germaine Greer recited in her book *The Obstacle Race*]. Historically, we can see some of what was missed and what women were up against in Maurine St. Gaudens' four-volume *A Survey of Women Artists Working in California, 1860–1960*.

Roberta Loach, *The Lonely Odyssey of the Artist*, 1995. Acrylic on canvas, 56"x50". "They [artists Frida Kahlo and Francisco Goya] spent a lot of time alone, and in what I've often observed as a choppy and dangerous sea full of sharks ... an artist's life is not like a song."

For Further Reading

Earlier Years

For more information about historical San José area arts development, including the Silicon Valley Arts Council, and an overview of San José institutional arts activity in the 1970s and early '80s, see Rindfleisch, Jan. "The First San José Biennial." *The First San José Biennial*. San José Museum of Art, 1986. janrindfleisch.com/History.html#SanJoseArt HistoryTo1985

Artist/educator Roberta Loach, Los Altos, published the quarterly magazine *Visual Dialog*, from 1975 to 1980, with essays, interviews, reviews and columns, expanding women's role in connecting Silicon Valley arts with Bay Area and national arts and arts activism.

In 1983, artist/professor Marcia Chamberlain published the seminal *CADRE '84* through the SJSU Art Department. In 1979 and 1987, she published the *Irregular Gazette*, "a once in a while publication of the SJSU Art Department," an opportunity to think about and understand women's contributions, cultural diversity, and entrepreneurship. 1987 articles brought forward emerging artists, the innovative textile design and humanism of Dorothy Liebes (1897–1972), the future for CADRE Laboratory, the fiber arts program (which she instituted), and the foundry program.

A Celebration of 100 Years of the Department of Art, 2013, Natalie and James Thompson Art Gallery—drawing from university archives—refocuses on the SJSU art department's past to "tie to larger cultural and social movements" of today, but creates a sense of a more diverse and diversity-welcoming past academic cultural climate than existed.

For understanding the making of art history and the times, including local activism, see Rindfleisch, Jan. *Staying Visible, The Importance of Archives*. Exhibition publication, Euphrat Museum of Art, 1981. Foreword "Artists and Archives" by Paul Karlstrom, West Coast Area Director, Archives of American Art, Smithsonian Institution. Commentaries included Michael Bell, Registrar/Cataloguer, Oakland Museum of California. Eleven articles involved researchers from various institutions concentrating on individual artists, all women, with a focus on putting material into archives. Karlstrom, Bell, and others brought project insight, guidance, and support, particularly important in our early critical days of discovery. The opening essay "The Importance of Archives" is available online. janrindfleisch.com/About.html

More Recent

Poetic Paradox, 10 Years of Innovation in Latino Art, MACLA, 2001, expands the region's cultural archives by examining innovation through the lenses of 19 exceptional artists who influenced the direction of MACLA's visual art program.

For information on arts activity beyond nonprofits, see Moriarty, Pia. *Immigrant Participatory Arts: An Insight into Community-building in Silicon Valley*. Cultural Initiatives Silicon Valley (CISV), 2004. Cultural anthropologist Moriarty examined informal arts groups in local immigrant communities. See also Alvarez, Maribel. *There's Nothing Informal About It: Participatory Arts Within the Cultural Ecology of Silicon Valley*. CISV, 2005.

For thinking differently about regional cultural policy and understanding CISV's final project, see "Bad Culture Interview: John Kreidler on *Medici's Lever*," (blogs.giarts.org/

kreidler/2010/07/22/bad-culture-interview-john-kreidler-on-medicis-lever/) or go directly to Medici's Lever (forio.com/broadcast/netsim/netsims/Medici/medici-home/index. html), an online suite of two games and one simulation laboratory. One of the games is entitled SJ Renaissance.

Some Art World Views

To have some sense of the gallery-industrial complex and the role of money, consider the viewpoint of NY Times art critic Holland Cotter on art, politics, and money in Cotter, Holland. "Lost in the Gallery-Industrial Complex, Holland Cotter Looks at Money in Art." *NY Times*. Jan. 17, 2014. nytimes.com/2014/01/19/arts/design/holland-cotter-looks-at-money-in-art.html?_r=0

See the Guerrilla Girls website, guerrillagirls.com/, or for a three-decade look, see Ryzik, Melena. "The Guerrilla Girls, After 3 Decades, Still Rattling Art World Cages." *NY Times*. Aug. 5, 2015. nytimes.com/2015/08/09/arts/design/the-guerrilla-girls-after-3-decades-still-rattling-art-world-cages.html

For viewing art and the art world, try *Meaning Maker*, a guided interactive tool to foster understanding and evaluation of specific experiences. Start with the *Art Viewing Experience Edition*, a simple downloadable brochure that is also art. meaningmaker.org *Meaning Maker* is the work of artists Kent Manske and Nanette Wylde, who have long offered wit, intelligence, spirit, and hands-on support to the art community through their PreNeo Press, Redwood City.

In General

The story of Silicon Valley arts is enriched by "human interest" arts stories in *Metro* and the *San Jose Mercury News* (and neighborhood affiliates) by writers such as Joe Rodriguez. Combining selections from these publications' archives along with alternative publications like *Visual Dialog*, could provide a very different view of Silicon Valley cultural life and its impact outside the area. Publications such as *El Excentrico* have augmented the big picture, as have *La Oferta, El Observador*, and numerous special-interest publications. *Low Rider* magazine started here. Silicon Valley arts have also been featured in the *World Journal, Hokubei Mainichi*, and countless small publications, including student publications like *El Aguila*, connected with Stanford's El Centro Chicano y Latino.

Written and visual records, including video, are easily lost for smaller operations, especially when artists and others edit resumes and remove references. Yet the archival foundation is what helps us understand origins, attributions, and down-the-line appropriations in the art world—understand how meaning and importance, also hype, can become imbued in an artwork, and see and appreciate a fuller circle of creation.

EARLY CULTURAL LANDSCAPES

A Spiral Through Time: Silicon Valley Arts and Culture from Ancestral Ohlone to Today

Building and sustaining a vibrant, innovative system of arts and culture in Silicon Valley has always started with engaging newcomers and transcending the divisions between art, history, cultures, economics, ethics, and other disciplines. It's helpful to have a sense of our diverse historical roots, as well as the forces of change and new ideas, as we ponder Silicon Valley's unique cultural development.

This exploration looks back 10,000 years to the ancestors of today's Ohlone Indians and considers their long and ongoing history; then examines the interwoven stories of 19th century pioneer Juana Briones and last century's Marjorie Eaton. The revelations provide an informative and provocative temporal bridge that spans from early Native American cultures to the contemporary local community and art stars like Consuelo Jimenez Underwood. The ability of these resourceful and generous women to honor indigenous heritage, draw from different sources, and shape new creative environments has left a timeless legacy.

A Natural Weave of Art and Community Life: The Ohlone

The indigenous Ohlone people hunted, fished, and harvested a diversity of plants and seeds. The elaborate adornment worn by a well-decked out, finely feathered elite and the

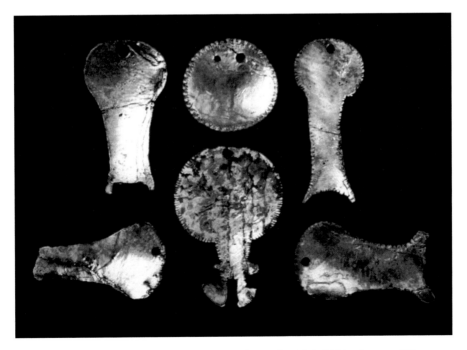

Kuksu ceremonial pendants, c. AD 1100, from CA-ALA-329 in Coyote Hills, similar to those found in downtown San José made of red and black abalone shells. Photo: Joe Cavaretta (Muwekma Tribe).

Ohlone's exquisite basketry showcased their social stratification and the artistic skills of the women. In sync with nature, they created fiber art with materials derived from the natural world and sustainable architecture, such as a *tupentak* roundhouse that could accommodate 250 people. They wove baskets for leaching acorn meal, cooking, fishing, and winnowing grain; as well as for storing ornaments of abalone, cut-and-drilled beads from *Olivella* shells, and complex feather dance regalia.

Certain art forms were owned, such as jewelry (shell ornamentation and regalia), which was associated with wealth and status based upon the family's lineage and ranking in the community. Other art had to do with shamanic visions and ceremonial religious performances. The architectural "shellmounds" of Coyote Hills were sacred landscapes, ceremonial burial grounds for nobility—California's pyramids.

Maria de los Angeles (Angela Colos), c. 1925, born in the Santa Teresa Hills in San José, at Alisal Rancheria between Pleasanton and Sunol, where her family found refuge in a shanty. The American conquest of California and the Gold Rush (1849), followed by statehood in 1850, ushered in an extended period in which indigenous Californians were robbed of their cultural heritage, homes, villages, and basic rights and had to hide out for their safety.

Once widely known for their fine basketry with geometric designs, Ohlone women lost much of their material and spiritual culture when they labored in the valley's emerging agricultural economy. At Franciscan Mission Santa Clara de Asis, Thamién Ohlone–speaking women turned to weaving cotton clothing, blankets, and carpets for the community. With the establishment of Spanish ranchos and a growing hide trade, the decimated Ohlone population became a hidden minority, their native way of life increasingly influenced by Spanish/Mexican culture. Their traditional arts often took a back seat to the arts of survival.

Installation image, California History from the Permanent Collection exhibition. Photo: Chuck Barry, © 2006 Santa Clara University. In 1986, Muwekma Ohlone tribal members and their children constructed a tule house (rúwwa) for the de Saisset Museum. The Museum recently launched its new iPad textbook focused on the early days of Santa Clara Valley and Mission Santa Clara.

Angela Colos, born in 1839, daughter of Indians who were married at Mission San José in 1838, was one of the principal linguistic consultants for many anthropologists.[1] A fluent speaker of the Chocheño Ohlone language, she shared her knowledge. Stating that "muwékma" means "la gente (the people)," she also passed along other traditions about the tribe. Her living descendants are enrolled members of the Muwekma Ohlone Tribe of the San Francisco Bay Area, which continues the traditional arts and gives precedence to new art forms for building community.[2]

---

[1] On October 16, 1838, two Mission Indians residing in south San José, married at Mission Santa Clara. A year later, their daughter Maria Asuncion de Los Angeles was born on the Bernal rancho. The family then moved to the Bernal-Pico-Sunol rancho between Sunol and Pleasanton. Maria Asuncion was later known as Maria de los Angeles Colos or Ângela Colos. She was interviewed by five anthropologists, starting in 1904. She died around 1929, before she was able to enroll with the Bureau of Indian Affairs. On October 12, 1929, John P. Harrington, a linguist from the Smithsonian Institution, interviewed Angela Colos and she stated, "The Clareños were much intermarried with the Chocheños [Indians from Mission San José]. The dialect(s) were similar. Muwékma, la gente *(the people)*."
Anthropologist C. Hart Merriam collected baskets from Ascencion Solarsano de Cervantes (died 1930) and her mother Barbara Serra (Mission San Juan Bautista) during the early 1900s, which are curated at UC Davis.

[2] For more information, see Rindfleisch, Jan. *Ohlone Art and Building Community*, 2014. janrindfleisch.com/Projects.html#OhloneArtAndBuildingCommunity.

The Art of Erasure

Today, we are learning more about how Ohlones have been denied their cultural existence and how their languages and place names were erased, replaced by Hispanic and Anglo ones. Contemporary art historians know well the art of erasure and also what anthropologists call "nominative cartography." Colonial systems have "remade, restructured, and renamed landscapes," literally transforming the map of the San Francisco Bay area. "Mapping Erasure,"[3] written by anthropologist Les W. Field with Alan Leventhal, Muwekma Tribal Ethnohistorian, and Rosemary Cambra, elected chairwoman of the Muwekma Ohlone Tribe of the San Francisco Bay Area,[4] is one of numerous articles in which Leventhal and Cambra describe and counter colonial systems and the widespread art of erasure.

An example is Moffett Field, a former naval air station, currently a joint civil-military airport whose airfield is leased to neighboring Google in Mountain View for 60 years. It is known for its tremendous Hangar One, one of the world's largest freestanding structures. Moffett used to be Rancho Posolmi, home of Lope Yñigo, who bridged three cultures. Born in 1781 in an Indian village near Mission Santa Clara, Yñigo was baptized at the mission in 1789 and served it from 1789–1839. He was given a land grant to the rancho, where he raised crops and livestock, defended his land grant for over two decades, and resided till his death in 1864. Yñigo was buried somewhere on this land, but at Moffett Field, there's no sign of any of this past.

Similarly, Stanford University lands incorporate former Indian villages, both in their archaeological preserve and at Jasper Ridge. In one article,[5] the campus archaeologist describes a place as possibly sacred, because there are tiny holes (cupules) in the rocks, suitable for grinding medicine and pigments used in rituals. She also notes the Ohlone nature-friendly style of human organization: "It's extremely effective—and low impact." Yet the Ohlone place names have disappeared from Stanford.

---

[3] Field, Les W., Alan Leventhal, and Rosemary Cambra. "Mapping Erasure." *Recognition, Sovereignty, Struggles, and Indigenous Rights in the United States, A Sourcebook.* Eds. Amy E. Den Ouden and Jean M. O'Brien. University of North Carolina Press, 2013.

[4] Rosemary Cambra is the elected chairwoman of the Muwekma Ohlone Tribe of the San Francisco Bay Area whose enrolled membership is descended from Missions Santa Clara, San José, and Dolores. A previously federally recognized tribe, the tribe is seeking reaffirmation as well as honoring their cultural traditions and identity. For ethnohistory and tribal recognition background in the context of a recent local reburial, see Leventhal, Alan, Rosemary Cambra, et al. "Final Report on the Burial and Archaeological Data Recovery Program Conducted on a Portion of the Mission Santa Clara Indian Neophyte Cemetery (1781–1818): Clareño Muwékma Ya Túnneste Nómmo [Where the Clareño Indians are Buried] Site (CA-SCL-30/H)." Leventhal, Alan, Rosemary Cambra, et al. Chapter 1: "Introduction: Project Overview." Cambra, Rosemary, et al. Chapter 10: "An Ethnohistory of Santa Clara Valley and Adjacent Regions; Historic Ties of the Muwekma Ohlone Tribe of the San Francisco Bay Area and Tribal Stewardship Over the Mission Santa Clara Indian Neophyte Cemetery: Clareño Muwékma Ya Túnneste Nómmo [Where the Clareño Indians are Buried] Site (CA-SCL-30/H)." CA-SCL-30H Combined Pres 3-8-2012.pdf, https://docs.google.com/viewer?a=v&pid=sites&srcid= ZGVmYXVsdGRvbWFpbnxlbnZzMTg1ZmFsbDIwMTRzc3V8Z3g6MzJjMDc3YTVmM2UyNzdlMw

[5] Softky, Marion. "Archaeology, Indian memories, and plodding through mission records flesh out lives of the original Californians." *The Almanac.* 5/14/2001. Quotation from archaeology professor and campus archaeologist Laura Jones.

A rare exception is Ulistac Natural Area near the new Levi's Stadium in Santa Clara, which may mean "place of the basket" in several Ohlone languages.

Reclaiming the Arts of Naming and Installation

With the renaming of the Tamien Railroad Station in San José, the Ohlone have reclaimed the arts of naming and installation. In 1777, Father Tomas de la Peña and an escort of soldiers and settlers arrived at the banks of the Guadalupe River, built an arbor of thatched tule reeds for a temporary shelter, and thus founded the Mission Santa Clara de Thámien. Peña mentioned in a letter to Father President Junipero Serra that the natives called the area of the mission Thámien. Shortly after the mission was founded, the Governor of Alta California, Felipe de Neve, sent instructions to establish a pueblo nearby. Commander Jose Joaquin Moraga of the San Francisco Presidio took a group of settlers and retired soldiers to the Guadalupe River to found California's first civil establishment, El Pueblo de San José de Guadalupe—now the City of San José. After construction of the railroad station uncovered a major ancestral archaeological site containing around 172 ancestors, the Muwekma Ohlone renamed it as Tamien Station to honor their ancestors and the memory of the thousands of Ohlones who had lived in Thámien. A permanent exhibition of "artifacts" found on the site has been planned but not yet constructed.

Regarding sacred burial grounds and cultural history, the Ohlone now work in a heartbeat alliance with archaeologists and anthropologists and use art forms such as performance art, installations, language revitalization, and public art. A close-knit community, the Muwekma employ Internet strategies as well as traditional gatherings.

One moving public ceremony occurred in 2010 when a Pacific Gas and Electric Company (PG&E) gas line replacement project within the Mission Santa Clara Indian Neophyte Cemetery required the excavation and then reburial of ancestral remains.[6] The reburial honoring ceremony included Native American spiritual beliefs and Roman Catholic religious traditions. Reburial layers interred the remains with associated regalia, sand, church-consecrated objects, and an abalone shell containing purifying sage and mugwort, or *estafiate*, turned upside down. The ceremony ended with the Lord's Prayer in the Santa Clara (Clareño) Thámien Ohlone language.

Noted artist/activist Jean LaMarr (Pit River/Paiute, Susanville), working with tribal members, counters the erasure of Ohlone presence. With her art, she speaks to the cultural identity and ongoing struggles of Ohlone people living today. LaMarr's 1995 mural (restoration and celebration 2013), *The Ohlone Journey*, located in Ohlone Park in Berkeley, celebrates Ohlone life and culture on four walls. The westward-facing panel, "Modern Life Transitions," honors individuals who lived in the 19th and 20th centuries. It depicts members of indigenous families, including Maria de los Angeles Colos, based on old photographs lent to the artist by their descendent family members.

---

6 Leventhal, Alan, Rosemary Cambra, et al. Op. cit. Cambra, Rosemary, et al. Chapter 11: "Reburial of the Muwekma Ohlone Tribe's Ancestral Remains from the Mission Santa Clara Indian Neophyte Cemetery: Clareño Muwékma Ya Túnneste Nómmo [Where the Clareño Indians are Buried] Site (CA-SCL-30/H) and Final Site Management Recommendations."

In terms of general Native American cultural history and concerns, the Indian Health Center (IHC) in San José has played a basic but significant role while undergoing multiple moves and divisions. The IHC was originally part of the Indian Community Center (ICC), established in 1969. Then it became San José American Indian Center in 1970, a gathering place that provided art exhibition space. At one point it sponsored ABLEZA: Native American Arts and Media Institute, which began in 1997.

Muwekma Ohlone Visibility

Makkin Mak Muwekma Wolwoolum, 'Akkoy Mak-Warep, Manne Mak Hiswi!
We Are Muwekma Ohlone, Welcome To Our Land, Where We Are Born!

Muwekma Ohlone visibility has benefited from a more focused multigenerational and multidisciplinary approach of dedicated individuals. Tribal Vice Chairwoman Monica V. Arellano's website updates cite activities from ceremonies to academic conferences.[7]

In spring 2015, Gilbert Martinez, a young active Muwekma tribal member, shared or reposted several pertinent touch points. The first of these was a 1930 recording of a Muwekma Ohlone language song sung by Muwekma Elder José Guzman, who lived in Niles and the Sunol/Pleasanton rancheria. Recordings of 27 songs from Guzman are currently housed at the Smithsonian Institution's Bureau of American Ethnology. The second posting noted the 2015 grand opening ceremony of the new Balermino Park in San José, which the tribe helped name for Ohlone ancestor Robert Antonio Balermino, a Mission Santa Clara Clareño-Thámien (Costanoan/Ohlone) who had been granted the land in 1844. Martinez also shared a link to an article by Stanford Ph.D. student Fanya Becks on Muwekma archaeology and ownership of the ancestral past.[8]

Through postings and actions like these, new or unfamiliar names arise and serve as an antidote to the repetitive recitals of the same names and touted accomplishments, which tend to bypass and decimate a rich history of borrowing, collaborating, and repurposing of sources and resources.

Changing Context: Mission-era Art

Regalia and cultural objects, integral to community life, were created and cherished by the ancestral Ohlone people. Subsequently, art and cultural objects in the valley were

---

[7] The Muwekma website, muwekma.org/home.html, cited two Muwekma presentations for the Society for American Archaeology 80th Annual Meeting in April 2015. For the Society of California Archaeology 2015 Annual Conference, plenary session organizer Kaely R. Colligan wrote that the meeting's theme "Beyond Boundaries" was chosen to emphasize "the influence of cultural and physical boundaries on our perspectives within the archaeological record. In the spirit of 'Beyond Boundaries,' we have built a plenary session featuring papers co-authored by Native Americans and archaeologists." The session included Leventhal, Alan, Rosemary Cambra, et al. "Meaningful Relationships between the Muwekma Ohlone Tribe of the San Francisco Bay and the Anthropological/Archaeological Communities: A Process of Reciprocal Benefits and Collaborations in Language Revitalization, Biological Anthropology." scahome.org/wp-content/uploads/2015/02/FINAL-2015-SCA-Program.pdf

[8] sfu.ca/ipinch/outputs/blog/tribal-archaeology-ownership-ancestral-past

increasingly created or acquired, displayed, saved, and contextualized by religious, academic, and public institutions with Euro-American roots and global networks and interests. The preponderant system of cultural values changed.

In 1851, Jesuits founded Santa Clara College, later known as Santa Clara University (SCU), at the mission site. Through their permanent collection, SCU's de Saisset Museum of Art and History offers a window to the diversity and global influences of Mission-era art. Their textile art collection encompasses opulent vestments from France and Spain (mainly 1650–late 18th century); brightly colored vestments embroidered in China, fabricated in the Philippines and distributed to the missions from Mexico; and somber matte velvet funeral vestments sewn by Ohlone living at the mission. In 2012, the de Saisset curated a historic display of Central Coast baskets and traditional Ohlone arts with select old ecclesiastical vestments from around the world found at the mission. The two collections complemented an exhibition of contemporary textile art, *Beyond Function: Fiber, Fabric, and Finery*, with garments that utilize, pay tribute to, and draw from the earlier forms.

Personal Freedom and Rich Interaction: Juana Briones de Miranda (1802–1889)

Living through the Mission era, the ever-inventive Juana Briones de Miranda set the stage for future cultural development in the valley. Briones was of mixed European, African, and Native American ancestry. Her grandparents immigrated to Alta California to escape a "racial caste system" and a deteriorating economic climate in New Spain (now Mexico). Her mother[9] was about five years old when her family came with the De Anza expedition to California in 1776, a year before Mission Santa Clara and the old pueblo of San José were established. Briones spent her early years in the Villa de Branciforte near Mission Santa Cruz, which set the tone for her life, including learning from Indians. When her mother died, her father moved the family to El Polín Springs, near the Presidio in San Francisco. After marrying soldier Apolinario Miranda, Briones and her husband established a farm nearby.

Through an archaeological project conducted by Stanford University at El Polín Springs, we find early information about Briones' relationships, values, and the pluralistic households she formed with her sisters. Professor Barbara L. Voss writes: "This ethnic pluralism may be reflected in the archaeological materials found at El Polín Springs,[10] which included groundstone, flaked lithics and glass, worked shell artifacts, glass trade

---

[9] Juana Briones' father was 12 years old and with his father at Mission San Luis Obispo, California when the Anza expedition passed through. In the 1790 California census (missions plus six nascent cities), 71% of the adults in Alta California originated in the Sinaloan/Sonoran/Baja California region. Briones' father had come from San Luis Potosi, her mother from Villa de Culiajan. In terms of the Presidio, not one of the original settlers was born in Spain; in modern terms, their national origin would be best described as Mexican. Voss, Barbara. *The Archaeology of El Presidio de San Francisco: Culture Contact, Gender, and Ethnicity in a Spanish-colonial Military Community.* Diss. University of California, Berkeley, 2002. P. 148.

[10] Ibid. For general information about the project and insight into the Briones sisters' relationship with presidial society, see Stanford University Research at the Presidio of San Francisco Tennessee Hollow Watershed Archaeological Project stanford.edu/group/presidio/juana.html, which includes an excerpt from Chapter 9, "The Presidio Landscape."

beads, and locally-made ceramics along with British-produced whitewares and other imported goods." Voss also provides discussion that gives insight into Briones' changing relationship with a patriarchal Presidio society.

Briones' history elucidates the ingenuity of successful women at the interaction of cultures. She became a businesswoman, humanitarian, and landowner. She raised eight children, including an adopted Native American girl, studied the art and science of natural healing from Mexican *curanderos* and her Native American neighbors, aided people in need during the smallpox epidemic, left her abusive, drunkard husband, and started new ventures. She moved her family to what we still know as Yerba Buena (perhaps named for the healing herb tea she used), developed successful cattle and vegetable businesses, and built community through her hospitality and healing as a *curandera*. The coastal site became increasingly known for celebrations and for meeting potential partners. Reflecting her reputation, it was highlighted on San Francisco's first map as *Playa de Juana Briones*— later to become the cultural hotspot known as North Beach, home of Little Italy, the San Francisco Art Institute, beatnik subculture, and City Lights Bookstore.

In 1844, Briones purchased the 4,400-acre Rancho la Purísima Concepción in the Palo Alto foothills from two Mission Santa Clara (Clareño) Ohlone men, José Gorgonio and his son, who then stayed on for years until they had to find safety. The two men had been given the first Native American–owned Mexican land grant after the breakup of the Santa Clara Mission in 1840.

Briones developed the cattle ranch and brought her creative vision to the land: a hilltop home for her family with a spectacular view, an architecturally rare type of redwood-and-adobe construction called *encajonado*, and an east wall arbor of wisteria.[11] Briones' rancho also served as an inn for travelers on a route that connected with Santa Cruz. From the wide-ranging art forms of Mission Santa Clara[12] to the cultural objects and ways of Ohlone or Chinese ranch laborers and various new immigrants, Briones lived in rich interaction with Mission art and the evolving arts of Ohlone, Spanish, Italian, Mexican, Chinese, and many other traditions.

Briones witnessed vast changes in traditional, liturgical, and secular arts. As a businesswoman, she saw the wins and losses in a changing culture and economy, and the strains on Indian and Chinese ranch laborers—the struggle for survival and for a voice amidst gender, racial, and class repression and abuse. Here's a partial local snapshot in

---

[11] In January 1848, surveyor Chester Smith Lyman observed the Briones household: "Find our quarters at Madam Briones quite comfortable. The family is composed of the Widow Briones 3 daughters (2 grown up) 2 or 3 boys, half a dozen Indians, 2 little pet pigs in the cook house & 15 or 20 dogs. The two older girls do the cooking; they are rather pretty looking, but like most Californians dirty & slovenly. There are two sick persons in the house, an Indian girl, of fever, & a man, a sailor, apparently a Portuguese, who has a very bad cough." californiahistoricalsociety.org/exhibitions/juana-briones/exhibit/#/cluster-585

[12] Briones, who lived at the Mission at one point, testified in favor of canonization of Padre Magín de Catala, who died in 1830 after serving Mission Santa Clara for 30 years. Catala baptized Gorgonio, as well as one of Briones' children (1827), and many children of her relatives. In her book *Juana Briones of Nineteenth-Century California*, Jeanne Farr McDonnell mentions that Gorgonio may well have been an assistant who accompanied Catala everywhere he went.

1873, a pivotal year for arts and culture in the valley. Briones would have been 71. Sculptor Edmonia Lewis, an African American working out of Rome in a neoclassical vein, became the first internationally known artist to travel to and exhibit in San José, with the support of San José leader and suffragist Sarah Knox Goodrich.[13] Several imaginative local activists sponsored her meaningful and lasting symbolism by purchasing three of Lewis' marble sculptures—the *Bust of Abraham Lincoln*, with its piercing, determined look, and the affectionate young duo in *Awake* and *Asleep*. The interactions with Lewis and the purchases of the sculptures by Knox Goodrich and the Friends of the San José Library illustrate these key individuals' shared dedication to the fight for basic rights and the betterment of their community. Their actions also help fill out a broader picture of racial relations, activism, and cultural activity at that time.

Briones' rancho home in 1880s or early 1890s. There's some speculation that portions may have been built over Gorgonio's house. Photo courtesy of M. Nott Ginsberg and Palo Alto Historical Association.

The year 1873 was two years before the start of the San José Art Association and eight years before an architectural phenomenon—the San José Electric Light Tower, a precursor to the Eiffel Tower and our first grand public art—touted San José as the only electrified city west of the Rocky Mountains. From all over the world, Santa Clara Valley newcomers brought with them cherished artworks, along with pens, brushes, needles, and tools to fashion more, to recreate meaning and cultural familiarity in an alien and hostile land. Chinese workers, who lived simply, started with baskets and kites. Later, they were enriched by the art in their temple, as well as costumed performances of Chinese opera in

---

13 The interactions with Edmonia Lewis (1844–1907) are telling in many ways. For further description, see "Mary Parks Washington: Motivated by History."

their large theater, a colorful blend of living art and architecture. However, anti-Chinese sentiment deterred these cultural activities, and in 1887, arson demolished the San José Market Street Chinatown and its businesses, homes, and livelihoods. Within weeks, the area was voted to be the site for San José's new city hall, a form of early urban renewal.[14]

Aerial photo of home (off Arastradero Road, Palo Alto) around 1925. Photo "Courtesy of M. Eaton" and the Palo Alto Historical Association.

Briones resided at the rancho for several decades. Then she moved to Mayfield (now south Palo Alto) to be nearer to her daughters.[15] Palo Alto author/historian Jeanne Farr McDonnell's 2008 biography of Briones brings the story and the times to life, even making the case for crediting Briones with the founding of the City of San Francisco.

Briones' home was demolished in 2011 after a long legal battle. It is difficult to believe that only a section of one of its uniquely constructed walls was salvaged. Plans are to make a permanent Briones exhibition, including the wall, at the Palo Alto History Museum. "The legend of Juana Briones grows by the year. All of us engaged in the long lost cause of saving the Casa can take heart in the fact that though we lost the house, we saved the persona and advanced La Causa."[16]

---

[14] For decades, historian Connie Young Yu, based in Los Altos, has researched events like this and offered unique perspectives on Chinese culture locally going back more than a century. Yu's stories elucidate historic dynamics of our economy, politics, and art: Chinese labor on the railroads; Chinese Exclusion Act; and Chinese art purchased by museums, collectors, and religious institutions. Portions of her family's historic art collection instruct patrons at Stanford's Cantor Arts Center. A recent project collaboration of Yu with historian Leslie Masunaga captures the joint history shared by San José's Chinatown and Japantown. See also Technical Reports of the Market Street Chinatown Archaeology Project (MSCAP), Stanford Archaeology Center.

[15] Briones died in Mayfield, at her home located at the corner of Washington and Second Street, an intersection now known as Page Mill Road and Birch Street. She was the first person buried in Holy Cross Cemetery in Menlo Park.

[16] Akatiff, Clark. Letter. *Palo Alto Stanford Heritage (PAST) Newsletter.* Nov. 2012. pastheritage.org/ JuanaBriones.html. See also brioneshouse.org, news.stanford.edu/news/2007/may30/briones-053007.html

Briones house hearth, 2007. The hearth was designed by videographer Susan Kirk, who lived in and loved the house, and fought its demolition. Photo: Linda A. Cicero / Stanford News Service. Photo taken as demolition was looming.

The persona of Briones has been reconstructed in recent years by storyteller Olga Loya. She created a one-woman Chautauqua where she becomes Juana Briones, which she has also adapted for performance as a more conventional, third-person narrative. For years, students from nearby Juana Briones School came annually to the Briones house to learn about the Briones legacy and to create art on site, which they would then display in an exhibition.

Stanford history Professor Albert Camarillo served as a guest curator for the 2014 exhibition mounted by the California Historical Society in San Francisco about the life and times of Juana Briones—*Juana Briones y Su California, Pionera, Fundadora, Curandera*. The remnant wall was prominently displayed. "The story of Juana Briones is important to us all as Californians for many reasons," Camarillo said. "She was a humanitarian and folk healer, a woman who cared for sick and needy people regardless of their ethnic, racial or class background, or whether they spoke Spanish, English or some other language. She was also a person of great integrity who persevered through tumultuous times in the 19th century and fought against great odds to protect her rights as a property owner, as a mother and wife, and as a businesswoman." Camarillo said the exhibition offered new perspectives and an "appreciation for a little-known historical figure whose stories reflect some of the best qualities we as people possess." At times Camarillo's students at Stanford have created projects related to Briones and an accompanying exhibition.

My thoughts about Briones and art go beyond the red lacquered Chinese chest given to her, the stone mortar and pestle found on site, the music in extended family gatherings, her dramatic recounting of events, or the dressmaking and sewing business in which she employed Indian women skilled from working in the missions. They go beyond the unusual construction of her homes, an architectural interest she may have first learned from Indian women who, having built their own homes, were construction experts. Rather, I think about her creating an environment that fostered innovation and freedom.

What is an art scene or a creative scene without personal freedom? More than once, Briones carved out a space and built on it—for herself and others—at a time when that was definitely not easy for a woman to do. I marvel at her mastery of the art of creative problem solving in multiple arenas, in part learned from Indians: the arts and science of using native habitat for food and herbs along with gardening, farming, and ranching; the arts and science of healing, setting bones, and attending births. Briones was known for her hospitality. In Briones' 1800s, social separations increased. A patriarchal military elite culture advanced in the Presidio and anti-indigenous practices multiplied. Yet Briones did not limit her cultural appreciation; rather, she valued locally made textiles and ceramics alongside imports from England, Mexico, and China. She valued people. With her openness to individuals across lines of race, ethnicity, gender, and class, she showed us the art of community building. Modeling courage and opportunities for women, she fought for her land rights up to the Supreme Court and won.[17] As it says on her gravestone, "She Cared."

Connecting Multiple Cultures and Art Movements: Marjorie Eaton (1901–1986)

Painter/actress Marjorie Eaton initiated a family-like arts colony in the Palo Alto foothills, on the stage Juana Briones had set with her home on the hill. Eaton was raised in San Francisco, but spent much of her life living in or next to the historic home of Juana

---

[17] Regarding rights, judge and historian Paul Bernal says many women were named in lawsuits because they were either grantees or heirs of grantees. In the transition from Mexican California to American California, there was a vacuum of law, a mishmash of approaches; this resulted in a lot of cobbled-together litigation between 1845–1860. Under Mexican law, women could inherit, while the U.S. had primogeniture. Bernal cites cases of Mary Bennett, "the Santa Clara Amazon," and her daughter Catherine, including the first custody case in the California Supreme Court. Mary McSwain Bennett Love would become a major landholder in Santa Clara, near the mission. In San José, activists Sarah Knox Goodrich and Sarah Massey Overton come in a little later (see "Mary Parks Washington: Motivated by History"). Knox Goodrich supported Clara Shortridge Foltz's study of law after 1876. Foltz pushed progressive legislation for women's rights in voting and legal fields. She was instrumental in securing passage of the anti-discrimination laws and section of the California Constitution. At the Chicago World's Fair in 1893, she expanded her networks; spoke at a sub-conference on labor chaired by Jane Addams, one of the most prominent reformers of the Progressive Era; and, after laying out how power can corrupt the judicial system, first outlined her concept of public defender, the basis for the public defender movement she founded. At age 81, she was the first woman to run for Governor of California. See Babcock, Barbara Allen. *Woman Lawyer: The Trials of Clara Foltz.* Stanford Press, 2011. See also Ginsberg, Ruth Bader. Rev. of *Woman Lawyer: The Trials of Clara Foltz.* Stanford Law Review Vol. 65, Issue 2, Feb. 2013 : 399. stanfordlawreview.org/print/article/woman-lawyer-the-trials-of-clara-foltz/. For an earlier more general view, see Beebe, Rose Marie, and Robert M. Senkewicz. *Testimonios, Early California through the Eyes of Women, 1815–1848.* Heyday Books, 2006.

Briones. In 1925, Eaton's stepmother, Edith Cox Eaton, a leading San Francisco dress designer and a key figure in Marjorie Eaton's life, purchased Briones' historic Palo Alto house, which had been enlarged by a Stanford botanist after he bought it from Briones's daughter. The 20th century brought new expansion and finery to the Briones/Eaton hilltop. People dressed for dinner. While Eaton's father, physician Dr. George Eaton, and Edith Eaton employed three generations of a Chinese family as household staff in San Francisco, the dinners on the hilltop were more a family affair, often gourmet meals cooked by Edith Eaton herself.

To understand the arts colony, we need to know and understand about Marjorie Eaton's art. Marjorie Eaton was a seminal figure linking multiple cultures, women arts leaders, and the proliferation of major 20th century art movements: Cubism, Expressionism, Social Realism, conceptual art, and abstraction. After completing her first oil painting in 1922 at the San Francisco Art Institute, she studied or worked in San Francisco, Carmel, Boston (Art Institute of Boston), New York, Taos, Florence, Italy, Paris, and Mexico, among other locations. Her independence and peripatetic experience were evident early on, laying the foundation for creating her complex artist colony, as we see in her recounting of how she befriended art dealer/collector/teacher Galka Scheyer in 1928:

> I recall vividly when I met Galka. She had come up from Los Angeles and was living at a little hotel on Sacramento Street near the Fairmont Hotel. She had with her all the paintings that she had brought from Germany of the German Expressionists, including Paul Klee. … This was the first trip, and she was showing to people [who] bought these things. I imagine she didn't go back for a couple of years at this time.

> I had taken a job as a [department store] stylist in Oakland, and I was commuting back and forth. I was so tired most of the time that I stayed at the YWCA—I couldn't make it back again.[18]

Fortunately, staying at the relatively new San Francisco Chinatown YWCA enabled Eaton to work and forge cultural connections.[19] Scheyer was giving lectures at the YWCA and "bringing her art right to the level of the people." As an energetic arts impresario who saw that art could make a change in people's lives, she brought fellow artists Paul Klee, Lyonel Feininger, Vasily Kandinsky and Alexei von Jawlensky together to form the Blue Four (so

[18] Except where noted, the basis of this early narrative is derived from: Estersohn, Betty. Interview with Marjorie Eaton. July 16, 1981. Audiotape. Estersohn, Betty, and Deanna Bartels. Conversations for "Marjorie Eaton." *Staying Visible, The Importance of Archives,* op. cit.

[19] Established in 1916 in an old saloon on Stockton and Sacramento streets, the Chinatown YWCA made a name for itself providing services sensitive to the community. White and Chinese-American leaders and activists supported the YWCA for rejecting stereotypes. By the mid-1920s there was a need for a new building; the designer chosen was Julia Morgan. Background information on the location and times can be found at Chinese Historical Society of America website chsa.org/exhibits/online/Julia-morgan-legacy-project. "Julia Morgan's status as a pioneer of women architects and her dedication to the women's movement shone through her work with the YWCA. Because Morgan embraced the Chinese-American community with an uncommon sensitivity for the needs of Chinatown, an amazing architectural achievement was created. It reflected the emergence of a distinct Chinese-American cultural perspective. The '20s and '30s were a time when Chinese-American social, cultural, and political identity were borne out of interactions with the broader society and a desire to create a community with sustainability and integrity. The Morgan-designed YWCA building is an iconic institution that celebrates the spirit of those collaborative times." Ibid.

named due to their association with the Blue Rider group of Munich Expressionists), and introduced their work to American audiences.[20] Eaton bought a Klee, her first acquisition.

Eaton was impressed by Scheyer's accomplishments and commitment. She invited Scheyer to her studio and showed her paintings. "She must have been in her early forties. She was German ... an artist, a poet, a painter herself. She had gone to Oxford." Scheyer's recognition and support meant a lot. "Galka was so enthusiastic about my work ... that she attacked my father for letting me ... waste my time, standing on my feet in a department store ... wasting my life on transportation."

Through a friend of a friend, Eaton was introduced to Lloyd Rollins, joint director of the de Young Museum and the Legion of Honor in San Francisco.

> He was young and full of ideas. In fact, I introduced him to Galka, and he had a big show of the Blue Four at the de Young Museum. They [Lloyd and Galka] came to blows a little bit, because she wanted to have one picture very high up and another picture low down, below the eye level, and another one at the ceiling ... diagonal movement on the walls.

Scheyer was clearly full of ideas, also. The standard museum eye-level installation, however, was not a convention Rollins felt he could challenge.

> I was very instrumental in Galka meeting people, and yes, she for me. You see, our lives were interwoven. They continued to be interwoven. And she would come down on the weekends [to Palo Alto] to recover from her wild life lecturing.

After meeting Eaton, Rollins offered, "Marjorie, if you go and give up being a stylist at this department store and settle down for three years and paint, I'll give you a show at the Legion of Honor." The offer was just what Eaton needed.

Eaton drove down to Taos and joined her friend, painter Katie Skeele. She saw "the most beautiful" Indian—"Leonardo da Vinci was right there in his face"—and asked him to pose for her. "Katie gave me some canvas, stretched a canvas for me, good canvas, and said, 'You can have my paints, but you can't have my brushes.'" So Eaton painted her first painting of Juan Mirabal with her fingertips. A friendship grew. She shared her arts knowledge with Mirabal, who would come to paint indigenous experience with a modernist interpretation and become known as one of three Taos Pueblo painters.

Eaton's favorite work, *Paulita Mirabal*, was done in Taos. Other Taos works include the oil paintings *Taos Girl, Corn Mother, A Dream, Juan Braiding*, and numerous drawings and watercolors.

At the end of 1931, Eaton submitted art for the juried Sixth Annual Exhibition of the San Francisco Society of Women Artists at the Legion of Honor. This exhibition included paintings by invited New York artists. Eaton's painting *Blue Lakes* had good company,

---

20 Galka Scheyer (1889–1945), who continued to have a close relationship with Eaton, is a complex art figure. See Tell, Darcy. "The Art Lover: Galka Scheyer's Higher Calling." *East of Borneo* Dec. 2, 2010. eastofborneo. org/articles/the-art-lover-galka-scheyers-higher-calling. In a 1936 letter from Scheyer to the artists, she reminded them that "the Blue Four was founded ... to share the spirit embodied in these works and to get away from art dealers."

including a Mary Cassatt, Agnes Pelton, and *Frida and Diego Rivera* by "Senora Frieda Rivera" of Mexico City.[21]

Eaton painted in Taos for three years. Rollins gave her a show at the Legion of Honor in 1932, featuring two rooms, one of drawings and one of paintings.

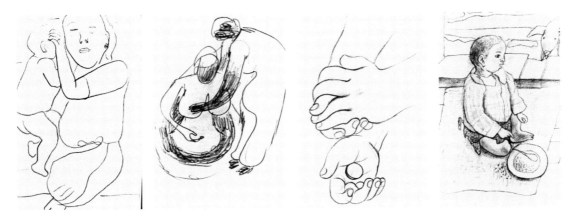

Marjorie Eaton pencil sketches from Mexico around 1935. In Mexico, Eaton made numerous line drawings of children and mothers, including *Five Indian Children, Concha and Baby, Xavier Eating Beans with Pig*. She got so involved drawing Xavier eating beans that she didn't notice how much he was eating—and he spent a very uncomfortable night. Eaton also captured the birth ritual in a sequence of gesture drawings that caught split-second actions, such as *Midwife Giving Carmen Her First Bath in Herbs After Birth*. She loved children, always wanted one. She drew them all the time.

Then Eaton left Taos and went to New York, although she really had intended to go to Europe to meet Klee, Kandinsky, and Jawlensky. "[I] had letters to them, and Hitler came into power in '33 and nobody was going there, you know." So she went to the Art Students League, studied with Hans Hofmann, and that's when "I met Louise Nevelson and I met Arshile Gorky and I worked with him … and I knew Diego Rivera already. I introduced him to Louise."[22] That year, 1933, Eaton and Nevelson came to share an apartment, with Rivera and Kahlo living above them. Nevelson worked a bit on murals with Rivera. Eaton learned new fresco techniques.

> He [Diego] invited me to come to Mexico to work with him there. So I did go to Mexico and spent three years there … painting. I used to take my work once a year to Diego, and he would

---

21 While earlier generation artists, like Impressionist painter Mary Cassatt (1844–1926), were well known, both visionary painter Agnes Pelton (1881–1961) and expressive painter Frida Kahlo (1907–1954) would only become widely recognized much later. Also exhibited were artworks by Claire Von Falkenstein and Lucretia Van Horn from Berkeley, Elizabeth Norton, Palo Alto, and Dorr Bothwell, San Diego.

22 First Generation (Deanna Bartels, Betty Estersohn, and Joan Valdes). *Marjorie Eaton*. Creative Women Over Seventy Series. California History Center, De Anza College, 1977. Video. Their timely research moved past stereotypes, including ageism. Interview filmed in 1976 at Eaton's adobe in Los Altos.

look at my sketches and my paintings. … There was never any patronage. … He just treated me as an equal. It was fantastic. … I went away to an obscure village, Pahuatlan, in the country, and lived there for a year with the … very poor people and the Indians…. All the young painters asked me to help them. … I did all that I could. … I came back, finally … and wept. I [was sad] to leave Mexico.[23]

Although after her father's divorce Eaton chose to live with her stepmother Edith, she ultimately wanted a space apart. In 1939, adjacent to the Briones house, with construction labor from Mexico, Eaton started building her own adobe house. The design honored the Briones home site, while combining her own ideas, giving a nod to Picasso, and employing modernist architect Gregory Ain. The home was built with adobe bricks handmade on site, the theater of action reminiscent of the manual labor for the Briones adobe almost a century earlier. Ain designed the home on a diagonal, based on Pablo Picasso drawings held by Eaton's friend, Galka Scheyer. All the adobe bricks had angles to them: a joining of heart and art.[24] The hillside became the amphitheatre; the house, a stage. Her home highlighted a large Mirabal mural. Despite long absences due to her subsequent acting career, she resided there until she died.

Eaton used the big house (the original Briones home plus later expansions) as her home base when she lived in New York and Southern California, working in film and on stage, including Broadway plays. Her film career included roles in *Anna and the King of Siam* (1946), *Mary Poppins* (1964), and *Street Music* (1981). During long absences, she rented out her new adobe, at one point to future U.S. senator Alan Cranston. One writer lived there for many years rent-free.

Eaton's colony never had a name. Its true years as an artist community began around 1941, when Eaton invited artist Lucretia Van Horn, who was having a difficult time in her later years, to come visit. She never left. Invited by Edith Eaton, the Nakatas, a Japanese-American family who had been interned, stayed in the cottage that had been the chicken coop for a decade after the war. The colony grew from Eaton's friendships and generosity, in part the result of a convivial sequence of dinners, visits short and long, events, and ultimately, architectural expansion. Some artists lived in the big house, which spanned the art vs. craft divide with décor that included painted furniture by Arthur and Lucia Mathews, who brought the spirit of the Arts and Crafts movement to Northern California in the early 1900s. Some stayed for years.

---

[23] Ibid.

[24] See "Marjorie Eaton," Staying Visible, op. cit. Estersohn interview, op. cit.
"The house I live in now … we started it in 1939 … and I went down with the first plans [for the house] to visit Galka [in Los Angeles]. … Hella Hammid was there, a girl of 17, who was mounting all the drawings by Picasso that were under her [Hella's] bed … Picasso sent all the drawings to Galka. Galka had arranged a show at the Stendahl Gallery [in Los Angeles] of the Guernica … These drawings were just in a box … beautiful drawings for the Guernica. They had never been matted, and Hella Hammid was mounting them. … And Gregory [Gregory Ain designed and built Eaton's house] came down … to look at my [house] plans. Gregory was so excited over these [Picasso] drawings with that diagonal thrust running through them—that that [along with a pre-existing planting of almond trees] started the thrust in my house. The Picasso drawings inspired Gregory … so that all the [adobe] bricks that had to be made for the house had angles through them. …
"Archipenko [the sculptor] might have been teaching at Mills [College] . … I knew him. … Hofmann, Schoenberg. … Oh yes! It was very alive."

Things were not always rosy. Consuelo Cloos, painter and opera singer, was so difficult, Eaton had a separate cottage built for her by a master carpenter from New York. It was essentially one huge room on poles, over to one side of the big house, and three-storied in back. Mosaicist Thomas Hunt came in 1956 and lived at different times in the big house and in a cottage at the rear of the compound (the Nakatas' former chicken coop-cum-cottage became his studio). Hunt took care of maintenance, did all the cooking after Edith's stroke, and grew into a devoted collaborator. He became the executor of Eaton's estate when she died.

Marjorie Eaton with one of her many godchildren. Photo by Hella Hamid, whom Eaton met in 1939.

Susan (Cox) Kirk, who grew up spending summers and holidays with her family at "the ranch," remembers the apricot and almond orchards, the aromas from Aunt Edith's fabulous cooking, dinners at the Arts and Crafts table, the music room with grand piano, the five fireplaces, the imposing wood staircase, and the gardens. She depicts a bohemian Marjorie seemingly at odds with her Victorian stepmother Edith. "Edith, San Francisco's leading couturier, traveled to Europe for fabrics every other year with large steamer trunks. Often Marjorie went along. Dr. Eaton had run off with his nurse, leaving Marjorie and Edith to fend together. Marjorie always strove for her father's acceptance. Her deep longing affected her trajectory in life." Kirk's father and Marjorie were raised side by side since the age of 12. Together, they took care of Edith in her wheelchair years. "For them, it was all about people," Kirk reminisces. "So many gathered around that table— artists, politicians, writers, family, friends—and held stimulating conversations about the times. I was raised to connect with people." Decades later Eaton told Kirk she envied her life raising two children, and called it "the real work." For Eaton, who had no siblings or children, the colony and the life she chose in the theatre after 1940 provided more than community. "I created a family," she declared in First Generation's artful documentary video of Eaton.[25]

In terms of architectural history, Eaton repurposed and built on the Juana Briones house, which had been modified by the previous owner; Briones herself had built on what appeared to be portions of an earlier structure, possibly Gorgonio's adobe house. The sequence hints at the repurposing cycles that flourished in the 20th century, when artists and other creative people took over neglected or ill-functioning architectural forms, often in

25 First Generation video, op. cit. Colony observations were also provided by Tom Hunt.

undesirable neighborhoods, and turned them into art spaces, re-envisioning what is possible.

It is easy for a multidisciplinary artist like Eaton, working in different geographies, to slip through the art-historical cracks. Eaton has not been featured in Maurine St. Gaudens' four-volume book *Emerging from the Shadows; A Survey of Women Artists in California, 1860–1960* because she painted primarily in Taos and Mexico, not in California. However, growing research places Eaton with the husband-and-wife team, architect Rudolph Schindler and activist Pauline Gibling Schindler, and father-and-son photographers Edward Weston and Brett Weston, at salons in Los Angeles and at Eaton's ranch. They belonged to a modernist coterie that exchanged ideas and contacts in the arts and architecture and led educational, labor, and social movements.[26] As editor of the Carmel-based progressive weekly *The Carmelite* in the late 1920s, Pauline Schindler had featured photographer Dorothea Lange on one of her magazine covers.

Eaton and her friend Pauline Schindler both had ideas regarding architecture, and offer less-discussed perspectives on architectural goals and purposes. Pauline Schindler had worked with social and political activist Jane Addams in Chicago's Hull House,[27] a successful center for social reform that provided arts-related and other opportunities for immigrants and the working poor. The continued influence of Addams' progressive communal philosophy found expression in Schindler House, aka Kings Road House (1922). This Southern California modernist architectural icon created by the Schindlers was an experiment in communal living, serving as an artistic salon and left-wing meeting house. While suitable as a work and social hub, it was not a great living environment. Galka Scheyer lived there briefly in 1931. After Rudolph's death in 1953, Pauline made changes for comfort and aesthetics, including audaciously painting her side of the communal house pink.[28]

---

26 Researcher John Crosse has been piecing together a story of the deeply intertwined lives of the Weston and Schindler families, who first met when Pauline Schindler began teaching at the Walt Whitman School in 1921 in Los Angeles ("The Schindlers and the Westons and the Walt Whitman School and Connections to Sarah Bixby Smith and Paul Jordan-Smith." Southern California Architectural History. June 22, 2013. http://socalarchhistory.blogspot.com/2013/06/the-schindlers-and-westons-and-walt.html). Crosse links articles on mutual friends and relationships, of which Marjorie Eaton is a significant one. Eaton and architect R. M. Schindler were close personal friends. Schindler and the de Young Museum's Director Lloyd Rollins met at Eaton's ranch in 1931, which eventually led to an architecture show of Schindler in 1933, at the same time as a photo exhibition with Edward Weston, Ansel Adams, Imogen Cunningham et al, at the de Young. Pauline Schindler was also a very close friend with Eaton. Crosse is at work on a book, *The Schindlers and the Westons: An Avant-Garde Friendship*.

27 Hull House was founded in 1889 by Ellen Gates Starr (1859–1940) and Jane Addams (1860–1935). Addams, a prominent Progressive Era reformer, co-founded the ACLU and was the first American woman to win the Nobel Peace Prize.

28 After studying California modernist architecture, a student declared, "It all looks the same." The differences in valuing systems struck me. As a student of ideas in the arts, I long for a fuller picture of California modernist architecture, of people involved both beforehand and afterwards in making a design not just impressive, but also functional and relevant—from early decisions like site choice to making a finished design radiate and breathe a personal or group identity. Briones and Edith and Marjorie Eaton made decisions that imbued the ranch with character, life, and history—a unique California architecture and living legacy to remember.

Pauline Schindler's own vision had a resonance with the family-like colony that Eaton would build:

> One of my dreams is to have, some day, a little joy of a bungalow, on the edge of the woods and mountains near a crowded city, which shall be open just as some people's hearts are open, to friends of all classes and types. I should like it to be as democratic a meeting-place as Hull House where millionaires and laborers, professors and illiterates, the splendid and the ignoble, meet constantly together.[29]

Artists Patricia Rodriguez and Marjorie Eaton in the exhibition *Staying Visible, The Importance of Archives* in 1981. Rodriguez, from San Francisco, resonated well with Eaton—both created art that was cultural and emotional, and both were activists. Rodriguez propelled Mujeres Muralistas, a group of Chicana/Latina artists in the Mission District that pioneered large-scale, woman-painted outdoor murals in the 1970s, when the mural tradition was overwhelmingly male. Their first mural was on a garage door in their alley—now well known as Balmy Alley. Twenty years later, the spectacular mural *Maestrapeace* (1994) turned the San Francisco Women's Building into one of the city's most distinctive and memorable architectural statements—educational, inspirational, and meaningful to the community. The multicultural, multigenerational collaboration of seven women included one of the Mujeres Muralistas, Irene Pérez. Both murals are prime examples of rethinking and repurposing. Photo (detail): Helen Carlisle Fleming.

---

29 Sweeney, Robert. "Life at Kings Road: As It Was 1920–1940." *The Architecture of RM Schindler*. Eds. Elizabeth A.T. Smith and Michael Darling. New York: Harry N. Abrams, 2001, p. 87. Exh. cat. Interesting observations about Pauline Schindler and the painting of her side of the house pink can be found in Lawson, Thomas. "Rhapsody in Pink: Stephen Prina Prints." *East of Borneo* April 11, 2013. eastofborneo.org/articles/rhapsody-in-pink-stephen-prina-paints

Other Eaton contacts include the Mexican muralists José Clemente Orozco and David Alfero Siqueiros, speaker/writer Jidda Krishnamurti, and artists and activists Henrietta Shore, Beatrice Wood, and Tina Modotti. Working with Scheyer, Eaton built a substantial contemporary art collection. At the time she bequeathed it to the Oakland Museum of Art, it was valued at approximately $2 million.

Eaton, born elite with a silver spoon in her mouth, lived relatively simply, but she traversed borders and supported diverse aesthetics morally, financially, and across cultural boundaries of social or economic status, gender, and ethnicity. "Try not to stop until something stops you."[30]

Shaping New Creative Environments

When I knew Eaton in the early 1980s, she was still running a small international arts colony from her property. Imagine the scene: Wisteria blooms from century-old vines blowing across the tile floors, piling near Briones' old adobe and redwood walls; Eaton, a slight woman with a dramatic air, playing host to a diverse and lively array of artists and others. Some, like Nevelson, would come and stay for a month; others, like artist Lucretia Van Horn, lived there many years. Mirabal visited from Taos. Photographer Imogen Cunningham came and took photographs of the ranch. An opera singer, an African American playwright, a French harlequin, and other artists lived on site in the early '80s. Salon-type events were a regular occurrence.

Kirk, a jazz singer who lived in the house on and off from 1945 to 1993, hosted elegant dinners and staged concerts. She recalled visits from notables across all fields, including scientist Linus Pauling, author Wallace Stegner, entrepreneur Steve Jobs, and the Palo Alto City Council. The Women's Heritage Museum (WHM), founded in Palo Alto by Briones biographer McDonnell, arranged with Kirk to conduct public tours at the ranch, telling the history and imagining what life was like there. With such tours, hundreds of local school children were able to get a flavor of the house's colorful history and its female visionary lead characters.[31] For decades, away from the confines of rigid systems, creative people developed new insights at the Briones/Eaton ranch on the Palo Alto hilltop.

Empowering People with "Thread Knowledge": Consuelo Jimenez Underwood

Contemporary artist Consuelo Jimenez Underwood wove baskets in 1971–1973 in Los Angeles as a young mother, having read a children's book about Dat So La Lee (ca. 1829–1925, Nevada), one of the last great Native American (Washoe) basket weavers. Understanding basketry allowed Underwood an easy transition to other textile arts, including weaving. Working with fiber to convey concepts sparked her creative process.

---

30 First Generation video, op. cit.

31 McDonnell, who started the WHM in 1985 and was its executive director for 10 years, envisioned the organization covering the California world. The WHM later moved to San Francisco to reach a wider audience, and changed to an international focus, becoming the International Museum of Women (IMOW), then merging to become the Global Fund for Women.

In 2005, her solo exhibition at Moviemiento de Arte y Cultura Latino Americana (MACLA) in San José, centered on *Tortillas in Basket* constructed at her nearby Cupertino studio: "The tortilla baskets celebrate the survival of indigenous culture."

Underwood's life and art span border issues and three cultures. She grew up crossing the U.S.–Mexico border, starting in 1949 soon after she was born in Sacramento, California.

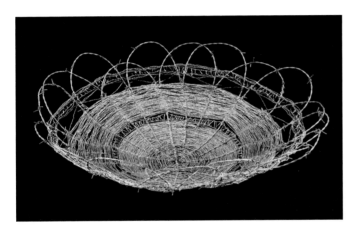

Undocumented Tortilla Basket, 2008. Barbed wire, aluminum wire, 9.5"x29" diameter.

Her mother, born in 1906, was a first-generation Californian, whose ancestral family had a connection with the Tarahumara of northwestern Mexico, the people who run long distances. It is from her maternal side that Consuelo draws "tenacity and strength of will." Her father, from Jalisco, was one of the first braceros during World War II. His mother was a full-blooded Huichol who married a Mexican and lived and worked on a hacienda in Jalisco, Mexico. Since she was never permitted to speak in her native tongue, Underwood's father never learned Huichol. Years later, when Underwood was a very young child, it was her father who introduced her to weaving and taught her the magic and mystery of life. He inspired Underwood with "songs and stories, where forces like wind and fire were main characters." While it is with her Huichol grandmother that Underwood connects, she never met her. Honoring her Huichol grandmother and all the Amerindian anonymous woman elders who wove with a backstrap loom, Underwood vowed in the 1970s, early on her artistic path, to always make art with a textile process or material. She insisted on focusing her artistic studies on learning how to spin, dye and weave with thread.

"I learned three ways of seeing and understanding the world—the English, Spanish and Amerindian, all very distinct." Underwood has spoken about the past, her Amerindian connections, survival

Tortillas in Basket, 2005. Reed, silk, corn leaves, thread, 20"x5' diameter. Part of her exhibition entitled *Tortillas, Chiles, and Other Border Things* at MACLA that commented on the "true American food that has survived 500 years of colonization— the *tortilla de maiz*. In 1992, the tortilla outsold 'white' bread in the U.S. That is incredible, when you consider that the tortilla was invented by the Amerindians."

skills, and the mixing of peoples and cultures. "There was no border in California, just two little stalls at the border crossing at Mexicali/Calexico."

Recalling the Chinese, Underwood recounts:

> They go way back. It was difficult for them in Mexico and the United States [due to the Chinese Exclusion Act]. In the late 1880s, they were sent back to China. Some were sent to Yaqui Land [the fertile valley on the banks of the Yaqui River in the Sonoran Desert]. They have burial grounds there. So there are Chinese descendants in Yaqui Land.

Underwood's husband, electrical engineer Dr. Marcos Underwood, is a Yaqui member of the Pascua Yaqui Nation in Tucson, Arizona. The Underwood family participates annually in the spring and fall rituals in Yaqui Land.

Consuelo Jimenez Underwood, *Undocumented Border Flowers*, 2009. Fiber, 17'x24'x5". Wall installation, Triton Museum of Art, Santa Clara. "My artwork is intended to alert the public about the devastating and irreversible environmental chaos that the US/MX border is creating on our southern homelands. My fear is that soon we will require even our state flowers to acquire proper documentation if they wish to grow on both sides of the border. Yikes!"

While others built an arts colony in Palo Alto or a Chicano movement in San José, Underwood worked the fields. She knows many would like to forget the borders and the struggles. Instead, she loves large walls as creative opportunities to rethink artificial divisions, see a larger picture, and imagine a more humane world where we don't need road signs warning of families running across the highway. Through her large, colorful and inviting fiber art installations, she has honored a strong connection with the land and living things, and countered the human tendency to use architecture and walls to create divisions, like the scar on our southern border.

Based in Cupertino since 1980, Underwood became a professor at San José State University. She went on to develop and head the university's Fiber/Textile Area for 20 years (1989–2009), where she took on the recurring arts vs. crafts division in the art world and empowered people with "thread knowledge." Respected as a star educator and internationally known for her fiber art, Underwood created a provocative and evocative solo exhibition of multiple wall installations in 2013 at the Triton Museum of Art in Santa Clara, entitled *Consuelo Jimenez Underwood: Welcome to Flower-Landia.*

San Jose Mercury News reporter Joe Rodriguez reviewed the 2013 Triton Museum exhibition. He noted how Underwood spoke with the Santa Clara University students: "I've learned the power of generational knowledge," she said. "When you pass knowledge to the younger generation, not everyone gets it. But if one, two, or three get it, then we won."

Winning connects with opening minds and hearts and, at its most basic, with survival for the marginalized. María Ester Fernández, curator of the *Flower-Landia* exhibition, elaborates:

> [Underwood's] indigenous heritage gave her the strength and purpose to infiltrate, play the game and survive. Trained as a child to cross borders real and psychological, Underwood walks between opposing issues. Living in the middle as an infiltrator, she has learned to navigate contested territories: as a picker in the fields, as a student in school, and as an artist using indigenous weaving tradition as fine art. This exhibition is an attempt to recreate that journey, to relive the tension of a highly volatile border region embodied by a young girl, and to re-imagine the border as a place where the spirit can roam free.

Regarding Underwood's self-portrait, *Tenured Petals*, Fernández adds:

> Ten is a magical number; the age at which Underwood realized that as long as she played the game and learned the rules; she could win. At ten, she created a life plan to free the spirit. It also touches on the artist's academic career, having achieved tenure at San José State University and retained her identity as a weaver after much pressure to succumb to a more traditional fine art practice.

Underwood is the subject of an individual profile that includes discussion of her stunning *Borderline Encounter #1*, a performance in the ocean.[32] Underwood's influence continues to grow. A 2014 Artist Laureate for Silicon Valley Creates, she has been interviewed by the Smithsonian Institution, had major installations in Reno, Nevada in 2015, and created

---

32 The performance was commissioned for an exhibition by MACLA and photographed by SJSU Professor Robin Lasser. See "Consuelo Jimenez Underwood: Thread Art Warrior."

a very large wall piece on site for a 2016 exhibition at The Textile Museum at George Washington University in Washington, D.C. Underwood was delighted to take her art to where they make policy, the political home of this nation. But the first six months of 2015 she dedicated to weaving a new *rebozo* (shawl) "for the *Virgen*."

Rebozos For Our Mothers, 2013. Woven wire, linen, silk, rayon, gold and silver threads. Left to right, *Mother Mundane, Virgen de Guadalupe, Mother Earth, Mother Moon,* and *Mother Ocean.*

Virgen de Guadalupe, 70"x20" (detail), 2013

Mother Moon, 70"x20" (detail), 2013

A Spiral Through Time

Underwood's baskets remind us of the workload women have carried, and her one-of-a-kind woven forms bear witness to the ongoing creativity, energy and innovation of Silicon Valley, and her unique spirit. Her gigantic fabric flowers also evoke spirit, transcendence, as well as the too long ignored, real world struggle to sustain natural habitats. Following Underwood's art and career yields stories that illuminate the realms of border crossing and take us on a beautiful spiral through time, starting with the early art of Ohlone women, through the intercultural appreciation and courage of Briones, followed by the expansive cultural and art-world connections of Eaton, up to today. Underwood's fiber art raises ongoing questions about local cultural development, about the nature and challenges of borders—geographic, generational, academic, social, and in the art world—and about imaginative travel through time. "I need the old ways." She speaks of the "ancient ones" as if they were intimate family members.

A convivial vision comes to my mind of a wonderful, intergenerational circle of women. All are admiring, perhaps with smartphones at hand, Underwood's exquisite woven *rebozos* for the "ancient ones," the first weavers: Consuelo with Dat So La Lee, Juana Briones and Marjorie Eaton; Angela Colos with Jean La Marr—sharing tales, touching the weave, nodding in approval, and smiling—a natural gathering of community in Silicon Valley, as it was in the beginning with the ancestral Ohlone.

Returning to real time, construction proceeds on the huge, synchrotron-like Apple Computer headquarters—a circular building echoing the Ohlone tupentak meeting space. The Cupertino site will have 85% open space, trees, an old barn, and a flavor of the agricultural past. Likewise, companies, organizations, educational institutions, and cities are choosing building sites with a hilltop or coastal view or the advantages of a nearby major transit artery—a good mix of art, technology, and community.

The dark, streamlined buses that ply routes from San Francisco to Silicon Valley bring workers who, like Briones before them, weave together cultural experiences, employment opportunities, and creative styles. Yet these fleets of black-windowed shuttles cause their own disruption and resentment. As in centuries past, travel, trade, and immigration have built new workforces and economies, brought class struggles and injustices, and engaged new ideas.

Our journey began with local indigenous people, examining changes in Ohlone art and lives in relation to socioeconomic and political changes that continue to this day. What do various creative—and caring—communities feel like in terms of architecture, institutions, and informal get-togethers? How do we connect with contemporary transmissions of values held most dear? These are ongoing questions that thoughtful leaders must address.

Additional information about the Ohlone and Indian tribes in California:
Field, Les, Alan Leventhal, Dolores Sanchez, and Rosemary Cambra. "Ohlone Tribal Revitalization Movement, A Perspective from the Muwekma Costanoan/ Ohlone Indians of the San Francisco Bay." *California History* 71 (1992) : 412–431.
Lightfoot, Kent. *Indians, Missionaries, and Merchants: The Legacy of Colonial Encounters on the California Frontiers*. University of California, Berkeley, 2005.

Additional information about Juana Briones life and times:
McDonnell, Jeanne Farr. *Juana Briones of Nineteenth-Century California*. University of Arizona Press, 2008.
California Historical Society, San Francisco. *Juana Briones y Su California, Pionera, Fundadora, Curandera*. 2014. Exhibition; californiahistoricalsociety.org/exhibitions/juana-briones/exhibit/. Includes Kristine

Samuelson's video of curator Al Camarillo narrating at the Briones site as the demolition loomed; and artist Rebeca Méndez's *Of the Earth 1*, a five-minute video portrait of the land where Briones' spirit resides.

Additional information about Marjorie Eaton and "the Ranch" arts colony:
Estersohn, Betty, Jan Rindfleisch, and Deanna Bartels, "Marjorie Eaton." Also, Holzgrafe, Carol. "Consuelo Cloos." *Staying Visible: The Importance of Archives*, Ed. Jan Rindfleisch. Euphrat Gallery, 1981.
Information about Tom Hunt: Holzgrafe, Carol. "Mosaics." *Art, Religion, Spirituality*. Ed. Jan Rindfleisch. Euphrat Gallery, 1982.
Kirk, Susan. "Growing up in 'History.'" PAST Newsletter, Vol. 21, No. 2. Fall 2007. Palo Alto Stanford Heritage (PAST).
Mayfield, Signe. *Marjorie Eaton: Paintings and Drawings from the 1930s*. Palo Alto Cultural Center. 1992. Exhibition catalogue.

Information about Consuelo Jimenez Underwood:
Rodriguez, Joe. "Artist weaves flowery tapestry of hope from thorny U.S.–Mexico border." *San Jose Mercury News*. October 29, 2013. mercurynews.com/breaking-news/ci_24412624/artist-weaves-flowery-tapestry-hope-from-thorny-u-s-mexico-border
Hernandez, Ester. Text panels for *Flower-landia* exhibition. Triton Museum of Art, Santa Clara. 2013.
Perez, Laura. "Threads." *Craft in America*. PBS. KQED, San Francisco. May 11, 2012. video.pbs.org/video/2230109016/
"Threads," *SPARK**. PBS. KQED, San Francisco. June 2003. Television. kqed.org/arts/programs/spark/profile.jsp?essid=4302

Mary Parks Washington: Motivated by History

Mary Parks Washington's art and actions interweave her Atlanta roots with her life in Silicon Valley. She stands out for her caring, gracious, and respectful ways, and her gift for remembering people from different walks of life, particularly those who have fought for social justice. I can only give a taste of the full Washington story—her decades of teaching, honors, and community service in Silicon Valley.

Washington's character and impact have been all-encompassing, reaping praise from artist/activist Ruth Tunstall Grant:

> She is one of our most prominent activists for African Americans in the arts and an amazing artist herself. I have the greatest reverence for all she has done. She's not looking for something [in return]. It's who she is—the best advocate for humanity, rising to do better, do good, make an impact for humanity, all the while thinking outside the box.

A Fighter for Civil Rights

Washington has an impressive activist and art background, including a M.A. from SJSU, independent study at the Art Students League in New York and at the University of Mexico. She studied at Spelman College with sculptor Elizabeth Profit and muralist Hale Woodruff, and then began to work at Black Mountain College in 1946, two years after the college accepted its first black students. There she established lifetime friendships with renowned artists Ruth Asawa, Gwendolyn Knight Lawrence, and Jacob Lawrence.

When Washington visited Ruth Asawa's School for the Arts in San Francisco, she recalls, "the janitor put his broom down and showed me the school—he was so proud of that school. I never thought about janitors before. I got interested in janitors because of her." So Washington did some sculptures, "sprayed some brooms gold," and did honor janitors with special skits at two schools. "I wanted to make kids aware. They throw paper on the ground and say, 'the janitor will pick it up.'"

Washington was featured in *Black Artists on Art*, Samella S. Lewis and Ruth Waddy's 1970 book. Locally, she advocated for naming San José's main library for Dr. Martin Luther King, Jr., featuring a Martin Luther King Room. With the San José Chapter of Links, Incorporated, she participated in the first Freedom Train from San José to San Francisco.

"In those days, to celebrate Dr. Martin Luther King, Jr. Day, there was a 7:00 a.m. breakfast in San José, with notables present. I made the Links banner for the march down Market Street in San Francisco." Washington has a scrapbook of the program and activities. She recalls people carrying paper bags with stains, mindful of the days when people carried chicken on a journey. San José's Freedom Train in 2015 was the last official ride of the nation's more than two dozen Freedom Trains commemorating King's legacy, the march from Selma to Montgomery 50 years ago, and the fight for equal rights for all races. San José's Freedom Train lasted three decades. Washington recalls trains from the past:

> Blacks couldn't eat [in the dining car] on trains except at a table with a curtain around it. Most blacks couldn't afford to buy the train's expensive lunch, and others didn't want to be behind a

curtain. When I finished high school in 1942, I was given a trip to Arkansas … changed three different trains. I ate behind the curtain. They had to set up a separate frame to surround my table. You know we [blacks] always had the first car [behind the coal car]. On a hot day, we caught the ashes and cinders coming in the window.

An Advocate for Equality in the Arts

With her congenial and enterprising manner, Washington has energetically collaborated with many people in building arts community. In the 1960s and '70s, Washington strategized with painter John De Vincenzi to guide and renew the San José Art League. They provided counsel as the art community branched out to found the San José Museum of Art and the Triton Museum of Art in Santa Clara.[1] Their archives tell many a tale.

Jacob Lawrence at Genesis, Sanctuary for the Arts—Washington seated to right of podium. Photo: Charles Alexander.

Washington and De Vincenzi radiated "community friendly." Washington took welcoming a step further and tapped the valley's diversity. At one point Washington recommended artist George Rivera to run the Art League. "John said he was too young, but I said, 'Try him,'" recounts Washington. Due to his success at the Art League, Rivera later became a much-loved director of the Triton Museum, lauded for invigorating community participation by featuring artists of diverse backgrounds and expanding the museum's youth and community programs.

In the 1990s, visionary artist Jacob Lawrence was exhibiting at the de Young in San Francisco. Washington wanted to give him a meaningful and memorable introduction to the community at a South Bay reception. Washington had been friends with Lawrence and painter Gwendolyn Knight Lawrence since their days at pacesetting Black Mountain College in North Carolina, where Lawrence was an instructor, and Washington a 1946 summer session student. She convinced Ruth Tunstall Grant to hold the reception in downtown San José at her Genesis, Sanctuary for the Arts, at 40 N. First Street, the studio and arts space Tunstall Grant founded to bring together different cultures.

---

1 Washington was a board member of the Art League, built up by a group of SJSU instructors, one of San José's first art organizations. She remembers how they met in De Vincenzi's home or banks until they could find a building (a two-story Victorian), how she supported George Rivera for director and how he brought so much to the arts, how they held what she believes is the first auction of instructors' art to raise funds—initially called a "Grab Bag" till she came up with a more respectful title, "Collectors' Choice." She remembers some members were interested in having a city museum, and how James Morgan separated off to start the Triton Museum because he wanted his art collection to be automatically included, something they didn't think right.

Using her contacts from years as an art chair of Links, Washington launched a program to spotlight Lawrence and his paintings, and provide a full, rich community experience. "The place was packed." Merylee Shelton, a communications instructor at San José City College, worked with a group of students on a spoken-word performance related to his paintings. Jamaican artist Tukula Ntama exhibited also; there were large murals and decorated wooden chairs. The reception went on all night, "went way above and beyond," including not just presentations, but also African art and materials available for purchase.

Washington has continued to enlighten us on exceptional artists who deserve more recognition, including Edmonia Lewis (ca. 1844–1907). Lewis' skills, perseverance, and success as a classically trained American artist working in Rome, as well as her views and content as a woman of color, prompted Washington to support her. Lewis, who identified as African American and Ojibway/Chippewa, was the first internationally known artist to travel to San José and exhibit there. As a result, three of her classic figurative marble sculptures were purchased in 1873: *Lincoln*, bought by the Friends of San José Library, and *Awake* and *Asleep*, purchased by San José leader and suffragist Sarah Knox Goodrich, who later donated them to the library. Lewis had been Goodrich's houseguest for a week during the 1873 exhibition.

Edmonia Lewis, *Asleep*, 1871. Marble. California Room, San José Public Library. In 2012, Washington was the keynote speaker at the Dr. Martin Luther King, Jr. Library in San José's celebration of the restoration and unified installation of their Edmonia Lewis sculptures.

The purchases were a big step forward for San José. Washington's dedication to promote the contributions of women and people of color to the arts are all the more remarkable in terms of the late 1800s, a time when women didn't have the right to vote and racial discrimination was rampant. In contrast, San Francisco's much-hyped 1915 Panama-Pacific International Exposition had a very limited understanding of this legacy: "Although women had executed some of the artworks within the foreign and state pavilions and the exhibit halls, of the more than one hundred commissioned structures, murals, sculptures for the main palaces, only three pieces were by women ..."[2]

A member of Friends of Edmonia Lewis, Washington has for years researched and written about Lewis and collaborated with others in studying the sculptor's life. She continues to maintain vigilance over Lewis's visibility to contemporary audiences.

> For 50 years, the three sculptures had been hidden behind a staircase in the old library. They didn't think they were anything of value. Then one was put at the top of the escalator [a dangerous position]. I got Links to pay $18,000 for three pedestals, and we had a program.[3]

Washington advocates for the accessibility of the Lewis sculptures, which are currently displayed only during the restricted hours of the library's small California Room. "Imagine three big pieces wedged together," she says. The Friends would like to "get them out so the public can see them. Now one has to go through a locked door, then the Beethoven Room, then another locked door."

Helping artists on a larger scale, Washington participated in efforts to secure a visa for painter Elizabeth Catlett, a victim of McCarthy-era anti-Communist persecution, to come to the U.S. from Mexico. "[Artist] Evangeline 'EJ' Montgomery organized it. ... All of us flew down to L.A. to meet her." Montgomery lived in Oakland; Washington and other African Americans in the arts would meet at her home.

A Preserver of History

Gathering information, history, and advocating for art in a living context, with a sense of its story, is Washington's full-time passion. She emphasizes:

> It's important to know more about the struggles. ... Today the history of many of Silicon Valley's cultural institutions isn't known or easily available to the public via websites; for example, the basic history behind the San José Museum of Art [included] the tremendous arts program for children that Ruth Tunstall Grant started, [and] a film department at one time. One year I was in charge of a two-week Black on Black Film Festival. What happened to the department and the films?

Washington encourages people to donate to archives. She has contributed papers and her husband's Tuskegee Airmen pilot uniform to History San José, envisioning the uniform in a case in the historic hotel at Kelley Park, so children can learn of the heroism of this all-black group of WWII aviators. She speaks about the ongoing segregation after his service.

> After WWII, my husband left the service. A graduate of the Atlanta University School of Social Work, he found in Atlanta he could only work with black people. So he re-entered the service. We were sent to Massachusetts, New York, and Japan, before coming to San José in 1958.

---

2 Ackley, Laura A. *San Francisco's Jewel City, The Panama-Pacific International Exposition of 1915.* Heyday, 2015, p. 110.

3 Washington, Mary Parks. *The San Jose Chapter of Links, Incorporated and the San Jose Public Library System honor Mary Edmonia Lewis, sculptor...* King California Room REF CAL 730.92 LEWIS Washington. Scrapbook with photos regarding the event.

For her own "histcollages," Washington integrates old letters, bills of sale, and contracts as she paints commemorative portraits, including one of the African American activist and janitor Jacob Overton, who inspired the purchase of the Edmonia Lewis sculptures. Recalling Overton, she relates, "He influenced Mrs. Knox Goodrich to buy the two pieces *Awake* and *Asleep.* He was also a caterer and

Mary Parks Washington, *Savior of a Million Soles,* 1989. Acrylic and collage on canvas. 36"x30". Washington's late father, A.W. Parks, with his shoe repair shop.

a musician … at Brohaska's Opera House [on Santa Clara, between 2nd and 3rd] during the 1870s." Washington's Overton portrait, along with portraits by artist Joyce McEwen Crawford, was displayed in San José City Hall in 2009–10 as part of the collaborative exhibition *Hidden Heritages: Six African American Families, 1860–1920*, which portrayed the legacy of early black settlers in San José.[4]

Washington dedicated the catalog for her 1996 one-person "homecoming" exhibition in Atlanta to her father, who believed that black Atlanta had a history worth cherishing. Fortunately for us, she moved here from Atlanta and gave our Silicon Valley arts scene a history that we can also be proud of. It's difficult to imagine our lively arts community even existing without her significant contributions.

---

4 A little sense of local race relations, activism, and cultural activity at the time: Sarah Browning Knox Goodrich (1827–1903) came to California by wagon train in 1850 with her husband Dr. William J. Knox and their baby. Knox was elected state senator in 1854. In 1863, they moved to San José. At his wife's urging, Knox promoted the rights of women in the legislature, e.g. giving married women the right to dispose of their property by will without the consent of their husbands. A suffragist, Sarah founded San Jose Suffragette Association in 1869. Susan B. Anthony and Elizabeth Cady Stanton came to her house on North First Street. She was a member of the Santa Clara County Pioneer Association, the San Jose Library, the Law Library and the Santa Clara Agricultural Society.

Jacob Overton and Sarah Massey Overton, two pioneers who would build San José's African American community, married in 1869; they lived on Eighth Street. Sarah was another activist community leader. She spoke out against racial discrimination in public schools, gave strong support to the Political Equality Club of San Jose, the Garden City Women's Club of San Jose, and women's suffrage; she was 2nd vice president of the San Jose Suffrage Amendment League.

In 1876, for the country's centennial, we see stark reality in a cultural event, a celebration march. Sarah Knox wanted to march "behind the Negroes and before the Chinese," because she thought that commented on the position of women in the society. With anti-Chinese sentiment, the Chinese at that time were being stoned.

Cozetta Gray Guinn: Keeping Culturally Connected

Artist Cozetta Gray Guinn is one of the pioneers in the development of a participatory arts community in Silicon Valley. Raised in rural Arkansas, Guinn attended segregated Julius Rosenwald Elementary School. As a champion of diversity determined to work in an inclusive setting, she taught in the Cupertino Union School District at Hyde and Kennedy middle schools after she earned a M.A. in social science from San José State University.

In 1968, with her physicist husband, Isaac "Ike" Guinn, Cozetta introduced different cultural experiences to a valley teeming with white engineers. The couple established Nbari Arts, a shop and museum-quality gallery in Los Altos, begun by connecting with students at Stanford and UC Berkeley. From a modest beginning on El Camino Real, Nbari Arts has shone for four decades as a cultural resource and a business featuring imported African art, African American art, locally made clothing, and Guinn's own paintings.

"Stylized version of a real dress I have," says Guinn.

Guinn has always been an avid researcher. In 1977, while volunteering for the National Museum of Nigeria, she helped to develop a booklet, *2000 Years of Nigerian Art*. For teaching, she researched "all cultures. We did Alaska to Peru." She is fond of reminding me, "I'm a blues fan," as she speaks of her 1967 story of blues in the Fillmore, *Reflections of Blue and Better Times*. In 2005, based on found documentation, she wrote several pages on the history of St. Mark A. M. E. Zion Church on Bay Road in East Palo Alto—now in their archives.

In her various roles as an artist, educator, and exhibition curator, Guinn calls on her experience to help others see and develop communal history. She has served as a volunteer and docent for The Mexican Museum, and since 1995 has served as a volunteer docent at the de Young Museum and the Legion of Honor. Guinn proudly asserts, "I taught Sheila Pressley, now director of education at the de Young Museum." Pressley glows as she describes how Guinn "specializes in interpreting our collections of art from Africa, Oceania, and the Americas. She has introduced literally thousands of visitors to the art and culture of these rich collections. [She] is an amazingly engaging docent with a huge wealth of information at her disposal."

A longtime instructor in the Intercultural/International Studies Department at De Anza College, Guinn is also a former board member of the Euphrat Museum of Art and the California History Center. The three groups collaborated on Guinn's 1999 exhibit and catalog *In Celebration of African American Art in Northern California Since 1860*, which she curated. Guinn was also a past coordinator of the Peninsula Book Club, an African American group promoting black authors since 1983.

Guinn's biggest project, *Californians Keeping Culturally Connected*, originally envisioned in 2002 as a catalog in conjunction with an exhibit of the same title, took 10 years to complete. An updated edition is currently in the works. A labor of love, it is exemplary as a creative exploration of community connections in historical context. The artfully constructed 140-page book is like a painting. Says Guinn, "As a painter, I tell stories on canvas and on paper … [a form of] social realism. …" While her quietly interspersed art, such as *Sunday Morning at Bethel Church* (1984), propels the story, Guinn emphasizes the contributions of others. She stresses the importance of knowing both the individual cultural strands and the larger woven tapestry, pointing out that we often don't know the people who live down the street.

Californians Keeping Culturally Connected was an ambitious community, arts, and educational tool, with suggested readings, history going back almost two centuries, and a timeline that went back even further. Published in 2012 by the California History Center and Foundation at De Anza College, *Californians Keeping Culturally Connected: A window for viewing art, crafts, and memorabilia within the African American and African Diaspora* included selections from the 2002 exhibition. In both the book and the exhibition, Guinn involved the college and community, including students in "their own words;" addressed major social issues; and shared her own paintings and stories of long ago.

From Guinn's introduction:

… Soon, it was evident that within the collection there were bits of information and memorabilia historically linked, revealing that Californians were literally "holding on to" cultural history.

Participants shared things that spoke to their identities, including such items as pottery, baskets, quilts, smoothing irons, tools, photographs, musical instruments, sheet music, books, legal documents, posters, and other cultural and utilitarian objects. … One commonality was that each item within the exhibit showed how tradition, customs and values were passed along to educate, inform and keep individuals connected to their pasts.

Among the items collected were authentic bills of sale for slaves … photographs and a recently written history of a black pioneer family who came … in the mid-1850s [and the] adverse social/political climate in the Bay Area at that time … a page from a replica of the newspaper *The Black Chronicle* of July 25, 1862, which described an event wherein a young slave, Robert Smalls, stole a Confederate gunboat and turned it over to the Union Navy …

Front cover, *Californians Keeping Culturally Connected* with Guinn's *Mother's Love*, oil painting, 1979.

Guinn explained that the exhibit was intended to expand the concept of the African American experience in the United States introduced in 1963 by Langston Hughes and Milton Meltzer in their *Pictorial History of the Negro in America* by "chronologically arranging documents, photographs, and three-dimensional objects" to create "scenarios of a complex story within a given time frame."

Contributors were an important aspect of the legacy inherent in the exhibit. In addition to telling individual stories that would merge into a single story, each lender, in his or her own way, has been a significant participant in the greater history of the place called Silicon Valley.

From Guinn's epilogue:

California Keeping Culturally Connected identifies factors that, when critically viewed, explain the importance of putting together this project conveying many stories ... having a common strand, one of self-identity and what it means to be who we are. It is in part a record that validates the existence of individuals who lived and moved within the confines of the communities surrounding De Anza College in 2001. The ... memorabilia ... were communiqués dealing with social issues from the past and present. They represented a variety of themes that focused on achievements, joy, pleasure, and pride, as well as atrociousness, sadness, struggles, and the fight for justice.

Reviewing the assorted images and stories in the exhibit has given me a broader insight into the social, economic, and political state of affairs that has permeated African American life for the past 300 years. Adding a chronology of events has been helpful in allowing me to see panoramically the time and context of the pieces displayed. ... The interconnected stories of war, slavery, freedom, economics, education, labor, lynching, music, theater, art and religion.

Back cover, *Californians Keeping Culturally Connected* with Guinn's *Yoruba Woman and Child*, oil painting, 1973.

Imparting culture is second nature to Guinn. At the 2013 "Hats of Distinction" luncheon sponsored by the Peninsula Bay Area Chapter of The Links, Incorporated, she was honored for her outstanding contributions made to and for people of color.[1] The elegant woman in her vintage chic couldn't resist sharing a recipe previously published in the Nbari newsletter that has accompanied the shop since its earliest days. This warm and communal gesture is just another example of Guinn's passion for shared cultural history.

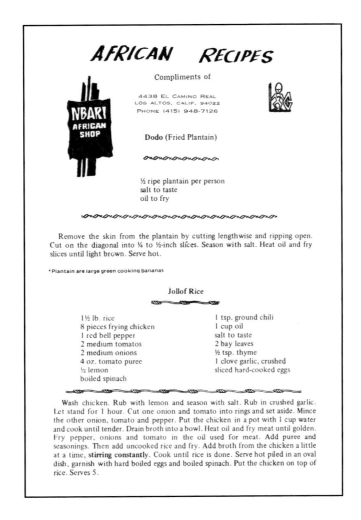

1 On April 20, 2013, participants at the "Hats of Distinction" luncheon sponsored by the Peninsula Bay Area Chapter of The Links, Incorporated recognized and honored five community leaders for their outstanding contributions made to and for people of color. More than 250 guests gathered to acknowledge Cozetta Guinn, a retired professor of African Art History and African American History at De Anza College; retired Judge LaDoris Cordell, the first African American woman to sit on the Superior Court in Northern California; Gina Sudaria, principal of Costano School; Dr. J. Renee Chapman Navarro, the University of California's first vice chancellor of diversity and outreach; and Dr. Jaqueline Copeland-Carson, USA executive director of the African Women's Development Fund. Scholarship recipient Devon Spence was also present.

Japantown San José, Jack Matsuoka, Roy and PJ Hirabayashi: Cultural Catalysts

Japantown San José has long been a catalyst for Silicon Valley art and community development. Its sense of cultural history and art and design sensibilities are reflected in preserved architecture, historical markers, thoughtful rest benches, festivals and grand community celebrations. A cultural destination just north of downtown, it is one of only three surviving Japantowns in the United States; the other two are located in Los Angeles and San Francisco. This excerpt from the exhibition *Pioneers of San Jose Japantown* illustrates its rough start:[1]

> The Japanese pioneers of San José were called the *Issei* (first generation). These immigrants were seeking an escape from their economic burdens in Japan. The agricultural industry drew them to the Santa Clara Valley in the late 1880s. As anti-Chinese exclusionary laws took their toll on the local Chinese population, white growers started to favor Japanese labor over the aging and numerically declining Chinese labor pool.

> San José's Japantown (also known as *Nihonmachi*) began in 1890 as the Valley's Japanese farming community became established. It was formed next to Heinlenville, a Chinatown that was created after the previous downtown Chinatown was a victim of arson. At one time, Heinlenville was enclosed by a high wooden fence topped with barbed wire to protect the residents and businesses from anti-Chinese elements.

I first worked on Japantown art and history with Reverend Hiroshi Abiko, minister of the San Jose Buddhist Church Betsuin, in conjunction with Euphrat Museum's 1982 exhibition *Art, Religion, Spirituality*.[2] According to Abiko, during World War II, many Japanese-American Buddhists interned in camps throughout the United States created beautiful homemade altars, often of scrap wood, in order to be able to continue their daily religious services. We exhibited one of three made by James Yoshio Kobayashi during his internment days at Poston, Arizona (1942–1945). Abiko said the fate of these altars (some quite large) varied, because it was only since the early 1970s that concerned Japanese Americans nationally began to advocate for libraries and small museums to store art, artifacts, literature, and memorabilia of pioneering Japanese in America.

Established in November of 1987, the Japanese American Museum of San Jose (JAMsj) grew out of the 1984–1986 research project by SCU professors Timothy J. Lukes (political science) and Gary Y. Okihiro (history , *Japanese Legacy: Farming and Community Life in California's Santa Clara County*, published by the California History Center in 1985.[3] Okihiro wanted a place to house the research and organized a meeting of four community

---

1 Japanese American Museum of San José website, jamsj.org/exhibit/pioneers-of-san-jose-japantown.

2 Rindfleisch, Jan. *Art, Religion, Spirituality*. Euphrat Museum, 1982, in conjunction with the exhibition. Abiko, Rev. Hiroshi. "Buddhist Home Altars." Ibid.

3 Lukes, Timothy J. and Gary Y. Okihiro. *Japanese Legacy: Farming and Community Life in California's Santa Clara Valley*. California History Center, 1985. Includes photographs by Duane Kubo, and foreword by Norman Mineta.

leaders to germinate the creation of JAMsj. The museum started in an upstairs room of the historic Issei Memorial Building, formerly the Kuwabara Hospital. In 2002, the name changed from Japanese American Resource Center/Museum (JARC/M) to JAMsj to better reflect the museum's archival focus. JAMsj now occupies the former residence of Tokio Ishikawa, M.D., two doors south of the Issei Memorial Building on North Fifth Street. In October 2010, the museum reopened after an ambitious remodeling and expansion project.

Jack Matsuoka—Fastest Pen in the West

Cartoonist Jack Matsuoka (1925–2013) lived in Japantown during his last years, sketching at community events, and regularly donating cartoons to raise funds for JAMsj. JAMsj curated a major retrospective for him in 2013, *Jack's Show—His Life and Sketches*. Artist/ activist Duane Kubo feels that "exposure to concentration camp art via Matsuoka inspired Sansei (third generation) artists to address the issue as well as expand on it. Nihonmachi Outreach Committee (NOC) did the first camp art show in the mid-'80s."[4]

For the 1986 Euphrat Museum book *CONTENT: Contemporary Issues*, we worked with Matsuoka, then editorial cartoonist for the *Pacifica Tribune*, whose works also appeared in *Hokubei Mainichi*, a Japanese daily in San Francisco, and in other Bay Area papers. An edited excerpt[5] from the article, with additional input from his daughter Emi Young, gives a feeling of the transitional times starting with World War II:

> Matsuoka grew up in Watsonville, California. One Sunday in 1943, his father was labeled a dangerous alien and taken to an internment camp in New Mexico. The rest of the family was sent to the camp ("really 'internment prison' or 'tar-paper housing' in the desolate desert") in Poston, Arizona. Matsuoka was in the first high school class to graduate from camp (1944). The education was poor. Cartooning became a way to pass the many empty hours of the day.[6]

> After graduation, Matsuoka went to the Cleveland School of Fine Arts "and was quite proud until a draft notice interrupted his training." Matsuoka served in the U.S. Military Intelligence Services in Japan; "each member of his group received a national medal from the President in 2013. The military wanted him back for another tour." His war memories include General DeWitt's "Once a Jap, always a Jap;" being denied coffee service even while in military uniform; and recalling a decorated Japanese serviceman with one arm who was denied a haircut.

> After completing his duties in MIS, Matsuoka studied Japanese history at the universities of Keio and Sophia in Tokyo. … He was beginning a career in cartooning for the newspapers in Tokyo. Matsuoka freelanced sports cartoons. He was the *only* bilingual cartoonist in Japan. He later moved to the Bay Area and began work for the *Berkeley Gazette*.

> Much of Matsuoka's work called attention to redress and reparation. Matsuoka also wrote and illustrated a book about his growing up in a relocation camp, partly motivated by the puzzlement

---

4 Personal communication with Duane Kubo. May 30, 2013.

5 Wood, Sharon and Gloria Rose Ott. "Cartoonists Garry Trudeau, Signe Wilkinson, Jack Matsuoka." in Rindfleisch, Jan. *CONTENT, Contemporary Issues*. Euphrat Museum, 1986.

6 Matsuoka, Jack. Camp II Block 211. Japan Publications, Inc., June 1974. Matsuoka, Jack. *Poston Camp II, Block 211*. Ed. Emi Young. Asian American Curriculum Project (AACP), 2003. The reissue was through the efforts of Matsuoka's daughter Emi Young. See rafu.com/2013/08/nisei-cartoonist-jack-matsuoka-dies-at-87.

of young people over his exhibits on camp life. One Arizona couple remarked that there had never been a place called Poston and suggested that some radical group must be behind his exhibit. The book, *Camp II Block 211*, is a light-humored look at an American tragedy and includes many cartoons Matsuoka had drawn in the Poston camp.

Matsuoka's comic strip *SENSEI* covered the exploits of a Nisei (second generation) teacher trying to survive in the Western world. Published in the *Hokubei Mainichi*, the main character, a Nisei teacher (*sensei* in Japanese), claimed to know all things Japanese but engaged in considerable cultural bungling.

Figures in Matsuoka's cartoons look Western, not Japanese. Matsuoka stated that he would like to feel American first, but that society refused to accept Japanese Americans as simply Americans of Japanese descent. According to his daughter, "his Asians did not have exaggerated features, whereas the Western faces had them."

Matsuoka, nicknamed the "Fastest Pen in the West," belonged to the Northern California Cartoon and Humor Association, joining one other Asian member, one black, one Latino, and just five female cartoonists. "He was also invited to join the National Cartoonists Society—his definition of success."

Matsuoka's book *Camp II Block 211* was originally published in Japan in 1974. His book *Poston Camp II, Block 211*, edited by his daughter Emi Young, a public school teacher, was published by Asian American Curriculum Project (AACP) in 2003 with a grant from the California Civil Liberties Public Education Program.[7] The new edition included sketches

Jack Matsuoka, *Executive Order 9066*, 1982. Ink, 12"x16".

paying tribute to the Nisei soldiers of World War II, photos, and an afterword by Sen. Daniel Inouye (D-Hawaii). Matsuoka and Young visited Bay Area schools and talked about his experiences, using art to educate. South Bay storyteller Megumi worked with Young to produce "Sketching Justice," a teachers' handbook to use with the book, and created a performance piece based on Matsuoka's cartoons.

Around 2010, Matsuoka participated in a teacher in-service program at the Stanford Program on International and Cross-Cultural Education (SPICE) under the direction of Dr. Gary Mukai. He came to the attention of a Salinas high school social studies teacher,

---

7 He supported Mas and Florence Hongo in their work to promote Asian American studies in our schools. Florence Hongo is president of AACP, which began locally in 1969.

Ignacio Ornelas Rodriguez, now with the Special Collections and University Archives Department of Stanford University Libraries and a doctoral candidate in history at UC Santa Cruz. Rodriguez spearheaded a City of Watsonville proclamation honoring native son Matsuoka in 2010, which in turn led to the cartoonist being honored by the California State Assembly in 2012, in conjunction with the passage of Assembly Concurrent Resolution 104 declaring February 19, 2012 a day of remembrance.

The sharing of cartoons by Matsuoka—including the Giants and 49ers sports cartoons he loved to draw, and the college sports programs with cartoon covers for Pac-10 games—was a key step to Japanese-American cultural resurgence in Silicon Valley and the Bay Area. Matsuoka's cartoons provided an accessible art form before taiko drumming and other art forms took off.

Roy and PJ Hirabayashi—Leading through Collective Intelligence

Japantown's artists, such as the indefatigable couple, Roy and PJ Hirabayashi, have helped put San José on the map through their leadership of San Jose Taiko and other endeavors.

San Jose Taiko

Taiko has a Japanese tradition in the U.S. as part of celebrations and events such as mochitsuki, the pounding of rice into cakes. Seiichi Tanaka and his San Francisco Taiko Dojo introduced it as performance art in 1968 for the Cherry Blossom Festival in San Francisco Nihonmachi (Japantown). Roy and PJ Hirabayashi pioneered taiko in a uniquely Japanese-American way. Their group, San Jose Taiko, mixed traditional rhythms of Japanese drumming with other world rhythms, including African, Brazilian, Filipino, Latin, and jazz—to "enrich the human spirit." Bridging styles, they created new dimensions in Asian American movement and music. Members composed, choreographed, designed and produced costumes, handcrafted the drums, and collectively led the group.

Photographers Curt Fukuda and Lissa Jones documented San Jose Taiko in the 1980s. Fukuda, who has also collaborated on a history of Japantown San José,[8] recalls:

> Reverend Hiroshi Abiko was the main inspiration for the creation of San Jose Taiko. In 1973, he encouraged Roy Hirabayashi and Dean Miyakusu to form a taiko group as a Young Buddhist Association activity. He had Roy and Dean go to L.A. to see Kinnara Taiko. The L.A. group showed how taiko was an art that the young generation can participate in. Roy and Dean returned to San José and started a taiko group. It attracted young people, including PJ. San Jose Taiko debuted at the 1974 Obon Festival.[9]

PJ Hirabayashi loved the strong role women played in taiko when she first saw San Francisco Taiko Dojo. "I saw a mother and daughter playing together and as powerfully as the men. No separation of gender. Everyone played equally as one." She noted, "Interestingly, San Jose Taiko started with equal numbers of men and women, but through

---

[8] Fukuda, Curt and Ralph M. Pearce. *San Jose Japantown, A Journey.* Japanese American Museum of San Jose, 2014.

[9] Fukuda, Curt. Personal interview. August 5, 2015.

most of its history, there was a higher ratio of women. Culturally, women didn't have the opportunity to have a ballistic voice, or unabashed expression."

Roy and PJ got married in 1975; together they guided San Jose Taiko until 2011, when they stepped down to transfer leadership to a new generation. San Jose Taiko is a consensus-based collective that supports a lifestyle with core values: respect and responsibility for the art form, for the audience and each other, for older and younger generations, and for the location in which the community is situated. Valuing process above product, the group builds a community of critical thinkers and wildly creative artists. The process of moving and sweating together reinforces their core values. In 2005, the Hirabayashis were the subjects of an extensive interview by Linda Uyechi, Stanford University lecturer in Taiko.[10] Exploring their full commitment to their community activist roots, PJ notes:

> Franco Imperial drew on his Filipino heritage and work with the kulintang to inspire compositions. Trish Wong uses taiko to tell the Chinese immigration story. Mike Fienen, from Minnesota with a pipe-organ-playing father, studied African drumming in college and taiko in Japan. Now Franco Imperial is artistic director and Wisa Uemura, his wife, is executive director. Culturally diverse, thoroughly immersed, both embody the values for the next generation.

Looking back, PJ expands on their leadership concepts:

> The organization is not top-down. It grew from grassroots organizing principles. There was no hierarchy, with one person on top to tell us what to do. We relied on the collective, group intelligence and set a framework. Everyone would have a voice, rotate leadership. We did not leave it up to one or two individuals to lead. We were consciously building community and developing leadership within the group. For those who wanted to join the group just to play taiko, we were the wrong group. We wanted them to understand "context." Learning a new song was NOT the point. We attempted to lead with flexibility, to develop the "leader" in each of us.

> San Jose Taiko was never a "made-in-Japan" group. We are an indigenous art form fertilized by our connection to San José Japantown and San José's diverse cultures. Relying on the powerful concept of self-determination, we can create the future that we want to see in our lives. We were one of the first three taiko groups to start in North America. Now there are over 350.

> With the burgeoning growth of taiko, the idea of creating a North American Taiko Conference (NATC) was launched in 1997, with biennial conferences to follow. It offers the chance for taiko players throughout the country to come together to share, exchange, learn, and celebrate our common passion and connection through taiko. It contributes to remembering taiko's cultural and historical roots in Japan and outside Japan. NATC affords an open system of sharing, prompting taiko players and taiko makers from Japan to observe and remark, "NATC could never happen in Japan, since most groups are so insular."

Over the years, San Jose Taiko has created the San Jose Taiko Conservatory to mentor other cultural groups, and collaborated with performing arts groups promoting cultural awareness, including Abhinaya Dance Company, a classical South Indian dance company founded in 1980. The pioneer taiko group is still going strong,[11] recognized locally and nationally for artistic and managerial excellence and community leadership.

---

[10] Uyechi, Linda. "Thinking Taiko: A San Jose Taiko Perspective." Asia Society, 2005.

[11] See San Jose Taiko website, taiko.org/history-traditional-japanese-drumming-rhythm-world-beats/.

Curt Fukuda and Lissa Jones, *San Jose Taiko*. The *San Jose Taiko* series was photographed from the mid-to-late 1980s. An enlarged reproduction became a section of the *Japantown Mural Project* (2012–2013) curated by Tamiko Rast.

PJ's path reveals the powerful potential of a multidisciplinary education that includes ethnic studies.

> Growing up in Marin County and the East Bay, I didn't want to be Japanese American. I wanted to be invisible because of the harsh prejudice I encountered going through school. It wasn't until my late teens at Irvington High School in Fremont that I had opportunities to become more visible and started to be more confident in my skin. I was a "Letter Girl" with the marching band. Then I became a cheerleader, more visible—yelling, shouting! Then "Spirit Queen" for my senior year. These experiences gave me the confidence and self-esteem to be in front of people.

> I studied math and computer science at Cal State Hayward, some art and journalism. In sophomore year I wrote a paper on the "Constitutionality of the Internment Experience," for which I interviewed my parents. I learned for the first time that the "camp" that I had heard them talk about when I was growing up was actually the incarceration camp for people of Japanese ancestry during WWII. Upon learning this, I became angry and indignant towards the "establishment," and felt an injustice that few resources presented "our" history. To fill the void of published material to learn about such events, the early Asian American studies programs brought in people from the community to speak from their own experiences. They were our first cultural history books.

> After two years at Hayward, I transferred to UC Berkeley and had Harry Edwards, a well-known African American sociologist, as a teacher for an ethnic studies class. I learned about the Third World communities, history, and about social injustice. It was ethnic studies and Asian

American studies that instilled the beginnings of my social consciousness—values, principles, and worldview—and how my education can serve and give back to community.

After I graduated from UC Berkeley, I went to Japan to live for one year, thinking that I could erase the pain of growing up Japanese in America and go back to my cultural roots where "my" people would accept me. However, I felt marginalized in Japan for being "different," as I was in America. I returned to the Bay Area to go into the Master of Urban and Regional Planning program at SJSU. I also became involved in the Asian American Studies program, becoming a lecturer and interim director from 1977–1979.

I wrote my master's thesis on the history and preservation of San José Japantown. There was nothing written like this before, looking at the past and imagining the future of Japantown. I asked small businesses, "What do you plan to do with your business in the future?" They had never given any thought to it and were just trying to survive as a small business in an economy that was all about shopping mall developments. At that time, San Francisco Japantown was fighting outside developers who would erode their cultural community. I didn't want that to happen in San José. I felt that we could design our own future. Mostly, my thesis was to open up the questions. Years later, the City of San José Redevelopment Agency referred to my thesis when launching a neighborhood development project in Japantown.

The 1970s was a pivotal time of awakening my social consciousness. After my return from Japan and settling in San José Japantown to attend grad school, I became involved with the early beginnings of the San Jose Taiko Group. It became my cultural touchstone to truly understanding my identity as a Japanese American. The word "Group" was essential to the name as it represented how we operated. In 1982, we incorporated as the first nonprofit taiko group and qualified to go for public funding. No funders at that time knew what "taiko" was and had a difficult time placing us into a category—is it music? is it dance?—especially the City of San José's Fine Arts Commission, as we were NOT the "Big 5," as they were referred to then—the ballet, the opera, the symphony, the museum, the theater. We were one of the first multicultural arts groups to emerge in San José, even before "multicultural" and "multidisciplinary" became ubiquitous.

In the early 1980s, PJ was a business partner with San Jose Taiko members Ellen Bepp and Linda Ito in Earthenwear, a contemporary ethnic-inspired clothing design shop in Japantown. Earthenwear and other small businesses expanded the horizons for young women who sought new avenues for making a living while still connecting to their culture and creativity. It was a non–art school entry to an artistic lifestyle, and to the world of arts and crafts. Festivals in Japantown helped these small businesses grow. Now Japantown is known for many small businesses and has a hip, arty flair, thanks to early commercial endeavors such as Earthenwear.

Upon her retirement as San Jose Taiko's artistic director, PJ founded TaikoPeace. It is a creative initiative that uses taiko as a tool "to open hearts and minds to new possibilities by unleashing our creativity, sparking new connections, and healing the personal and collective wounds that have fractured our human community." The TaikoPeace initiative can be activated by anyone to amplify positive social change. According to PJ's website,[12] "The TaikoPeace experience integrates taiko drumming with artistic modalities such as Japanese butoh dancing, chanting, and spoken word in order to activate and awaken self-

---

[12] pjhirabayashi.com/?page_id=157.

expression in disruptive, yet positive ways." TaikoPeace has held intensive workshops to foster this awakening, and asks people around the world to sign the Charter for Compassion and make a lifelong commitment to live with compassion and gratitude. PJ's latest endeavor shows that taiko drumming is not just for the elite to experience its musical excellence, but it is also a powerful tool to build awareness of how we connect with each other as a world community.

Roy Hirabayashi has also fostered and mentored other artistic leaders, with an incredible track record for art and community involvement, going back to the early 1970s when Asian Americans gathered together to affect positive change in their community.[13] More recently, from 2004–2013 he was a founding member of 1st ACT, an initiative to bring together regional leadership to advance downtown San José as a creative center that integrates art and technology to fuel creativity and entrepreneurship, and to leverage its multicultural uniqueness. He was an advisory committee member (2011–2013) and then a board member (2013) for the School of Arts and Culture at the Mexican Heritage Plaza. In terms of multicultural leadership, he served as a board member of First Voice, a multicultural arts coalition in San José, from 2004 to 2008. In 2007, he helped found 1st ACT's Multicultural Arts Leadership Institute (MALI), which trains Silicon Valley artistic leaders to engage their community and strengthen their business management skills. Roy is an American Leadership Forum Silicon Valley (ALFSV) senior fellow, an Asian Pacific American Leadership Institute (APALI) senior fellow, board member of the California Japanese American Community Leadership Council, a James P. Shannon Leadership Institute alumnus, and board member of the Japantown Community Congress of San José.

In 2011, the Hirabayashis were named as National Endowment for the Arts National Heritage Fellows in Folk and Traditional Arts. They also received the 2014 Silicon Valley Creates Legacy Laureate and the National Japanese American Citizens League Japanese American of the Biennium award. In 2015, Roy received the ALFSV John W. Gardner Leadership Award.

A Social Center and Art Space

Multiple cultures have lived in Japantown. Italian Americans arrived during and after WWII. The Chinese Ken Ying Low restaurant building was also the site of the Puerto Rican Club for 50 years. Okida Hall now is home for the Orthodox Ethiopian Church. The Northside Community Center was a center for Filipinos that later included the Indo-Americans.

The JAMsj 2012 exhibition *On Common Ground, Chinatown and Japantown, San Jose* focused on the story of Heinlenville, San José's last Chinatown. Guest curators Connie Young Yu and Leslie Masunaga brought to light the area's history and interactions between the Chinese and Japanese communities. In 2015, to celebrate the 125th anniversary of San José's Japantown, two individuals who made the existence of Japantown possible were

---

13 His early affiliations included Asians for Community Action, San José (1971–1974) and Asian Americans for Community Involvement, Santa Clara County (1973–1975), both organizations founded by Asian Americans to better their communities.

honored: John Heinlen and J.B. Peckham.[14] Heinlen built a Chinatown out of brick after the Market Street Chinatown was destroyed by arson fire on May 4, 1887.[15] New Japanese immigrants in the 1890s built nearby, feeling safer there than elsewhere. Peckham bravely supported Japanese families and property ownership in Japantown prior to and during internment.

Over decades, Chinese, Japanese, and Filipino families and stores were side by side, and people interacted with each other. Traditionally, "Chinatowns" included all Asian cultures. As Japanese, Filipinos, Vietnamese, Indo-Americans, and other Asians came to San José, they formed their own towns within this city.

For the Filipinos, their original Filipino Community Center was a brick building adjacent to the Hip Sing Tong Building in San José's current Japantown. Filipinos began living and owning businesses in Japantown in the late 1920s, though at the time it was still referred to as Chinatown. In 1933, a Filipino Community Center was formed as a special gathering center unifying the Filipino communities of the South Bay. Hard-working Filipinos from the fish canneries on the coast, hotel workers, farm workers, and builders took notice of the San José center. On weekends, families and single men spent time together, sharing with music, dancing, and traditional Filipino food potlucks. They reminisced about their times in the islands, and shared stories of immigration and initiation into the American ways of life.

In 1975, Jacinto "Tony" Siquig led the Filipino community and lobbied the city to obtain funds to purchase land and later rebuild what is now the eponymous JTS Northside Community Center that is integrated into Mabuhay Court Senior Housing. An important goal was to incorporate art and culture—including dance and art exhibitions—in the building and its programming. Bay Area artist Diana Pumpelly Bates' sculpture of the ancient folk bird, the *Sarimanok*, graces the front of the building. At the intergenerational center, one could find traditional dances for the adults, as well as Filipino youth-organized mobile DJ music battles. In 1994, the Filipino Heritage Festival, a.k.a. Street Jam, was born.

Around the same time, artist Terry Acebo Davis served as an art consultant to the Northside Community Center. She taught printmaking to seniors there, and told young street artist Abe Menor, "I'll teach you and you'll help me." Their work became part of the expanded exhibition *Never Too Late*, organized and funded by artists Jean Yee, Yeung Ha, and Acebo Davis. In 2002, Acebo Davis won a Community Foundation Silicon Valley grant to do a documentary film on Filipino-American veterans, *Mabuhay with Equity Project—Filipino War Veterans of WWII*. She worked on the project with Menor and Independence High School. Accompanying exhibitions at San José's Northside and Eastside senior centers included her life-size print of four Filipino WWII veterans.

---

14 Yu wrote the essay on Heinlen for the program, and Norman Mineta wrote on J.B. Peckham. Speakers at the event included Yu, author of *Chinatown San Jose, USA*, who highlighted Heinlenville Chinatown before Japantown (1887–1930s), and Robert Ragsac, local Filipino-American community historian, who spoke of the Filipino-American community in Japantown (1920–1940s). Since Heinlen has no descendants, Yu accepted the commendation from the Assembly and a glass trophy from the city, which she will bring to JAMsj. The celebration was sponsored by Japantown Business Association.

15 In the documentary film *Digging to Chinatown*, 2016, Yu and filmmaker Barre Fong tell the story of the original Chinatown buried under today's Japantown.

Acebo Davis has bridged worlds in multiple ways. As a Filipino American growing up in Fremont, she had come with her family often to Japantown to buy rice. As an artist and graduate of SJSU, she chose to live in Palo Alto, a midpoint between the arts centers of San José, San Francisco, and Oakland. "We had to reach out as Asians and Filipinos." At the time of the International Hotel evictions in San Francisco, she was there protesting. "My dad knew the old-timers there."[16] Activism against the I-Hotel's planned evictions and redevelopment in the late 1970s spread through the Bay Area arts community, boosting cultural awareness and helping to build networks between students, tenants, and community activists. Acebo Davis was inspired by Nancy Hom's silkscreen posters and the collaborations across cultures, and by artist/educator Carlos Villa's determined pursuit of multiculturalism. She has lectured about these events and Filipino identity at the Smithsonian and numerous universities.

Acebo Davis is an early member of Asian American Women Artists Association (AAWAA), a principal artist of Diwa Arts, a Filipino collective, and an advocate for Bay Area artists of color. As a Palo Alto arts commissioner, she pushed for Mildred Howard's bottle-house sculpture at City Hall, working with then–city council member LaDoris Cordell. Acebo Davis has maintained a full-time nursing career at Stanford Hospital to pay the bills, and understands the importance of culture and language in working with patients and families. Her 2016 exhibition recreated her mother's skilled nursing facility room. "I can walk all those lines."[17]

The Filipino American National Historical Society—Santa Clara Valley Chapter (FANHS) will be uncovering more local art and activist history. It is now led by Ron Muriera, a performing artist in dance, music, theater, and comedy, and an organization and grants consultant.

Terry Acebo Davis, *Filipino Veterans WWII*, 2002. Print on vinyl, 72"x120". Part of Mabuhay with Equity Project exhibited at San José's Northside and Eastside senior centers.

---

16 The "I-Hotel" was a low-cost residency hotel at the corner of Kearny and Jackson streets, in San Francisco's Manilatown. The majority of its tenants were elderly Filipino men living on Social Security. Kearny Street Workshop, an artists' collective, was also evicted from the building, along with other storefront groups. See foundsf.org/index.php?title=The_Battle_for_the_International_Hotel.

17 See also Alba, Victoria. "An Interview with Terry Acebo Davis." *(detail)* Vol. 6, Number 1, Fall 1998: 6–9.

Over 125 Years of Creative Energy

In the 1980s artists formed an arts colony at the Citadel, first located on the edge of Japantown in the old Tri-Valley warehouse on Taylor and North Tenth streets. There, many artists rented space and developed a camaraderie that propelled their art careers, and in 1985, artists Estelle Akamine and Glen Rogers began Open Studios. In 1995, Dr. Jerry Hiura, Steve Yamaguma, and Miki Hirabayashi created Contemporary Asian Theater Scene (CATS), which in 2015 hosted the first annual San José J-Town Film Festival.

Terry Acebo Davis, *Dahil Sa Yo* ("because of you" in Tagalog), 1994. Tableau, life-size. An installation about drawing support and inspiration from women, family, and one's adopted communities. Near life-size images of her mother, who was originally from the Philippines, are screenprinted on a checkered plastic tablecloth Acebo Davis once used for a celebratory dinner with artist Mildred Howard. Below are produce crates, such as those used by her father, relating to farm workers and the manongs—the labor force of single men coming from the Philippines earlier in the century.

Davis always learned, "First came the men," but she wondered why we don't look at the women. So she created an artwork about her mother—and later an artwork from photos of hands and feet of older Filipino women, "people who have mothered people," who made sacrifices, like Gabriela Silang ("similar to Joan of Arc"). "They always want me to eat with them ... a nurturing, caring-for sense." As a member of DIWA Arts, Davis has found "aunts and uncles" in the Filipino community and "brothers and sisters" in the art world, often bonding around shared food.

The alternative WORKS Gallery presented exhibitions in a warehouse at the northeast corner of North 6th and Jackson from 1990–1996. Acebo Davis, the first non-white person to serve as president of WORKS, worked with others to involve the Northside Community Center "just down the street."[18] She opened opportunities for young artists and added diversity to WORKS programming. In 1995 and 1996, WORKS, known for all manner of innovation in art, included some artists who have spent years working for positive change in Silicon Valley. In 1995, Acebo Davis co-curated *Rice*, increasing recognition for the AAWAA, and Carlos Pérez curated two shows on gang violence. The following year featured *Inside Out*, art by youth in four special programs led by artists Frances Paragon Arias, Pérez, Phil Rosenthal, and Flo Oy Wong. It was followed by a show curated by writer Therese Harlan examining issues around Indian casinos.

Rising rents and redevelopment have been problematic for Japantown. Demographics of the neighborhood have changed. Over the years, individuals like historian Leslie Masunaga have spoken up for preservation. In 2001, Senator John Vasconcellos authored Senate Bill 307 (SB307) identifying the three remaining U.S. Japantowns and requesting funding to preserve their cultures—a pilot for other ethnic communities in the state. Groups like the San José Japantown Community Congress, NOC, and Yu-Ai Kai Senior Center have been formed, with different interests working together. While growing and changing, Japantown has preserved and promoted diverse culture, history, and a welcoming small-town feeling.

Recent murals have addressed community building, such as the *Japantown Mural Project* (2012–2013), a joint effort of the brother-and-sister team behind Japantown-based rasteroids design, Tamiko and Miles Rast, and the City of San José Public Art Program. Featuring art by 50 local artists who celebrate the multicultural spirit of this historic San José neighborhood, more than 60 large panels of color covered the chain-link fence that surrounds the barren land of the city's former 6th Street maintenance yard known a century ago as Heinlenville, the early San José Chinatown. The works portray both Chinese and Japanese-American community history. The project's website[19] gives details of participating artists and businesses. In addition, Carlos Pérez created a digital mural portraying the Japanese-American community's history in Japantown for the interior of the Yu-Ai Kai Senior Center.

Japantown art spaces currently include sculptor Ken Matsumoto's Art Object Gallery, spotlighting Bay Area artists since 2000, and Empire Seven Studios, which "represents artists determined to make something out of very little to nothing." Local San José painter Juan Carlos Araujo and partner Jennifer Ahn, a photographer and painter, established E7S in 2007 in a warehouse near the corner of Empire and Seventh streets. The gallery hosts art exhibits every second Friday of the month, focusing on "urban contemporary" work often rooted in "street" subcultures like graffiti, skateboarding, or comics created by both

---

18 Acebo Davis lauds the leadership of Ben Menor in rebuilding the Northside Community Center and promoting the arts; one of her most prized recognitions is the Dr. José Rizal Community Hero Award, founded by Menor under the auspices of the Filipino American Opportunities Development Council.
For more art and more information, see terryacebodavis.com.

19 See rasteroids.com/japantown-mural-project/.

self-taught and academic artists. However, their tenure in Japantown will soon come to an end, as the entire block of Seventh Street where the gallery is located was recently sold to a developer.[20] Araujo and Ahn also direct the E7S Mural Project, a collaborative effort of local artists to spread awareness of San José's artistic riches and bring art to the streets of Japantown and the nearby Northside neighborhood.

JAMsj offers historical walking tours through Japantown. The books *Chinatown San Jose, USA* and *San Jose Japantown, A Journey* give detailed local histories with different cultures, small business, sports, and arts connections. J-Town Community TV is a recent YouTube channel where video artists like Duane Kubo (*Cruisin' J-Town*, 1976 documentary), bring personalities, events, "news and views" to life.[21] Japantown's range of traditional festivals, boutique shops, and contemporary restaurants, along with arts, scholarship, and activism has made it a Silicon Valley cross-cultural draw.

---

[20] See metroactive.com/arts/Silicon-Valley-Housing-Empire-Seven-Japantown-Art-Gallery.html

[21] See jamsj.org/japanese-american-history-museum-san-jose/japantown-walking-tours and jamsj.org/japanese-american-history-museum-san-jose/j-town-community-tv.

Flo Oy Wong: Reclaiming History

Since the 1980s, Sunnyvale-based artist Flo Oy Wong's art activism has spanned cultures, disciplines, and generations. Spirited and no-nonsense, Wong's voice lowers and her back straightens when she makes a point. She throws her head back when she's having fun, bursting with delighted laughter. The indomitable artist began her career in the 1980s at the age of 40, and has become an important force in the local and national arts scene.

Silicon Valley Arts Activist

Wong's arts activism started locally in Silicon Valley. She was a founding member of the Sunnyvale Arts Commission (1982) and helped to organize the city's public art policy. As a member of the board of directors of Arts Council Silicon Valley, Wong helped to build the popular Hands on the Arts family arts festival in Sunnyvale. In 1984, she began a six-year involvement with the Asian Heritage Council, organizing two major shows encompassing Asian American experiences. Besides exhibiting at Euphrat Museum, she has also had solo shows at the Triton Museum and San José State University.

Education Advocate

Viewing education as key, Wong has participated in college symposia in the U.S. and China, worked with local at-risk junior high students, taught elementary students, and served on the board for the Euphrat Museum of Art. Setting a pace through her advocacy with Sunnyvale School District and workshops at Resurrection School, she was honored as an early "unsung hero" in art education in conjunction with Euphrat's exhibition and publication *The Fourth R: Art and the Needs of Children and Youth* in 1992.

Champion of Ordinary People

Wong sees the extraordinary in the ordinary; the unusual person in the common predicament; the people who battle racism, sexism, and discrimination resulting from sexual orientation, neglect or eradication of history. "My work honors working-class families, who were so important to the building up of America," she asserts.

Her seminal project *made in usa: Angel Island Shhh* exemplifies her dedication to this point of view. Commissioned by Kearny Street Workshop, an Asian Pacific American arts organization in San Francisco, *made in usa: Angel Island Shhh* began as a series of rice sack flags that revealed the identity secrets of 25 former Angel Island detainees. These detainees, known as "paper people," were immigrants who had assumed false identities in order to enter this country due to the passing of the 1882 Chinese Exclusion Act.

To create the flags, Wong recorded the often-suppressed stories of family members and other people detained and interrogated at Angel Island Immigration Station; then incorporated their stories, including their true names, in the artwork. She worked with Nancy Hom, then executive director of Kearny Street Workshop, who suggested premiering the work onsite at the Angel Island Immigration Station. The project involved many community partners, including the Angel Island Immigration Station Foundation, Angel Island staff, and the cybergroup Save Our National Archives. Many of the former detainees had never gone back to the island, nor told their children about the experience; yet Wong's project encouraged them to return to the detention area with their children and grandchildren, transforming the place of shame to a place of healing. The exhibit drew significant attention from the media, including a segment on *The NewsHour with Jim Lehrer* (now known as *PBS NewsHour*).

After its successful debut, parts of *made in usa* were exhibited in various venues in the Bay Area, including Evergreen Valley College and Euphrat Museum of Art. The show traveled to the Japanese American National Museum in Los Angeles and culminated in 2003 in an exhibit onsite at Ellis Island, entitled *Tin See Do: The Angel Island Experience*, which included *made in usa* and other works. There, she worked with the Ellis Island National Monument, Angel Island Immigration Station Foundation, Kearny Street Workshop, and OCA-NY (Organization of Chinese Americans, New York Chapter) to bring this project full circle.

Wong continued to create new flags. In 2011, Euphrat Museum showed some of the flags and premiered a new flag honoring California Assemblymember Paul Fong and his family, who have historic ties with the Santa Clara Valley's floral industry. The presentation included remarks by historian Connie Young Yu:

> We are at the confluence of the arts, of history, education and civic engagement. This event is about more than unveiling of an art piece: It provides a forum for the history of Chinese exclusion laws and the struggle for civil rights ... and the inspiring narrative of our own Honorable Assemblymember Paul Fong and his family. ... It took years of struggle, hardship and civil disobedience before all forms of exclusionary policies stemming from the Chinese Exclusion [Act] were overturned and declared unconstitutional; and many more years for our society to recognize that excluded communities existed.

> The California Assembly [enactment] [Assembly Concurrent Resolution] ACR 42 introduced by Paul Fong is called a "request for an apology," but he intended it as a call for recognition and resolve: [that] these terrible wrongs happened; *never again* a law that excludes a specific race from American society and deprives people of their civil rights. What Paul Fong did was create a forum for education. It was a teaching opportunity that Americans badly needed. And Flo Wong continues that step forward. Her work connects us, illuminates our stories in an aesthetic form, and puts history back into our souls.

Advocate for Women

Gender issues surface in Wong's art and activism. Wong is acutely aware of many injustices to women and girls in Eastern and Western cultures, being "an artist from a traditional transplanted Asian culture—which did not support self-expression and which denied the value of females."

In 1989, she began a project with artist-activist Betty Kano from Oakland that resulted in the founding of the Asian American Women Artists Association (AAWAA), around the same time that Godzilla, an Asian American arts organization was founded in New York. AAWAA continues to promote inclusion of Asian American women as a vital part of American art history. The group invited the feminist art activist Guerrilla Girls to an AAWAA meeting, where they had frank discussions with them about the politics of color and its hierarchy, pointing out that Asian American women were a missing component.

Ruth Asawa, center, with four "unsung heroes" in art education honored at a Euphrat benefit for arts and education in January 1992, hosted by George and Judy Marcus. Left to right: Nancy Marston, founder, the Los Altos Art Docents program in the Los Altos School District; Flo Wong, advocate, Sunnyvale School District, Resurrection School, workshops; Ruth Asawa, renowned leader in art, art education and public sculpture, SF Art Commissioner, collaborator, advocate, alumna of Black Mountain College; Talala Mshuja, founder of Nairobi Cultural Center, East Palo Alto; Marie Franklin, advocate and teacher at Stocklmeir School in Cupertino Union School District. Photo: E.C. Wisner.

In 1989, Wong also became involved with the national Women's Caucus for Art (WCA) and proceeded to help develop the Women of Color in Art slide series, a tremendous benefit for arts institutions, art teachers, and others who had not had access to the breadth and quality of art produced by women of color. Wong served on the organization's national board of directors from 1991–1997, and attended the International Women's Conference in China as part of the delegation from WCA in 1995. There she moderated a nongovernmental organization panel on the experience of Chinese-American women in the arts, and co-coordinated the group's color Xerox art exhibition.

Advocate for Inclusion

Wong wrote an essay titled "There's More to Being Chinese in America than Chop Suey" as part of an anthology of different approaches to art criticism. She is acknowledged by the establishment, yet is not afraid to take it on. In 1997, a curator of the de Young Museum asked her to focus on their collection and help develop an exhibition on "identity." Wong suggested that he include more women and people of color. In this collaboration, Wong addressed identity issues for artists and the identity of the de Young itself, offering ways to improve its permanent collection and make it more representative of American culture.

Relationship Builder

Wong's approach as an artist has been largely focused on reclaiming histories and bettering relations between peoples. Rice is a common element in her art, whether using the sacks that the rice came in or the rice grains themselves. The staple is shared with other cultures, and she often uses it as a metaphor for spiritual nourishment, whether at a dinner table with friends and colleagues or in the art itself.

Wong weaves the personal and the universal in her work. The Wong family history is complex, because half of her siblings were born in China, half in the United States, and there were many "paper" relatives and family secrets which are still coming to light. A key piece in understanding her life's work is *Eye of the Rice: Yu Mai Gee Fon*. Still a work in progress, it measured 15'x26' in 1997. Wong began sewing on rice sacks in 1978 and started her ongoing *Oakland Chinatown* series of graphite drawings in 1983, but it was in 1986 that she combined the idea of recording Chinese-American history with sewing and altering rice sacks, often donated by friends. The work originally was intended as a tribute to Chinese immigrants and their struggles, but after several years she realized it recalled her childhood memories of Chinatown in Oakland, where her family owned a restaurant.

From these early memories a huge patchwork of rice sacks, images, and ideas flourish through the decades, as Wong charts her journey and family history and in the process, addresses politics, gender, and race. She now identifies as a poet as well as a visual artist, and looks forward to more projects in both mediums. With an unstoppable spirit, Wong continues to expand her artistic horizons, collaborating in numerous ways that build community.

Parts of this article are adapted from the author's 1998 essay "Flo Oy Wong: Honoring," written in conjunction with Wong's receiving the 1997 Media/New Genre Award from the Arts Council Silicon Valley for the quality of her work and professional achievement.
For more information:
"Flo Oy Wong: AAWAA Biography." *Women Artists of the American West: Asian American Artists.* cla.purdue.edu/waaw/asianamerican/Artists/WONGbios.HTM
"Flo Oy Wong." *SPARK*. Season 4, *The Influence of Memory*. KQED, San Francisco. 2006. http://ww2.kqed.org/spark/flo-oy-wong/

Connie Young Yu, 2011, speaking in front of Flo Oy Wong's *made in usa* art. Photo: Bob Hsiang.

Flo Oy Wong, *made in usa,* 2000. Photo: Bob Hsiang.

BUILDING NEW FORMS

Gen Guracar and Connie Young Yu: Democracy Engaged

In the 1970s, artist Gen Pilgrim Guracar from Mountain View and historian Connie Young Yu from Los Altos reached across cultures and disciplines to create a colorful patchwork quilt that truly represented the diverse peoples of America. Overcoming patterns of racial, ethnic, class and gender exclusion, they brought together people from different walks of life—teachers, household and agricultural workers, health care workers, community organizers, artists, liberals and conservatives. They even incorporated this country's founding documents and new technology in their art. Guracar organized the women who created squares for *The People's Bicentennial Quilt* (1974), and Yu wrote the book that tells the story behind each square, *The People's Bicentennial Quilt: A Patchwork History* (1976).

"We made this [Bicentennial] quilt," wrote organizer Guracar, "in answer to those who would commercialize our Bicentennial celebration ... leaving us without a spiritual link to those who struggled so hard for the rights that we have now." In her foreword, Connie Young Yu wrote: "We felt there was much in American history that could unite us and inspire us in a cynical time. ... We hoped to inspire other community groups to celebrate American culture and history in a true revolutionary spirit."

The quilt squares began with early slavery and indentured servants, continued to the Declaration of Independence in 1776 and The Bill of Rights, then memorialized movements and struggles, concluding with the contemporary ecology movement and "Women Hold Up Half the Sky." Yu's square "Chinese Labor on the Railroad" commemorated her great-grandfather, Lee Wong Sang, who worked on the "Iron Road" in the 1860s.

Jane Benson, Nancy Olsen and I wrote about the *Bicentennial Quilt in The Power of Cloth: Political Quilts, 1845–1986*. We placed the quilt in an art historical context, from the *Eagles and Rainbows* quilt, c.1845, created by an unknown artist, to *The Purple Quilt*, 1986, by contemporary artist Faith Ringgold, who was inspired by author Alice Walker. We also described the slow acceptance of quilts in the art world. Until the 1970s, the art world, with its emphasis on paintings and sculpture, ignored the artistry of women who created elaborate, sophisticated works of art out of the materials they had at hand, expressing their own geometric and aesthetic values. Quilts were considered "women's work." The San José Museum of Quilts and Textiles, the first in the country to focus on quilts and textiles, was not founded until 1977.

The Bicentennial Quilt pioneered the use of the quilt as a complex research and educational tool, but its subject matter was not always well received. Guracar and Yu spoke about *Patchwork History* at KPFA, a progressive radio station in Berkeley. "We were also interviewed by the local CBS station. They didn't want to hear about child labor." Mainstream media's interest did not include recalling that a large part of America's wealth was built on child labor in textile mills and mines, let alone slave labor on plantations.

The quilt traveled to multiple community gatherings before final placement in the International Quilt Study Center & Museum (IQSCM) at the University of Nebraska–

"The Abolition Movement"   "Chinese Labor on the Railroad"   "Child Labor"

Lincoln in 2006. As the duo explained:

> We weren't sure The San José Museum of Quilts would survive. It was moving around, looking for a permanent place. We heard some quilts were being stored in garages. Also we sensed conservatism. In contrast, the Nebraska center, while conservative, was affiliated with a university, had a student program, and we found a radical person there.

Yu wrote about their inspiration to republish in 2010:[1] "It was Alice's [Alice Keesey Mecoy] talk on being a John Brown descendant at the Saratoga History Museum that inspired Gen and me to create a color edition of the 1976 *Quilt* book. We wanted to update and make this people's history alive and true, and show we're descendants, all."

In her new introduction, Yu wrote that some of the women quilters had "lived through the bloody battles fought over desegregation and the right of black people to vote." She described an American tradition: women coming together to create from scraps of cloth. "By our stories and handiwork we strive to fulfill the ideals and the dream of our nation, word by word, stitch by stitch."

Guracar now remarks about the "precedent setting" of addressing "issue-oriented" content in the quilt projects.[2] She calls attention to its early and lasting impact by citing that the IQSCM started the new millennium with what has become biennial symposia on "Making and Mending: Quilts for Causes and Commemoration." "The IQSCM had a whole symposium in April 2015," she reports. Yet galvanizing institutional respect, meaning, and significance is still a struggle.

How the Collaborations Began

After earning a bachelor's degree in art and design from the University of Michigan, Guracar lived in Ohio with two small children. A friend gave her an elementary book on quilting. Bored, she taught herself. Guracar's political education also began in Ohio.

---

[1] See also Mecoy, Alice Keesey. "The Quilt That Changed My Life." Introduction. *Patchwork History, The People's Bicentennial Quilt*. By Connie Young Yu. Saratoga Historical Foundation, 2010.

[2] Additional information:
Guracar, Gen Pilgrim and Jan Rindfleisch. *The Women in Struggle Quilt Project*. Euphrat Gallery, 1983.
The Women's Quilt Project. Dir. Terri Esther. 1983. Video. Collection of IQSCM.
Women in Struggle Quilt poster. UP PRESS, 1984.
Keller, Audrey and Gen Guracar. "The Ribbon and the Quilt." *CONTENT: Contemporary Issues*. Ed. Jan Rindfleisch. Euphrat Museum of Art, 1986.
Benson, Jane, Nancy Olsen, and Jan Rindfleisch. *The Power of Cloth, Political Quilts 1845–1986*. Euphrat Museum of Art, 1987.

> Kennedy killed. George Wallace. An Oberlin [College] student called up and asked me what I knew about the Vietnam War. I said, 'They must know what they're doing,' but later I thought about it more. Also I was deeply shocked in 1968 by Daley's Chicago and [the 1971] Winter Soldiers' testimony.

The political violence, the civil rights movement, the peace movement, and the antiwar movement awakened her social consciousness and led to her activism. She came to California in late 1968.

> I first met Connie at the Peace Center in Palo Alto. [Yu was a co-founder of the Palo Alto Peace Center in the mid-1960s.] … I was from the Midwest, hadn't seen Asian culture. Meeting Connie opened another world. … Now here is a real person sitting across from me. I learned about the extension of Chinese-American culture in this country. Connie took my kids to see historical parts of San José; she took them to Angel Island. I introduced quilting to her—and Bea Keesey (a John Brown descendant), Lolly Font (whose mother worked at age 12 in textile mills), and older women from the African American community in East Palo Alto—Hattie Kelly, Vernell Halsell, Mary Hyman—who could talk about culture in the South. … The quilt involved young hippies, housewives, and grandmothers.

> It was a culture clash when I first visited the Peace Center and UP PRESS. I looked "establishment professional." The PRESS [an alternative, woman-run collective] was all young women. I worked with Becky Sarah, did my own [*Patchwork History* book] pre-print and binding. It saved me money. The press lasted from the 1970s to around 1985.

Yu was transformed also. "The [*Bicentennial*] quilt project was how I learned about American history—with a personal connection!" The quilt square "The Flint Strike, 1937" commemorated the autoworkers' strike against General Motors during the Great Depression. "I love the Flint story, the 3D, [mothers holding up] the children, throwing food [to the striking men] … ."

The *Bicentennial* was not the first quilt the pair worked on. In 1974–1975, they created a signature anti-war quilt with "congresspeople, labor people, artists, [and] people who would sign the Declaration of Independence." Guracar recalls, "This was a time when Richard Nixon had an enemies list, yet people were willing to sign quilt squares." It was raffled to raise funds for the Peace Center. A young man won it and wanted to ride across country on a motorcycle, using the quilt as a blanket. Concerned that the quilt might be endangered, they felt it deserved a venue that would protect it. "No way!" He understood and kindly gave it back. It too went to the IQSCM. [3]

---

3 Guracar, Gen. Correspondence with author. August 14, 2015:
  The Vietnam Era Signature Quilt was made in 1974–75. I sent a letter to people who had spoken out against the war in Vietnam, stating that the quilt was a fundraiser for the Palo Alto Peace Union. A piece of cloth was enclosed with the letter for their signature. People [and groups] such as Joan Baez, Vietnam Veterans Against the War, Leonard Bernstein, Pete Seeger, George McGovern, Cesar Chavez, Gloria Steinem, Pete McCloskey, Justice William O. Douglas, Kate Millet, Mary McCarthy, Daniel Berrigan, Ralph Abernathy, Bella Abzug, Shirley Chisholm, Daniel Ellsberg, and Mike Gravel, who got the Pentagon Papers into the Congressional Record, to name just a few. Names that were signed on the cloth were then embroidered.

Guracar's Art Path

I worked with Guracar—aka edgy cartoonist Bulbul, the nightingale—on several pathbreaking exhibitions. In 1981, she spearheaded the Euphrat showing of *Pork Roasts, 250 Feminist Cartoons*, the engaging exhibition curated by Avis Lang Rosenberg that probed values through humor. Guracar also lectured about women in cartooning, still a rarity in the field.

In 1983, she coordinated 43 women for *The Women in Struggle Quilt*.[4] They wanted "to discover the deep concerns that move women to organize, and to affirm women who actively shape their world." Many of the quilters who worked on this quilt were immigrants from countries such as Turkey, Australia, and the Philippines. Each researched a topic, designed and sewed a square, in order "to know about strong women who have fought injustice." Topics included the struggle against chemical and biological warfare, campaigns against toxic wastes, and women's resistance to apartheid in South Africa.

A video of the quilt, *The Women's Quilt Project*, was produced and directed by Terri Esther, who studied video production at Laney College in Oakland.[5] This quilt was part of the Euphrat Gallery 1983 exhibition, *ARTECH and Art by Hand*. Guracar and I collaborated with others to print a small book partially sponsored by the gallery, *The Women in Struggle Quilt Project*, with an early dot-matrix printer. Several contributors' names were withheld to protect the artists or their families from retribution by oppressive governments or violent groups. One of the tech artists in the exhibition was Trudy Myrrh Reagan, who started YLEM, Artists Using Science and Technology, in Palo Alto in 1981, which went strong for decades. Reagan, who worked on both quilts, said, "It was a yeasty time."

---

4 Additional reflections of Gen Guracar on *The Women in Struggle Quilt* project, excerpted from *CONTENT: Contemporary Issues*, op. cit.:

> In September 1981, eight of us from the Bay Area wrote a letter to women's groups in many countries, proposing to collectively sew a quilted artwork to celebrate women and their struggles throughout the world.
>
> Why did we decide to do a quilt—when the initial impetus occurred in the middle of high-tech Silicon Valley and I, one of the prime movers of the project, earned my living as a technical illustrator? The form had to be a quilt. *The Quilt* affirms women's creativity. Quiltmaking is a gentle, unthreatening art form. It's an activity of working together and directly related to traditional women's work, sewing. A quilt would have a strong cross-cultural appeal. It could travel in a duffel bag. It could be touched (very important). It could be washed when it got dirty—three times now (a horrendous task!) after three trips across the Atlantic. ... The idea spread, and over 100 women from around the world became involved ...
>
> *The Women in Struggle Quilt* was first displayed at La Peña Cultural Center in Berkeley. ... It was displayed at the International Peace Conference in Czechoslovakia, at women's centers in Denmark, Switzerland and Poland, the New Song Movement Festival in Ecuador, the International Conference of Black Social Workers in Egypt and Kenya, at the United Nations End of the Decade Conference on Women in Nairobi ... and at many other places.

Everywhere, *The Quilt* has been received with tremendous enthusiasm. Many women promote the quilt project—which, in an art sense, is a continuing performance piece. ... For its inspirational purpose, *The Quilt* has had the most relevant and reverent installations—hanging between two trees at Greenham Common, and being spread on the ground before Kenyan tribal women who subsequently created a dance about it.

5 All three collaborative quilts and the video were given to the IQSCM. Though *The Women in Struggle Quilt* was a group quilt, it came to have only Guracar's name on it. In December 2014, Guracar told me, "The sweet woman I worked with died soon after the quilt was given." This demonstrates how accurate institutional memory can be fragile.

Today, Guracar creates editorial and social commentary cartoons for labor publications in the U.S. and Canada through the Worker Institute at Cornell University in New York. Her cartoons appear in *Drawing My Times: Cartoons by Bulbul, A Thirty Year Retrospective*.[6] She makes and exhibits quilts with a message, such as *Women Standing Tall*, 2012.

"In the quilt world, few take on issues. I do my quilts and enter them in shows: *Refugee, Poisoning of Bees,* and *Madame Defarge Knits up the Tax Dodgers*." Guracar still encounters challenges in presenting her work. In a recent conversation, she remarked how often people ask what big publications print her cartoons, implying that her work is not valid unless she has received mainstream recognition.

Yu's Art Path

Yu understands the power of cloth from her own family history. Her parents collected exquisitely embroidered historical garments and textiles from China and bequeathed them to Stanford University's Cantor Arts Center (one robe was displayed in the center's 2013–14 exhibition *Border Crossings*), the Tacoma Art Museum (TAM), and other institutions for the purposes of better relations and understanding between cultures. These magnanimous gestures were their family's response to many decades of anti-Chinese sentiment and devastating exclusion and expulsion, including the burning of West Coast Chinatowns.[7] Unfortunately, institutions can inadvertently forget the significance of historical holdings: in 2013, the Tacoma Art Museum tried to deaccession the collection without realizing the history involved.[8]

---

6 Bulbul. *Drawing My Times: Cartoons by Bulbul, A Thirty Year Retrospective*. Arachne Publishing, 2001. See also bulbul.com.

7 The Chinese at that time were also being stoned. The women that were in San Jose Chinatown, a predominantly bachelor society, probably hid when a census was done, but by 1880, at least a few seamstresses and even a milliner braved the times and were counted.
Given this dismal background of the 1870s and afterwards, stories of early Bay Area Chinese women are still being collected. In a letter to the author dated September 10, 2015, Yu recounted the following stories:
  Gene Chan on his great-grandfather, a railroad worker on the Central Pacific: "One night in San Francisco (1870), he saw a girl [Hel Shee] crying in the street. He talked to her and learned she was trying to escape from her master. So he went to her owner and bought out her contract. He married her and they settled in a farmhouse in the [Sacramento–San Joaquin River] Delta and raised eight children."
  My great-grandfather Lee Wong Sang after working on the railroad had saved up money and sent for his betrothed from China. My grandfather was born in 1878 on Dupont St. (Grant Ave.) in SF Chinatown and was delivered by a *Chinese midwife* (name on the birth certificate).

8 Seattle alternative newspaper *The Stranger* describes how Tacoma "kicked out its entire Chinese population on a single rainy night in 1885" in what came to be known as "The Tacoma Method." thestranger.com/seattle/chinese-treasures-shipped-out-of-tacoma/Content?oid=16173402
Yu, November 15, 2014 correspondence to the author:
  TAM did succeed in deaccessioning most of my parents' textiles and all the jades. Great pieces were sold in the first auction at Bonhams. The selling of the red robe (shown in the photo worn by my mother) broke my heart. ... In the yearlong battle, I gained a whole new vista ... found many friends and allies in the Northwest community, folks who "get it," making the connection with history, art, culture, race. Northwest Indian tribes came out in support of us. Our attorneys were two African American men and a Japanese-American woman, who did pro bono work, as they believed it was a civil rights case, the driving out of Chinese culture by Tacoma, which drove out the Chinese people 130 years before.

Yu's recent personal textile collection of Chinese children's hats and dolls, often stitched together from pieces of old garments and then further embroidered, includes a grandmother doll with bound feet and a grandfather doll. The collection reveals much about women's art forms, their affection for and dedication to their children, their skills, values, and social status.

Cartoon by Bulbul, 1994.

Self-portrait cartoon by Bulbul, title page for *Drawing My Times*, 2001.

Yu currently writes, speaks, and consults on historical and cultural issues, projects, and exhibitions. She was a longtime hands-on Euphrat Museum board member, and continues her support of and collaboration in the arts as a trustee of the Hakone Foundation dedicated to preserving and enhancing its historic buildings and gardens in Saratoga. Her publications include *Chinatown, San Jose, USA;*[9] more projects are in progress. Her 1976 quilt square on "Chinese Labor on the Railroads" was a calling out. It took until 2014 for the Department of Labor to recognize and induct 19th century Chinese railroad laborers into the Labor Hall of Honor; Yu was there for the 2015 ceremony. Recently she edited *Voices from the Railroad.* Yu feels in awe of her ancestors' moral courage. "I'm recording [their actions]. Will I be tested?"

A Three-Way Conversation on Art

Collaborations can be exhilarating and affirming. Guracar's and Yu's creative, dynamic friendship is an enlivening influence. Both women, with strong inner drives, persevere against injustice, individually and collectively. Both have an intense interest in labor issues and feel that knowledge of our forerunners' struggles and survival gives us strength to survive adversity.

---

9 Yu, Connie Young. *Chinatown, San Jose, USA*, 4th edition. History San José, 2012.

At a 2014 lunch at Yu's, over stir-fry and persimmons, the pair began reflecting on early life-altering art experiences. Guracar described her amazement at a Tut exhibition she saw when young: "That my species can rise to such beauty! A human endeavor." Yu spoke of the impact of seeing in San Francisco's Legion of Honor a bronze statue of a Chinese worker with a braid, cast in France around 1800—"a Chinese worker in France!"

Children/hats c.1895 in Heinlenville, San José's last Chinatown (1887–1931). Chinese children's hats could have amazing stitchery and refinement (blind stitch, use of gold for nobility, special symbolism) or could be quite whimsical with large eyes and faces with symbolic animal attributes. China Central Television (CCTV), the national TV station of the People's Republic of China, recently came to Yu's home to video the hats, revealing the country's current hunger for certain aspects of their history. Image courtesy of Connie Young Yu.

Thinking of the stunning art of these two women, I put forth my view that art is composed of form and content. Anything we make or do can be art. Art encompasses it all—installations, performance art, interventions, the art of hospitality, the art of cooking, the art of healing. While we may instantly notice obvious form and content, there is also hidden content, such as the use of very low-wage labor, slave labor, or child labor in the production of many classical/historical and even contemporary artworks. Hidden content is also integral with the story around a work of art, the words that go along with it, and its social function—but it is rarely acknowledged or discussed. Taught about the rectangle on the wall and the hunk on the pedestal, most of us limit our conception of what art is, let alone its larger meaning.

Our three-way conversation encompassed the art around us, including quilts, cartoons, garments, children's hats, dolls. Bits from San José's archaeological history were included: historian Leslie Masunaga's discovery of ceramic shards from early San José's Japantown and Chinatown, found together in the Heinlenville excavation; a small European doll found in the excavation of San José's First Street Chinatown—now the site of the Fairmont Hotel. These discoveries illustrate cultural exchange back in the 19th century—interactions, values, ways of doing and being—and show how San José has been a multicultural society since its inception.

As Yu picked up, she spoke about food service—a form of installation and performance art, so often the art of women—highlighted in Judy Chicago's collaborative *Dinner Party* (1974–1979), which utilized individualized textile runners, sculptural plates, and a large triangular table. Yu mentioned how Chinese like to eat at a round table, with more equal access to conversation and food for all members, different from the "reaching and trading" promoted by a rectangular table.[10]

Yu pointed out that her *Bicentennial Quilt* square on Chinese labor on the railroad was based on one of 12 paintings of Chinese life in California by Jake Lee featured in one of her favorite Chinese restaurants. A Stanford art historian once said of Lee that he was "just an illustrator," that the paintings were "not worth much."

After the restaurant closed, the art disappeared. Later, the Chinese Historical Society executive director wanted them and found 11 in an auction. While Lee died broke, bids on these works were starting at $5,000 each, even though they had suffered moisture damage. The twelfth, in good condition, was found in an auto repair shop. Coming out from under a car, the shop owner said, "You want it?" and gave it to them.

Yu expressed our shared awareness of the continual struggle for exhibition time, funding, publicity, and storage. For the exhibition *On Common Ground: Chinatown and Japantown, San José* at the Japanese American Museum of San José in Japantown, volunteers did the work, and many items could not be saved. For an exhibition at San Jose's Dr. Martin Luther King, Jr. Library, "[we were] putting it up ourselves."

---

[10] Both Chinese and American table service can become complex. Some Chinese explain that the host sits in a particular place at the table and the honored guests are on the right or left side of the host. The protocol about who eats what first can also be very complicated.

Yu described local development of the *Lazy Susan* we know today:

> Johnny Kan suffered racism in the 1950s and said, "When I have a restaurant, we will get respect." He brought in a great cook from Hong Kong. My uncle devised the ball bearings for the central platter, so one could avoid reaching and trading. Johnny Kan's Restaurant opened in 1953, then Ming's in 1955 in Palo Alto. Every table had a Lazy Susan. It caught on even in Hong Kong and Taiwan. Last month in China, I saw the biggest one, made in glass.

See Gross, Daniel A. "The Lazy Susan, the Classic Centerpiece of Chinese Restaurants, Is Neither Classic Nor Chinese." *Smithsonian.com*, February 21, 2014.

smithsonianmag.com/arts-culture/lazy-susan-classic-centerpiece-chinese-restaurants-neither-classic-nor-chinese-180949844/?no-ist A serving problem is fixed with a functional object that then opens design and art opportunities.

It was Kan's Restaurant that featured the paintings by Jack Lee mentioned in the subsequent paragraph.

Guracar hands me a large poster of one of the early collaborative quilts, along with some individual postcards: "It's good we got the *Women in Struggle Quilt* video!" We all agree it's definitely time for a new focus on both the *Bicentennial* and *Women in Struggle* quilts. Even today, many admit they have never heard of half of the subjects portrayed by the *Bicentennial Quilt.*

Lunch conversations meander. For me, the takeaway is twofold. Broadening the definition of what art is and being able to see art around us brings color to our lives. It spurs our creative energies, and helps us to appreciate the story around the art and see past the hype and exclusion that would minimize our rich, real-life experiences. The other issue concerns the challenge of keeping the treasures of a particular period—particularly those of minorities, women, and excluded groups—and of keeping records of their struggles and contributions to modern life.

It's so easy for our understanding of who we are and how we got here to slip away, lost to future generations who would benefit from that knowledge. We must pay attention to whose histories and creations are preserved and valued, and whose are brushed aside and forgotten. The quilt and book projects prevent erasure of the energies and passions for creativity and expression that have not been recognized or supported with any consistency by the corporations and institutions that influence our art history.

Both Guracar's and Yu's work stands outside standard academic studio art practices; yet they built early collaborative public art models that embody inspiration, innovation, and engagement, the goals of major contemporary art spaces. In a time of great racial divide, they unified people. They joined forces against the exclusivity of the elites that continually try to monopolize and narrowly define the legitimate forms of expression. Their projects both affirm life and renew its challenges.

Euphrat Museum and Early Community Building

Euphrat Museum played an unusual role in the valley's early cultural development. From my first years as director, I was committed to building community, engaging democracy at ground level, and pulling together publications as a community voice and tool. Ensuring equal opportunity was a priority.

The Euphrat was founded as the Helen Euphrat Gallery in 1971 by way of a financial bequest and the vision of E.F. and Helen Euphrat. Resembling a long modernist bunker, the building opened out to a courtyard shared with adjacent Flint Center for the Performing Arts. Prior to 1978, about two-thirds of the original gallery had been converted to classrooms. Proposition 13 passed, resulting in the elimination of funding for the Euphrat, which had been supported by Community Services. For years afterwards, Euphrat Gallery faced the constant threat of having its already truncated space turned into a computer lab.

The 33 years of my leadership (1979–2011) were an exceptional time of growth and achievement for the Euphrat. We began building our concept of a forum, drawing people together for broad-based discussion and consciously creating the foundation for a unique partnership between the college and the community. Fellow visionaries asked how they could help.

A trope of the time predicted that in the future, people would create their own jobs. We ran with the idea. Together, our loose cohort of dedicated idealists explored the political and cultural milieu and invented job titles to describe our efforts. Two of these intrepid explorers were artists Lucy Cain Sargeant and Kim Bielejec Sanzo. Given the token and infrequent remuneration, we would never have survived and succeeded in the early 1980s without the on-the-mark professionalism and eye of Sargeant or the creativity of Bielejec Sanzo. Support from district trustees Franklin Johnson, Dr. Gerald Besson, and Dr. Raymond F. Bacchetti, the latter two serving on the first Euphrat board, was also essential. In 1992, with the expertise and ideas of art historian Patricia Albers, then director of special programs at the Euphrat, we became the Euphrat Museum of Art. The Euphrat board would grow, champion innovation and help build programs, outreach, and the new museum building. This was a most unusual challenge for a community college.[1]

Building Community as a Small Organization

The '80s were full of joining forces in a distressed cultural landscape. We sought out other fledgling organizations to amplify our alternative voices. We spoke up for a chance to

---

[1] Euphrat Board Presidents—Charles Newman, Joan Barram, Jim Jackson, Jane Reed, Nancy Newton, Robert Gonzales, Helen Lewis, Margaret Kung—provided terrific leadership and guidance. The museum also owes an armful of gratitude to early Euphrat supporters and a plethora of ever-inventive, inspired Euphrat staff in years when there was no money. We will never forget artist Nancy Calhoun's designer receptions and student Tom Carson bringing in artworks from L.A. at midnight one weekend. That wasn't the plan, but the unexpected happens.

expand arts venues and programming, and definitions of art in Silicon Valley and beyond. As the Euphrat got off the ground, government arts infrastructures were also in the early stages of development. For example, the Arts Council of Santa Clara County started in 1982, but its focus in the '80s was on supporting San José's "big five" arts organizations; small organizations waited their turn. From 1985–1988, smaller groups met monthly, often at the Euphrat, forming the Arts Alliance, an Arts Council advisory group. Some of us reached out to Business Volunteers for the Arts, a new Arts Council program (1985–1986).

Since we were located in Cupertino near the crossroads with Sunnyvale and Los Altos, we sought partnerships with these cities, partnering with three very different Silicon Valley civic bodies. With Euphrat's board, we initiated the establishment of the Cupertino Art Commission in 1986–1987 to boost a local presence for the arts. Our work with the City of Sunnyvale led to the Euphrat accepting responsibility for curating a decade of exhibitions at the Sunnyvale Community Center.

Nothing was easy. To reach families and communities, we formed art education partnerships including city councils and staff (which was out of the norm for all of us) and developed ongoing programs with school districts. During the '80s we worked with faculty, staff, and trustees of the Fremont Union High School District and Cupertino Union School District. We initiated the installation of FUHSD student shows in a professional art setting at the Euphrat to spotlight the strong artwork and bolster the case of the beleaguered high school arts programs. We formed a Euphrat Board Art Education Committee, and later connected with the SJSU art education department so we could train new graduates in community work. We immensely benefited from in-depth conversations with Ruth Tunstall Grant and Maribel Alvarez, who shared their energy and experience. They offered a wealth of ideas to our education program and vision of a diverse arts community, including the understanding of the needs of underserved populations and at-risk youth.

Slowly, the idea that responsive regional governments, schools districts, and other public entities could benefit their constituencies through partnerships with arts organizations— even a small or dedicated upstart arts organization—gained traction. The notions that everyone, regardless of age, had a stake in the arts and that some sectors of the community had special arts needs also came to be acknowledged.

Enlightened corporate and small-business leaders would become key community partners—a learning experience for all. Vice presidents from Apple, Hewlett Packard, and Tandem Computers and presidents of small companies like Allied Medical Laboratories and Capsco Sales served alongside community leaders, artists, and activists on our Euphrat board. Euphrat created art exhibitions at Hewlett Packard, Tandem, and Apple. Lili Butler's dramatic, larger-than-life sculptures reminiscent of chess pieces, *The White One* and *The Black One*, graced Apple's main lobby in 1985, the year of the clash between Steve Jobs and the Apple board of directors.

A community breakthrough for small and mid-size organizations came in 1989, when the Euphrat was the site for a press conference sponsored by the Community Foundation, Santa Clara County Arts Council and National Endowment for the Arts to announce the creation of a major new endowed fund for small to mid-size arts organizations in Santa Clara County. These small grants, like California Arts Council grants, had disproportionate importance because they required the arts organizations to undergo extensive peer review. The awards and recognition spotlighted the functioning and stature of smaller organizations as movers and community builders able to engage public and private sectors.

Apple was our neighbor down the street, with its own struggles, views, and impact on our community and creative culture. In 2011, Jobs presented Cupertino City Council with designs for Apple's new circular headquarters nearby. That same night, the council deliberated the annual city budget and art appropriations, which both recognize and support the role of art in making a community people want to live in. Our exhibition at the time was *Learn to Play*, about video games, computers, and life—probing moral and ethical dimensions of our lives through games. Jobs, on his last legs with terminal cancer, knew our plight. "Everyone needs money," he said.

Democracy Groundwork

It's hard to build community with a questioning, forum-based organization, which requires the exchange of ideas and views, if basic knowledge and understanding of the human condition are lacking. A long time ago, a student asked me about the meaning of a small printed word that was part of a large collage sculpture. The word was "apartheid." I think of the ideas presented over the years in artworks exhibited in the Euphrat. Through art we learned in unique, unexpected ways of the Tuskegee Airmen, lynching, the Nanjing Massacre, the Cherokee Trail of Tears, refugees, very short people, and mental illness. *Looking for the Creek on Stevens Creek Boulevard* examined watersheds and creek restoration, while eating disorders were addressed in *To Your Health!* Other Euphrat shows shed light on AIDS, the paper bag test for determining admission to a segregated

Deborah Kennedy, *For Freedom*, 1991. Mixed media installation for exhibition *Freedom Views: 1991*.

place ("If your skin was lighter than a paper bag tacked on the door, then you could enter."), the I-Hotel, gentrification, gender issues, bullying, human trafficking, the Chinese Exclusion Act, Manzanar, global warming, veterans' issues, high student loan debt, and extinction of native languages. Artists are often bellwethers of hidden trouble spots, human rights and social justice work, focusing on life that others have passed by or swept aside.

Democracy depends on questioning and informed citizenry; yet it had not often been emphasized as a prime mover of art museums or art education. We made sure democracy came up repeatedly in Euphrat exhibitions. For *In the Public Eye: Beyond the Statue in the Park*, 1990, Thomas Marsh and anonymous students shared their *Goddess of Democracy* sculpture fashioned locally after the one used in the Tiananmen uprising in China. *Freedom Views: 1991* featured a large *Four Freedoms* installation about freedom and responsibility by artist/educator Deborah Kennedy.

Publications: A Community Voice and Tool

Euphrat publications through the 1980s were extremely low-budget community projects. They shared an underlying emphasis on questioning assumptions and examining all sides of an issue, even when it might be difficult or uncomfortable to do so. These early, concrete examples of the "open door" afforded needed opportunities not only for critical debate, but also promoted visibility and civic engagement. People could create together and support each other—leaders, thinkers, and inquiring students of all ages and backgrounds. When in 1982 a student asked why there was never religious art in a modern art gallery, we created the exhibition and book *Art, Religion, Spirituality*, with over 30 contributing community writers.

In 1985, we published *Content Art: Contemporary Issues* in conjunction with two exhibitions, the first installed at Southern Exposure Gallery, San Francisco. At that time, overt content was frowned upon in the mainstream art world, and strong establishment-challenging content was especially avoided. Curators typically organized group exhibitions by medium, style, or standard themes, such as landscape. The second exhibition entitled *Content: Contemporary Issues... Points and messages... Making a point... spelling it out... and talking about it!* was installed at the Euphrat in early 1986. The name change reflected an art class experiment followed by discussion about how difficult it was to get an idea across, even with images and words.

Two projects included a broad swath of the Bay Area's immigrant communities, giving a sense of what they were going through and what they had to share. The probing and expansive publication *Art of the Refugee Experience*, 1988, researched in collaboration with the United Nations High Commissioner for Refugees when there were 12 million refugees worldwide (compared with 50 million today), was expanded further conceptually with the publication *Coming Across: Art by Recent Immigrants*, 1994. The latter project was developed in collaboration with the Bronx Museum of the Arts with funding from the Rockefeller Foundation and the NEA.

Drawing from Experience: Artists over Fifty, 1990, and *The Fourth R: Art and the Needs of Children and Youth*, 1992, brought in writers, artists, and groups, some with experimental grassroots programs tailored to needs, giving voice and opportunity to young and old.

In all, over a dozen early Euphrat publication projects included hundreds of participants of diverse experience, not just arts people, from the Bay Area and around the world. Early publications, poetry series, and music presentations later grew to multiple community and academic endeavors and a rich variety of events.

Mao Sith, 19, and Thangkam Chhom, 18, build a traditional Cambodian kline-ite from bamboo, rattan, plastic, beeswax, palm fronds, and twine in the Euphrat, January 23, 1988. Photo: Doug Cloud.
Introduced to us by writer Linda McKinney, a consultant to refugee community organizations, Sith explained that the large kline-ite or singing kite was once "the radio of the countryside." Upon completion, when the well-heeled Saturday-night Flint Center audience was inside watching a performance, Sith tried out his new kite outside. On this quiet night, he created musical magic above Euphrat's courtyard for a lucky couple of Euphrat staff to witness.

We opened our new museum with a Shorty Fatz bike in the front window to encourage more inroads/opportunities for Greater Bay Area arts, sports, and community to support each other.[2] We followed it the next year with a basketball installation for short people with the right shoes and moves, then the collaborative, encompassing *Learn to Play* exhibition,

---

2 Arts and arts education, like sports and sports education, can bring out personal best and build teamwork. While long in different camps and at opposite ends of a campus, Greater Bay Area artists and creative athletes have been forerunners, pushing at boundaries and prejudices by joining arts, sports, and community—from creative bike culture to detailed skateboards and surfboards, to star performances by a determined Brandi Chastain on and off the soccer field. It's fitting and exciting to see a middle-school or high-school choir sing the national anthem and provide a cappella halftime entertainment at Stanford women's basketball games. We share the same anticipation: Game day! Surf's up! Bike party! Art walk! Chalk fest! Yarn bomb!

with its huge streetwise *Control Freak* mural by Sean Boyles,[3] and Yunan Cao's *Ping Pong Diplomacy* installation. A joyful moment was purchasing her bilingual, binational ping-pong table for the museum—art as a teaching tool you could actually use and have fun with!

A Let's-Do-It Spirit

Change of pace, the unexpected, and especially flexibility were Euphrat hallmarks. Innovative practices with curators and maverick experts in other fields, our flexible space arrangements (within and outside museum walls), and adaptable scheduling enhanced our ability to allow programming to overlap and evolve as we presented untold stories, became an early participant in larger social movements, and addressed inequities. We supported people and startup organizations doing something different, like the initiators of Computers in Art, Design, Research, and Education (CADRE) at SJSU, the South Bay Chapter of Women's Caucus for Art (WCA), and Asian American Women Artists Association (AAWAA). We developed exhibition programming in the community and created collaborative public art projects. The Euphrat also collaborated with the California History Center and Intercultural Studies. We progressed from teaching museum studies classes to initiating class projects across disciplines. We presented workshops and offered local and state conference sessions. We also participated in international exchanges.

Our emphasis on flexibility guided the design of the new Euphrat—its high external and internal accessibility, with sliding doors and movable walls, and capability for multiple interactive exhibition formats with dedicated space for countless and sometimes spontaneous student and community projects.

This formative groundwork paved the way for new visions in the new millennium, such as McTate M. Stroman II's popular First Thursdays that featured open mic, poetry, and music, and innovators like Donna Fung. Fung, a counselor, was that rare individual who cared about a neglected student population; developed heartfelt, maverick programs from scratch against tremendous odds; challenged countless institutional barriers that leave little wiggle room; and inspired multiple community partners. Fung and I worked to develop the Euphrat Multidisciplinary Arts Bridge Program for Foster Youth, in conjunction with her De Anza Summer Bridge Program for foster youth near emancipation. Fung's community celebrations revealed more of her imagination and artistry. They were masterpieces. The graduating youth spoke of personal challenges, sang, and recited their poetry, and community members stood up to read "snippets" of the youth's lives.

Early efforts opened creative opportunities for thousands of participants of all ages and changed many lives. Our multifaceted work at the Euphrat shared a single focus: to integrate an expansive view of art—full of questions and caring—in the very foundation of the community and each person's life. Countless testimonials attest to the success of our goal.

---

3 When the exhibition was over, I left a hint of the Sean Boyles mural—a flying duck—untouched at the top of a high wall, what I hoped would be a long-lasting remembrance and a reminder to rise above the controlling elements of our lives. The mural will ever live with me. Yet museums revert to floor-to-ceiling pristine walls. Maybe one day a restoration expert will remove a few layers of paint, so people can smile as a duck flies free.

Tony May: Playing for Real

Much has been written about artist, master woodworker, conceptualist, and San José State University professor emeritus Tony May. Here are just a few examples of his extensive art and community building actions that stood out for me beyond his contributions in art,[1] education, alternative spaces, and collaborative public art projects.

May has been playing the art-and-life game a long time. Back in 1985, we conversed about "Improving the World, the Process and the Growth."[2] While some artists beautify corporations, he has targeted deteriorating buildings and promoted an awareness of the city and the effort, however small, to affect it.
May reflects:

In the fall of '84, I taught a class called Town Improvements. The premise was that art should do something to improve the world, rather than make it worse. The students and I decided to make nondenominational art shrines, inspired by Shinto and European street shrines. It became a performance and was politically complicated. We revealed our intention to use a doorway on the back of an abandoned downtown building too early. A couple of the students had gone ahead to prepare the doorway at night and painted the area black—nice and neat—but in the process tipped off the owner. Negotiations followed, but permission to proceed was denied. Finally, early on a Sunday morning, we just did it anyway— a polychromed spectacle: gold leaf, mosaic tile, mirrors, like a David Best or Lois Anderson sculpture. Anarchy was involved; it was a process development piece. Nice contrast: a five-story building, five floors of scum contrasted with polychrome tile on the stairs, copper, Mylar, mosaic door covering—like an entrance to an exotic private club. The building still stands at 3rd and Santa Clara but has long since been renovated, and the artwork no longer exists.

Downtown San José doorway project nearing completion

1 Pritikin, Renny. "Why Aren't You Famous Yet?" *Tony May: Old Technology*. San Jose Institute of Contemporary Art, 2010. Exhibition catalog essay.
Critic Kenneth Baker included *Tony May: Old Technology* in his list of top ten art exhibitions of 2011: "The San Jose Institute of Contemporary Art honored a half-hidden treasure of the Bay Area art scene, a 'conceptual craftsman' whose art emerges—sometimes not very far—from house renovation." Baker, Kenneth. "Kurt Schwitters display dazzled Bay Area art scene." *San Francisco Chronicle*, Sunday Datebook, December 25, 2011, p 10. sfgate.com/cgi-bin/article.cgi.

2 Rindfleisch, Jan. "The First San Jose Biennial." *The First San Jose Biennial*. San Jose Museum of Art, 1985. Exhibition catalog essay. Details expanded and/or clarified by Tony May.

I think the *Tumbleweed Topiary Garden* (1980) was one of my favorites. My Special Projects class constructed it next to the Fox Theater—"the fox hole," a transient-haven kind of place with one part at basement level. We built a formal garden out of tumbleweed with arches and walkways—trimmed it with hedge clippers.

Once, my class was invited to produce a show on very short notice for the main gallery at SJSU. We had earlier been exploring the Guadalupe River area, marveling at well-organized homeless lodgings under bridges and collecting interesting debris from the creek bed. In the show called *Recent Acquisitions*, these items were presented as rare museum pieces. We used Plexiglas cases for such items as newspaper logs, set them up in the dark gallery with dramatic directed lighting. We had a black-tie reception with highbrow music.

May enabled us to see downtown San José in a new way and taught us about place naming, cultural history, and sharing. In 1978, May gave a group of us a ceramic fish from his temporary public installation *Milagro de los Pescados (Miracle of the Fishes)*, created for the Paseo de San Antonio fountain in conjunction with the San José Museum of Art's *The San José Exhibit*. The modern art installation, comprised of 28 ceramic fish floating with their heads out of water in a downtown fountain in a semi-abandoned plaza, commemorated a legendary sermon given by St. Anthony of Padua. It was mind-bending, so unexpected. I still have my ceramic fish.

Tony May pioneered collaborative public art in San José. In 1982, artist Valerie Patten wrote:[3]

> [His] group projects ... constitute a highly evolved contribution to thought about process, about values which can be allowed to consciously or unconsciously predominate in process, and the relationship of process to product.

> ... Ideas were arrived at through group discussions and brainstorming, [with May's position] something closer to [that of] discussion leader.

> Anyone who has ever tried to work democratically with other artists on a project knows how difficult it is to learn when and how to compromise aesthetically or ideologically and when not to ... one must first define one's own values and imagine a way to make them function optimally when meshed with the ideas of others. Occasionally, confusion in May's groups is preferred ... initial confusion is always overcome by the

Tumbleweed Topiary Garden entrance

3 Patten, Valerie. "Tony May's Projects: Values Embodied in Process." *PRESENTENSE*, San Jose Institute for Contemporary Art, June 1982.

participants themselves … they rethink and recreate themselves to deal with the situation. This involves each person in a humanistic dialogue with themselves and the rest of the group, supported by May's attitude.

… May's sensitivity to dialogue, his ability to create an atmosphere for groups to function in and to believe in their own viability is radical….

[May:] "The only way you can make people change their mind is to just show them. One tries to find some little truth, and if one finds it, one wants to convey it, to show it to others, to come up with some happy coincidence that will allow one to elucidate or present that truth to others."

May taught the Art in the Community class at SJSU for decades and created collaborative public art projects, often with no budget other than what the group could scrounge together by their own devices.[4] An exception was a project funded by the City of San José: a large memorial to San José community activist and spiritual leader Father Mateo Sheedy, pastor of Sacred Heart Parish from 1988–2000. Sheedy rebuilt the church damaged by the 1989 earthquake and created hope and opportunities for his low-income community. Working with a group of SJSU students, May completed a monumental-scale memorial umbrella for Parque de Padre Mateo Sheedy, a City of San José park. The sculpture, entitled *El Paraguas del Padre Mateo*, was dedicated in September 2008.

May doesn't sugarcoat the trials of a community action process in a university setting. "It's a struggle. Torture. Endless wrangling. It worked with a class size of 12, but not when the minimum class size was increased to 18 students. Some students found the collaborative process too much chaos, or tedious—some would freak out or walk out." If both people and structures in academia and government were more flexible, it could ensure a more vital educational experience and better understanding of what it means and entails to find community consensus.

Many of May's students went on to bring new dimensions to art and community. Hawaii-based artist Lonny Tomono, schooled in Shinto temple restoration in Japan, collaborated on a project with May called *A Transient T. Tree House* in 1999. Artist Margaret Stainer, with contagious enthusiasm for art and investigation, developed the Ohlone College gallery in Fremont over three decades. She researched part of our *Staying Visible* publication in 1981. Patton, who went on to teach in the prisons, commented that May could

… get [us] past the pomp and circumstance of art to genuinely and spontaneously respond to ideas … [He was] a subversive force within the college art department … offer[ing] the

---

4 Ibid. "It is hard to imagine a neighborhood more disrupted by redevelopment than downtown San José. People living in the older sections of town have had to put up with large pieces of unfinished freeway ending abruptly in their backyards, demolished lots, and empty city blocks collecting refuse in their neighborhoods. In this chaotic and humanly depressing environment, May organized the following series of group projects: Snow-cover in St. James Park, 1968; the handmade Adobe House built on a neglected lot near SJSU, 1971; *Curtis Place Park*, 1971; the *Hercules Club*, 1972; paintings of historical beds under Guadalupe Creek bridges, 1973; *Rat Lab Mural*, on campus, 1974; the *Julian Café*, Julian Street, 1975; the *Chiechi House*, a restoration project, 1977; the *Temporary Tree*, SJSU campus, 1979; *Billboards*, 1979; the *Rubber Baby Bentons*, hundreds of miniature Fletcher Benton sculptures made out of foam rubber, 1980; *Joining*, a fence constructed by joining individually made sections, 1980; and finally, *Laundry Hung Out to Dry*, succeeded by the *Simulated Topiary Garden*, 1981."

alternative of an exploration of conceptual art. … Some of [the] temporary artworks produced collectively by students (and other collaborators) were this artist's best legacy of all.[5]

What stands out is his nonhierarchical collaboration and team play.[6] It wasn't all about him, even from the earliest days of the alternative space, Works, which he helped found. May laments the all-too-common simplification of art history and its negative impact. "So many were involved in the founding of Works. Somehow it has boiled down to a couple of people. It's not fair. It's actually annoying and not accurate." Others working with May could take the lead and the glory. He encouraged his collaborators to step out of rigid, sometimes petty institutional systems. He told them to challenge themselves fully so they can develop, shine and grow. In this way, May fostered a true communal spirit of sharing.

El Paraguas del Padre Mateo. Steel, concrete, ceramic tile, c. 50' tall.

---

5 Patten, Valerie. "Tony May: The Meager Retrospective (Work from the Basement Archives)." Essay accompanying the Ohlone College Louise Meager Art Gallery exhibition of the same name, 2006.

6 For more general information, art, and articles, see www.tonymay.net.

Ruth Tunstall Grant: Artrepreneur

The Beginning Years

It's spring 2012. Ruth Tunstall Grant and I are talking in her studio, connecting past and present, exploring values and ideas. In full sight is a large painting Tunstall Grant has started, filled with eight blue circular brushstrokes. More bold color and brushstrokes will come. For now, there are just hints of her earlier canvases, the *Warrior Princesses*, filled with the colors and the I-can-do-it-all joys of childhood.

In her youth, Tunstall Grant's interests were art and architecture. "Only guys were interested in those subjects then," so she was often the only girl. A straight-A student, she went to college at 16 and lived on her own. Today in her studio, we talk of the late 1970s and early '80s, when some of us, including Tunstall Grant, decided to build an alternative arts community in the South Bay. She was there at the beginning. So was I. The past? "It's all OK. Even the bad political stuff." It gives her strength and perspective.

Overcoming Barriers

Tunstall Grant has had to deal with barriers and hostility in her struggle to build community. Talking about the past brings up memories of pain and anger for her. In the late '70s and '80s, it was difficult to join the art world in San José. Being a black woman and also not a graduate of San José State made Tunstall Grant an outsider. The aesthetic was narrow, fairly rigid. She was told, "You are not cutting-edge. Too ethereal." We both agreed that anger could be a strong motivator for creative action. Tunstall Grant persevered. Somehow, like water, she can find a path and make something beautiful grow along the way.

Tunstall Grant ultimately developed a strong exhibition history. An early success was her 1981 exhibition with sculptor David Middlebrook in the San José Museum of Art under director Albert Dixon and curator Martha Manson. She had a prime spot in the new annex. Russell Moore, subsequent director at the San José Museum of Art, featured her in the late '80s, when he opened three Allegra Galleries in San José. Tunstall Grant's work was featured as the inaugural show at all three sites. The exhibit in the Dorman Building on First Street had one of the biggest openings ever in San José. It was across from Eulipia Restaurant, a white-tablecloth restaurant with poetry readings upstairs. "We took over all of Eulipia—over 600 people. The *Mercury News* did a good job of coverage. That was 1990–1991." Tunstall Grant's artwork was purchased for numerous collections, including the Presidential Suite at the Fairmont, where her work hung alongside the art of painter David Hockney.

Now she was a star artist. But recognition from the "in" crowd, a circle of establishment art academics and dealers, came late. "I was doing trailblazing on my own." It was only after her work was placed in the Presidential Suite that an arts leader told her that her work had "grown and changed. Maybe you should have been shown earlier." Commenting on the discrimination encountered at that time, Tunstall Grant says flat out: "Quiet, unseen stupidity" happens at every level. People at the top "have a lot of shit, too." Those were the times when curators, directors, dealers, and academic committees made little effort to "encompass all of humanity, not just Anglo-Saxon men."

Tunstall Grant has two ongoing projects. One is a watercolor picture book for her new granddaughter. She calls it a "Tunstall Grant Aesop Fable," a tale about how to deal with life and what it means to give out joy. "Like a butterfly, joy comes back to you." The other project is about a father she never knew, but learned about through Google. He was one of the Tuskegee Airmen during WWII, America's first black military airmen. She says of her research, "That's for my son and his family. It fills in gaps."

Curatorial Trailblazing

As we begin to touch on various aspects of the arts in Silicon Valley, we remark on how the history of Silicon Valley from a get-past-the-barriers arts standpoint has not been told, and we proceed to add pieces to the puzzle, tracing Tunstall Grant's footsteps.

Tunstall Grant and I connected early on at Works Gallery, a trailblazing space for emerging artists. She was on the first board of directors for Works, starting when it was housed in a former meat store on Auzerais Avenue in San José. For meetings we would often sit on the bare wood floor. San José State University art professor Tony May was president of the board.

Various curators took turns organizing early exhibitions. I was one of them, taking my first curatorial opportunity to address a wider perspective. At a storefront on First Street, Tunstall Grant went all out and created the first official graffiti show, *Off the Streets*, in summer 1986. She also advocated for one of textile artist Consuelo Jimenez Underwood's early shows. A professor emeritus at San José State, where she developed an innovative textiles program, Underwood would go on to make a big impact locally and internationally. Underwood's powerful images are widely acclaimed and she is featured in the 2012 PBS special *Threads*.

Bringing Art to the Schools

We often talked about going beyond mere lip service to encompass a broad spectrum of humanity, and took action to realize this over the decades. Countering exclusion was a shared impetus behind our work—mine as executive director at the Euphrat Museum of Art, and Tunstall Grant's as director of education at the San José Museum of Art and later at the Santa Clara County Children's Shelter.

In the late '80s, Tunstall Grant and I often met at the onetime Good Earth restaurant near Santa Clara University, where we had many conversations about the needs of the art community and the need for programs for children. We both realized that creating an art community meant building it from the ground up, and at all levels simultaneously, from families to school district leaders and city government officials.

While the Euphrat Museum of Art had been working with school classes for years, I wanted a program that took art creativity, skills, ideas, and a diversified history to the school sites. Tunstall Grant helped me develop the Arts & Schools Program for the

Euphrat. We began our Educational Committee in 1988–1989 as part of the Euphrat board. Tunstall Grant was our first consultant. We brought a few other heavyweights to join her, such as Maribel Alvarez, who was simultaneously co-founding MACLA (1989). Tunstall Grant, Alvarez, and I shared a deeply felt commitment to social engagement. We aimed to reach at-risk youth, and to add new cross-cultural perspectives.

Museum Outreach Program to Neighborhoods and Downtown

Tunstall Grant triumphed in developing unusual, new programs within mainstream systems, such as a uniquely engaging outreach initiative to build the San José Museum of Art School up to 3,000 kids. There were only 28 children when she started in 1979: 14 for Jeanne Aurel Schneider, then education director, and 14 for Tunstall Grant as teacher. This was a huge accomplishment in the growth of the arts in Silicon Valley. It was "the first outreach program ever for the museum." In contrast to fee-based classes in the museum, this effort would go to the schools and reach kids where they lived—in their neighborhoods, including the museum's downtown district. Tunstall Grant chose schools in impoverished, struggling San José neighborhoods, such as the Eastside, Alviso and Berryessa. She applied for a Community Development Block Grant for seed money. Tunstall Grant recalls: "In the '80s, around '84, I told my outreach idea to Al Dixon [then San José Museum of Art director]. He didn't think it made sense." But the new director Russell Moore thought it did. Tunstall Grant persevered, and real collaborations were formed with the school districts.

Beyond Art: Relating to Children at the Shelter

In the late 1980s and 1990s, Tunstall Grant began her long stint as director of art education at the Santa Clara County Children's Shelter with a $2,500 grant. Over 15 years, she grew it to a $1 million program with funding from the California Arts Council, National Endowment for the Arts, and others. At the end, she employed 12 teachers to work with abused youth, foster youth, and runaways.

> I've always loved kids. I'm a queen of pop culture. You have to be to deal with a seven-year-old. You can't speak [the kids'] language unless you are willing to go into their reality. It is part of being a good educator.

She pauses, reflecting on her experience teaching maltreated children and youth at the shelter.

> Society is being torn apart. Take the abused child. Every line has been crossed in a negative way: verbal abuse, lack of food, beatings, and sexual abuse. We are not just teaching art, but re-educating. For example, you are sitting in your chair. You don't lean over, take another kid's pen, and draw on his paper!

Tunstall Grant believes you have to send straight messages so the kids will learn about consequences.

> My granddaughter is like any child in the world. Joy in; joy out. But one needs to make the lines clear. There's no negotiation with a toddler, a preschooler. Art is about discipline, setting a goal, doing it over and over. Then you can stretch the rules because you know them. You have

to know even the basics, like how to get away to a safe place. Ultimately, you are by yourself. There is not someone else always calling the shots.

A Visionary Leader

Tunstall Grant has been an energetic, visionary leader. She was one of the first board members of the Santa Clara County Arts Council [later called Arts Council Silicon Valley]. Serving as chair of education, she created Hands on the Arts, an annual participatory, fun-filled arts weekend event to reach and include more children and families. The Euphrat participated in the early years in what would become a signature event for Sunnyvale.

> The first one was at the County Fairgrounds. Then the City of Sunnyvale wanted to be involved [c. 1985]. Sunnyvale still has the program. It's going strong.

Nurturing the Arts

Tunstall Grant started Genesis/A Sanctuary for the Arts from scratch in the same time period that she began at the Santa Clara County Children's Shelter, and continued with both simultaneously for well over a decade. She would tell people, "The shelter is my day job." After working all day at the children's shelter, she'd pick up her son and go to Genesis. "He grew up at Genesis, listening to the music."

The nonprofit, full-of-life studio and art space was housed at three sequential locations in San José that she renovated and developed. The first, on Ryland Street, was a huge warehouse transformed into art and music studios, with a gallery plus rehearsal and performing space. The second space for Genesis was at 40 First Street; it occupied the whole second floor, with use of the fourth floor for huge performances.

The third location on The Alameda took seven months to clean out and convert to exhibition and artist spaces. It later transformed into ArtWorks, the current fine-art studio complex dedicated to helping students of all ages tap into their artistic capabilities and realize their artistic goals. Figurative painter George Rivera, director of the Triton Museum for many years, had a studio there.

Concerts at Genesis included India Cooke, the renowned jazz violinist, and others. Current United States Poet Laureate Juan Felipe Herrera performed there. Tunstall Grant even brought the legendary painter Jacob Lawrence to Genesis.

Relationship Building

Tunstall Grant's outgoing, encouraging manner has helped her build substantive relationships across the valley. In the midst of our conversation about the growth of the local scene, the phone rings. The friend/colleague on the phone had worked with Tunstall Grant on the Children's Shelter's Quilt Project, which Tunstall Grant started with a volunteer around the year 2000. This program spanned her last 10 years at the shelter and involved 23 women, all quilters, working from an artistic perspective. There were various exhibitions. "A lot of quilts! Many still hang at the courthouse on Terraine Street."

A long-time San José Art Commissioner, Tunstall Grant was chair of public art for six years. In recent years, she chaired the City Hall Exhibits Committee, in which I had the pleasure to participate. Tunstall Grant developed wide-ranging, compelling City Hall exhibitions, starting with San José's early history and *Hidden Heritages: Six African American Families 1860–1920*. Throughout her tenure, she worked closely with the former director of the City of San José's Public Art Program Barbara Goldstein, who put San José public art on the map and brought it to prominence. In addition to the City Hall shows, they worked together on art at community centers and at the new Norman Y. Mineta San José International Airport. Having come from public art programs in Seattle and Los Angeles, Barbara Goldstein understood what Tunstall Grant has been trying to accomplish in these last decades.

Crossing Rivers and Cultures

On Tunstall Grant's studio wall is a large meditative painting of China that she did around 1988–1989. She received a fellowship to teach painting and drawing at the Children's Palace in Beijing and was a special guest at the University of Shanghai because she had written a paper entitled "Creativity and Discipline," feeling at the time that U.S. education was lacking in the discipline department. The scene is a little village outside of Xían, before it was totally excavated, before tours—mountains, a river, and a small boat. Tunstall Grant sees this "crossing-the-river" landscape every morning. While I ponder river-crossing metaphors in Tunstall Grant's life, she tells me about the African work the University of Shanghai held, and about blacksmith teachers brought from Benin and Ghana in earlier centuries. Tunstall Grant, who easily crosses from one culture to another in the course of a day, uses this moment to make the connection between cultures, even ones overseas.

Artrepreneurship

As Tunstall Grant and I consider life directions, she muses:

> My creative journey? It was like [being] an 'artrepreneur.' The first thing an art student would be told then was, 'There are no jobs in art. If you are a woman, there are no jobs in art. If you are a minority, there are no jobs in art.' But I was determined. If you can create things, you can create jobs. You see openings. You see voids … where one could make a living.

The creating-the-job part was true for me also; there was no funding at the Euphrat when I started. For both of us, our art forms involved job creation, not interviews for established positions.

On Mothering and Mentoring

We talk about mothering and Tunstall Grant's son. When he was young, she says, she was clear: "I'm an artist. I got to go to the studio." When her son was asked what stood out from his childhood, he mentioned the time she had the cheese, crackers, and celery out and said, "Let's snack up and go to the museum." His other friends' moms made cookies. Tunstall Grant said to him, "I'm not a cookie [and] jello mom. Know who your mom is. Don't have expectations."

We talk about her students.

> I'm not a pushover. Clear expectations. Non-negotiable. If they act up, it ups the ante. Their time-out increases. One student asked, 'How long is my time-out?' I asked, 'How old are you?' 'Seven.' 'OK, seven minutes time-out.' That's a long time.

> I never met a really bad kid. Many have seen a lot, experienced a lot, so that is how they act. I always liked teaching kids, even the worst of the worst.

Some of the youth she mentored have gone on to develop their art, poetry, and community awareness, but mostly it is about their own personal growth. "No matter what, you need to start with the basics. Talk about art. You don't give illusions."

An Advocate for Creative Power

Bougainvilleas bloom outside the window. Tunstall Grant is cutting silhouettes of girls walking and playing for her "Tunstall Grant Aesop Fable" book project. The letter "A" is for African girls. We speak of power, something so many people want. Tunstall Grant says:

> I don't have the power. I'm trying to empower [others]. This is a hard spiritual, moral lesson for people to learn. … I am an advocate for the arts, an educator. I happen also to be an artist.

For Tunstall Grant, it has always been about "being an advocate for the creative power we all have, bringing back creativity and light into people's lives." The art goes off the canvas into daily life. "There are no wasted moments. All moments are magical, gifts." Like the time I have spent with her today—truly a gift.

Ruth Tunstall Grant, *Breaking the Chain of Abuse*. Acrylic on canvas, 6'x8'. From the series *Breaking the Chains of Abuse*. Originally designed to be a billboard.

Consuelo Jimenez Underwood: Thread Art Warrior

Consuelo Jimenez Underwood is a pillar of our vibrant Silicon Valley arts scene. She confronts barriers by probing, researching, teaching, and inspiring. Her art and words power new views about the importance of art engaging community, the borders in our lives, and the too often unchallenged separation of academia from community.

One of Underwood's biggest contributions to the Santa Clara Valley cultural scene was her role as professor and the chair of the Fiber/Textiles area at San José State University, where from 1989–2009, she developed the program and powered new views of the "craft vs. art" division.[1]

> For over 20 years, I "seeded" the notion that the "needle and thread" is a valid artistic practice, way more than "craft." Many students, staff, and even fellow professors that ventured into the fiber studios would encounter an environment of textile and contemporary art. My personal mission was to infiltrate the art world with threads. Everyone who entered the SJSU fiber studios would leave empowered with "thread knowledge" to be able to join the ranks of the "Thread Art Warriors."

Underwood tackles basic art and life concepts and gives them a twist:

> Crossing borders and negotiating between two perspectives has always been a fundamental aspect of my persona and the basis of my creative process. … Over 30 years ago, when "craft vs. art" was the most divisive issue in the arts, I discovered and established my "authentic artistic voice," refocused my artistic studies from the paintbrush and pigments to "needle and thread." Empowered by the voices of my indigenous maternal ancestors, I began to cross the intellectual borders that separated the hand and the mind from the "fine" art spirit.[2]

She prods people to observe, think, feel, and act as engaged citizens.

> My work is a reflection of personal border experiences: the interconnectedness of societies, insisting on beauty in struggle, and celebrating the notion of seeing this world through my tricultural lens. Thus, when I weave, sew, or embellish, the *viejitas* (the old ones) seem to express their encouragement and support of my creations.

> A central message [of my work] is that a binational environmental travesty is occurring, a result of the physical barrier that is under construction between Mexico and the United States. … More importantly, perhaps the viewer will become more engaged in her/his civic duties as a

---

[1] Underwood's early contributions supported the valley's fledgling arts organization and art education endeavors. In 1984–1985, she served as publicity director for Gallery 9, a cooperative gallery in Los Altos. Then, as a SJSU graduate student (1985–1987), she connected with Associate Dean of Humanities and Art Dr. Jose Colchado; was an educational enhancement task force organizer, co-directing Big Brother–Big Sister Day; and exhibition director for the Museums of Los Gatos' Sixth Annual Santa Clara County–Wide High School Art Exhibition and Competition. From 1987–1988, Underwood was a member of Works/San José's artist selection committee and served as an exhibition director.

[2] Underwood, Consuelo. Written bio for Silicon Valley Creates, 2013. Remaining quotes: Rindfleisch, Jan. Personal conversations with Underwood. 2013–2015.

citizen when confronting or engaging in border politics, whether it be on a political, social, or personal level. Whether or not the viewer is an immigrant or a descendant of immigrants, we all have to learn how to merge our cultural differences and biases and view our environment as one place. As a society, we need to reassess our notion of borders and nations and consider the long-term ecological damage that our current political policies are achieving.

When one does nothing, the saints cry.

Robin Lasser, documentary photographs of Consuelo Jimenez Underwood's *Borderline Encounter #1, Tortilla Meets Tortilla Wall*, 2005, a performance in the ocean with 43" diameter tortilla made of dyed and sewn maize husks, commissioned by MACLA in conjunction with *Tortillas, Chiles, and Other Border Things* exhibition. Imperial Beach, Alta California/Tijuana, Baja California. Photo sequence by artist and SJSU professor Robin Lasser, who initiated the collaborative art event and organized the border interventions at Border Field State Park on the U.S. side of the border fence jutting into the ocean. The event also included Lasser's art and interpretive border documentation by SJSU graduate photography students.

Underwood has taken her multilayered art and life installations inland. In *Mountain Mama Borderline Blues*, a 35-foot-wide wall installation at the Nevada Museum of Art, a jagged line of nails, barbed wire, beads, and fibers representing the U.S.–Mexico border juts across a wall painting resembling Nevada's Black Rock formations. Large fabric flowers pay no attention to the artificial limitations. Safety pins "hold together" her nearby *Home of the Brave* woven textile.

Migrant labor and women's labor have traditionally been given low status. "My process pretty much follows my philosophy," Underwood said. "Little is great and great is small. Hence, the 'low' becomes 'high' [and] then the world is beautiful."

For her 2015 exhibition *Mothers—The Art of Seeing* at the Nevada Museum of Art, she made her philosophy clear, whether about the art world or real world: "Find joy in the struggle. Find strength in weakness. Find spirit in the mundane."[3]

---

3 Horn, Amanda. "Artists moving beyond the borders of tradition." *Reno Gazette-Journal*, March 26, 2015. rgj.com/story/life/2015/03/27/artists-moving-beyond-borders-tradition/70529528/

In 2016, Underwood was featured in the U.S. Textile/Contemporary Art Museum at George Washington University in Washington, D.C. For *Stories of Migration: Contemporary Artists Interpret Diaspora*, she could create a new borderline piece for a 31-foot-high wall of her choice. The artist loves working on large walls and happily took her art to where national decisions are made.

Underwood's artwork is stunning and provocative on its own merits, but she has also given talks, consulted, served on panels, committees, and boards, with an extensive and substantive résumé of local involvement. She was willing to come to SJSU on a cold autumn night for a personal talk with a class on social justice. She satisfies our craving to learn, whether through demonstrations, dialogue, or video, such as her June 2003 SPARK interview for San Francisco PBS station KQED. Being tricultural, she relates to Silicon Valley in multiple ways and has electrified museum, gallery, academic, and community audiences from venues all around the valley, reaching young and old. Simultaneously, her international involvement has brought increasing recognition of Silicon Valley as an arts center, and enhanced interchange and knowledge locally.[4]

In my earlier "Spiral" narrative, Underwood spoke about her Amerindian roots; growing up working in the fields, while others locally built the Chicano movement; making baskets as a young mother, inspired by Dat So La Lee (Washoe);[5] indigenous struggles; spiritual renewal in Yaqui Land; and a big differential in experiences in the larger society.

In this vein, Underwood reflected on artist José Antonio Burciaga and his 1989 mural at Casa Zapata dormitory at Stanford University. For *Last Supper of Chicano Heroes* in the Casa Zapata dining hall, students of the dorm filled out a survey about who their heroes were; then Burciaga placed these figures in a traditional Last Supper image. It is part of the larger mural *The History of Maize*. Included were people such as Cesar Chavez, Sor Juana Ines de la Cruz, and Dr. Martin Luther King, Jr. Underwood had insistent questions for Burciaga:

> How could you? How could you not put Zapata in [the front-and-center chair in] the Amerindian component? How could you put Che Guevara from Europe there instead of Zapata? We would always get into it.

Burciaga stood up for the process. Underwood would argue the subject matter. Yet Underwood admired Burciaga greatly.

> A good man. He understood. … I loved him. He respected who I was. It was all for the cause, and not about him. He was an incredible warrior. A Texan. I understood more after I went to Texas.

---

[4] For more information including art, articles, and multiple videos, see consuelojunderwood.com. One video lecture at SJSU gives the story of her political work, starting with her undergraduate years in the '70s. Underwood's international presence has included a cultural exchange visit to Taiwan in 2009 and participation in the U.S. Department of State's Art in Embassies program.

[5] Dat So La Lee (ca. 1829 – December 6, 1925), whose birth name was "Dabuda," meaning "Young Willow," (English name, Louisa Keyser) was a renowned American basket weaver and one of the most famous Native American artists of the 20th century. A member of the Washoe people in northwestern Nevada, her basketry came to national prominence during the Arts and Crafts movement of the early 1900s.

Underwood learned about artist/poet/writer Burciaga and his mural, and Vice Provost Cecilia Burciaga—along with the couple's powerful yet contested presence at the university—through her daughter, who was a law student at Stanford. The Burciagas served as Casa Zapata Resident Fellows from 1985 to 1994, and mentored Underwood's daughter.[6] Underwood sighs when she remembers indigenous struggles at the school. "For warriors, what else is new? It's been 500 years here, thousands of years in Europe. They're still at it."

Regarding local art world and academic barriers, she quips in a manner recognizable to many Silicon Valley workers stifled by organizational structures or milieus:

> Let's write a novel, so we can do the movie. A mystery. The day some mind-numbing administrators left town, let go, and turned in their badges.

> This [endeavor could be] like driving three stagecoaches: documenting historical coffee-table book, collected stories, a novel. *Rebozities in the Silicon Valley*. Who were the instigators again?

Underwood switches from the mystery novel to real life:

> We need to recreate the energy of the '80s. It was so alive. Spontaneity was allowed; [there was] electricity in the halls at San José State. They even hired me. Then the '90s came. Not as beautiful. By 2000, nothing beautiful. Only the résumé.

> The change—it had been so radical, so extreme. It vibrated before. Now it [the spirit] goes dead. No magic or electricity—[in] people and things. The Internet sucked it up. In 2000, it wasn't there. Money [took over].

Thinking back to the beginnings of her art career, Underwood reflects: "I thought [creating art] would be like [being in] the caves. People take things away, bring me things." But after an early exhibition, one of her instructors "threw me to the wolves. … [Now I have] to think of publicity, remember things, go to banquets, send out packets. And I just want to thread this silver *rebozo*!!"

I recall Underwood's preparing in May 2012 for her 2013 Triton Museum exhibition. She was making *rebozos* for the mothers, starting with the mothers of the earth, then moon, then water. She had the wires for the weaving, with "bronze for earth." She had her locations for work, fashioning the moon rebozo at her northern California getaway, the earth at her home in Cupertino. Making progress, she became sad as the series was nearing the end. But then in one of her inimitable creativity moments, she thought of multiples. "Can you imagine—one for each of four seasons? My goal is for 60 or 70!" That's a lot of weaving. It takes two seasons to weave a rebozo, two hours to weave just an inch.

She planned two *rebozos* for the Virgen de Guadalupe. There was a man in Japan getting rid of old kimono looms. He had gold and silver threads, and brought back warps, enough for her to do five *rebozos* in "different golds … yellow, red-orange ..." Like the *rebozos* she creates, Underwood weaves the fabric of her life, illuminated by threads of different colors.

---

6 Underwood's daughter has since become a legal advisor to the Yaqui Tribe.

OPENING DOORS

Mary Jane Solis: Onward from El Centro

Mary Jane Solis is one of several Chicano students who came together to co-found El Centro Cultural de la Gente in the early 1970s.[1] Referring to El Centro Cultural, she says:

> We just started providing programs and the community came and Chicano artists came to present their works. We had no money and no training on how to do it, but we had passion. We got a building from the city that was about to be torn down for $1/year, and since there was no heating, families would come with their blankets to watch theatre.

Adrian Vargas, founder and director of San José's Teatro de la Gente (1967–1977), was a co-founder and first executive director of El Centro.[2] When the group went to the city "fine arts" commission for funding, they were told the commission did not fund "folk art." So they brought a class action suit against the city through Casa Legal and a recently graduated lawyer from Santa Clara University. An application form was forthcoming. The first grant was $15,000, but it opened the door for other multicultural funding, and ultimately the commission dropped the "fine" out of "fine arts."

Solis was also a founding member of Movimiento de Arte y Cultura Latino Americana (MACLA) in 1989, and served as vice chair of the San José Arts Commission (and chair for Multicultural Arts Development 1987–1995). To this day, through her work at Santa Clara County's Office of Human Relations (OHR),[3] she continues to promote art as a vehicle for building community and for promoting human rights. Solis remains a stalwart art activist through her involvement with organizations such as Teatro Visión and the San Jose Multicultural Artists Guild.

Solis sees "arts and culture as a foundation for cultural visibility, framing political and social ideas, and building pride in our community." Yet it's "still a battle" for funding, support, and involvement. "In the '70s and '80s, we began to see how important it was to have Latinos at the decision-making table, and so several of us, including myself, sought appointment to the San José Arts Commission." Solis felt that it was important that the commission foster a more multicultural perspective, and this began her long history in multicultural

---

[1] Drawn in part from "Performance, Art, and Activism," a panel discussion on the legacy of El Centro Cultural de la Gente, September 25, 2013, Dr. Martin Luther King, Jr. Library, San José, in conjunction with exhibition by photographer Jesús Manuel Mena Garza, and additional conversations with or writing of Solis.

[2] For more description of the times and the participation of Adrian Vargas, see Jimenez, Francisco, Alma M. García, and Richard A. Garcia. *Ethnic Community Builders, Mexican Americans in Search of Justice and Power, The Struggle for Citizenship Rights in San José, California*, Alta Mira Press, 2007. The book has a section on "Culture and the Arts," including artist/activist Mary Andrade, co-founder of the weekly bilingual newspaper *La Oferta*.

[3] Solis has been a force for decades, creating art, exhibitions, events, programs, and even award ceremonies—wonderful support and recognition for what is oftentimes a difficult struggle and scarcely visible. Not only has she worked on OHR annual Human Relations Award ceremonies, but also on Women of Achievement awards in the '80s and '90s, when the Commission on the Status of Women was part of OHR. Artist/activist Ruth Tunstall Grant recognizes Solis's contributions: "What she has done for the Office of Human Relations—she put it on the map, so people noticed. She brought in spoken word, performance, panels, and symposia. She's a quiet, unsung hero."

El Centro Cultural de la Gente, 1974. Photo: Jesús Manuel Mena Garza.

arts development. Because of their ingrained mentality, it took several years to make real changes regarding the way the commission funded local arts groups, but it made a big difference to the arts community. She recalls an incident when a city commissioner once questioned funding for multicultural arts and stated, "Don't you think that it's tantamount to welfare?" She observes, "He obviously wasn't thinking of the buildings and large subsidies given to San José's 'big four' arts institutions at that time."

On the San José Arts Commission, Solis worked closely with other activists: Jerry Hiura, Pua (Lillie) Takamoto, and Susan Marsland.

Gil Villagran, educator/social worker, and the last president of El Centro Cultural, was on the first Santa Clara County Arts Council board. When he questioned the small amount of funding that was granted to multicultural arts organizations, he was told, "Everybody benefits from funding the symphony." "I guess it was the trickle-down theory mentality that was so popular at that time," commented Solis. Playwright Luis Valdez also encountered prejudice at the California Arts Council. "It was a knock-down, drag-out fight," he stated.

Elisa Marina Alvarado joined Teatro de la Gente in 1973 and became the first full-time staff of El Centro Cultural. She would curate exhibitions and program the black box—"It was a way to talk about what was going on in the streets," such as the shooting of a black man, then a Chicano. Alvarado, later founder/director of Teatro Visión, felt empowered, and felt the need to challenge traditional gender roles in theater and in the arts in general. It was difficult being a part of a paternalistic organization with a man at the head, particularly since women kept it going. Not only did women curate programming and perform on stage, they also cleaned the bathrooms, brought food, and made sets and costumes. The changing gender roles were a huge challenge at that time. Without experience and the skills for dialogue, discussions became polarized; other women were afraid to speak up. Alvarado was censured, had to leave, and felt "punished for her outspokenness."

As a woman, taking leadership was difficult because the group also wanted a united front. At El Centro however, Solis was able to take the visual arts lead because men didn't want it.

> It gave me the opportunity to utilize my organizational skills and to learn how to curate exhibitions. I went to exhibitions at the Galeria de la Raza in the San Francisco Mission District, where I got inspired by Latina artists such as Carmen Lomas Garza, Las Mujeres Muralistas, and Lorna Dee Cervantes. Artists Jesús Garza, Art Cadilli, Jaime Valadez and others came to teach each other techniques, beginning with a silk-screening class. The idea was to teach ourselves and then the community how to make posters to promote community events. Eventually we worked with CETA (Comprehensive Employment and Training Act) programs for at-risk youth who had artistic talent. However, at first there were no girls in the program, and so I went to the school and found five girls in one day.

Solis stood up to the men, and the girls saw that and did great work. Once, a quiet, shy Vietnamese artist who was in the program was razzed by the Chicano youth. When he did a silkscreen of boat people drowning, they asked him about it. He said it was his family. Their response was "You're a *mojado* like us," and the youth drew him into their circle. He became welcome as one of the guys.

Solis sees El Centro's legacy as a model for what is possible, as a place to come together and feed the community spirit. She recalls learning more there than at San José State University (SJSU), where social justice art was not encouraged or accepted as real art. Social justice art[4] has since become a "new thing," more acceptable.

> We need to provide youth with opportunities in music and art. They need support to strengthen their identity and cultural expression. Unfortunately, so many organizations have fallen. Even today, 90% of San José's Arts Commission funding goes to four groups. Major organizations get a building and a lot of funding to leverage other funding. They have qualified and experienced staff because they can pay them. But it's crumbs for the rest! Funding hasn't changed … It's a cultural equity issue, particularly when our county is at least 66% immigrant or children of immigrants.

Solis is originally from the San Joaquin Valley, where she began producing art under the tutoring of her mother when she was three years old. She moved to San José to study fine arts at SJSU. Since serving as El Centro Cultural's gallery curator and mural program manager from 1978–1981, Solis has been involved in many social justice–related art and

---

4 Solis emphasizes the early context of El Centro—UFW, Central America, Vietnam, crises, police brutality—noting "without context [e.g. a larger awareness, discussion, and mobilization around issues affecting the community], there is no live culture." El Centro was founded at the time of the Chicano Movement and a need to mobilize around issues like racial profiling. Solis relates how in 1974–75, they became aware of immigration issues, particularly through the canneries and deportation. *La Migra* was the "first *acto* [improvised dramatic skit] on immigration ever in an analytical way," from the cannery perspective.

community causes.[5] She educates the community, including leaders and funders, and gives presentations on the Chicano Art Movement and the impact of the Mexican Muralist Movement on Chicano art. Alvarado also notes that Solis, with her tremendous personal insight into the experience of being an artist and activist, has encouraged and supported many young artists. Solis served on the board of directors for Teatro Visión, and for many years has collaborated with the San Jose Multicultural Artists Guild as curator for their annual Dia de los Muertos arts exhibitions and festival—a joyful community celebration and remembrance of those who have brought us this far.

Written with Mary Jane Solis.

---

[5] A painter and designer, in the early 1970s she also created illustrations for labor activist and educator Ernesto Galarza's Mini Libros Series.

Paul Pei-Jen Hau: Quiet Leadership

When renowned artist Paul Hau, 99, speaks at a reception, he is often in his red quilt coat, smiling and joking as he tells stories that recognize the contributions of others. At times he will raise a finger and his voice will get serious. His presentations, interlaced with Mandarin, are always warmly received.

Hau, born in Liaoning Province in northeast China in 1917, is a pioneer in the growth of our Silicon Valley arts community. His community impact is unusual because he came to the U.S. at age 39, both steeped in traditional Chinese painting, an exacting art form, and shaped by large-scale political and cultural change.

Paul and Mary Hau at the opening of Paul's 2013 solo exhibition at Zhejiang Art Museum in Hangzhou, China.

After studying sociology in Japan from 1940–43 and returning to China during the Japanese occupation, Hau's remarkable story includes service in the Nationalist Government as a senator.[1] Disinterested in politics after the Kuomintang/Communist split following the war, he transitioned to fulltime artist/writer and moved to Hong Kong. In 1956, married and

---

1 Friends helped Hau escape from Japan by boat. He could have been killed. When asked if he was scared, he shrugs, "I was young." He worked in the Chongqing foreign affairs department, was promoted as a Japanese expert, moved to Shanghai, and joined the constitutional group, a Kuomintang-Communist collaboration.

with a young family to support, Hau came to the U.S. under the Refugee Act as an artist, writer, and scholar. At first, the Haus were stung by anti-Chinese prejudice here. In 1956 in Palo Alto, not selling a home to Chinese was "common, but people were mostly kind." The young couple found a welcoming haven in Los Altos in 1961.

Hau sensed the importance of making good China–U.S. connections. He taught at the Palo Alto Art Club (now Pacific Art League). In 1956, the first class he taught had "all American students," including a Stanford professor. They asked: "What is brush? What is ink?" After the '60s, the class composition changed to mostly Chinese students. He continued to inspire students for over 50 years, challenging them through conversation that continually crossed cultural borders between China and the U.S., antiquity and modernity.

American Society for the Advancement of Chinese Arts group photo, 2013, with Paul and Mary Hau (green coat). Paul Hau exhibited with members of ASACA at Silicon Valley Asian Art Center (SVAAC) in December 2013. Photo: Karen Tseng.

The newly built de Saisset Museum at Santa Clara University (SCU) presented Hau's first museum exhibition in 1958, when Joseph Pociask, S.J., was director. Hau's first art show had been at St. Mary's Church in San Francisco's Chinatown, "the biggest hall in Chinatown," where he met a lot of old friends. He recalled the show was written up in the *San Francisco Chronicle*. Through this exhibition, Pociask became acquainted with Hau's art. Pociask taught art history at SCU and talked about Chinese art. Students asked typical questions, "like 'how?'" While *Chinese World* published news, there were not very many Chinese artists known in the U.S. then. In 1958, many westerners at Santa Clara University were "shocked by the art," which felt completely different. The focus on water and ink, black and white contrast, line, masterful brushwork, and the use of small traditional trees and houses in commanding Chinese landscapes, felt worlds away from either classic Western realism or 20th century modernist geometric abstraction.

In 1963, the de Young Museum awarded Hau a solo exhibition. Over time, Hau became internationally famous for his colorful splash-ink landscape paintings (the splashing of certain color areas is done on a table or, if large, on the floor), which are innovative visual bridges between cultures of East and West. Paintings of Los Altos, Carmel, and Yosemite play off paintings of childhood memories, nature, and dramatic landscapes in China.

Paul and Mary Hau became a dynamic Peninsula art couple. Theirs is a longtime, deep-rooted love story. Mary Hau understands nuances of Paul's art and process. She has run the Chinese Fine Arts Gallery featuring her husband's art on State Street in Los Altos since 1973, and continues today on a limited basis. Cordial and knowledgeable, elegantly dressed, the former clothing designer has educated viewers and developed collectors for over four decades, contributing to Silicon Valley's cross-cultural appreciation and understanding.[2]

The establishment of a formal diplomatic relationship between the U.S. and China in 1979 propelled discussions in Hau's Palo Alto Art League class. "One day after class, a proposal to form an organization advancing and facilitating Chinese and American art exchange" was enthusiastically embraced, and the American Society for the Advancement of Chinese Arts (ASACA) was born. Like a proud papa, Hau cites an old Chinese saying when he speaks of ASACA's 35-year growth from "youth" to a "respectable man" (or a mature organization), noting the ASACA–sponsored lectures, classes, exhibitions, and travel to China.[3]

Hau draws praise for his quiet leadership. Historian Connie Young Yu's 1985 biographical sketch of Hau described his contributions to Silicon Valley, his "graciousness and depth as a person," and his stature as a Chinese master when he was a "young" 68-year-old. Palo

---

[2] The religious connection was personal and historic. Hau became Catholic in order to marry in 1946. Mary Hau's uncle was a priest, and her family, from Hubei province, had been Catholic for 300 years, since the Ming dynasty. San Francisco's Old St. Mary's Church, the first building erected as a cathedral in California, was built in 1854–1891 with Chinese labor, granite stone from China and bricks from New England. St. Mary's became increasingly involved with nearby Chinatown, a crowded community struggling for survival. St. Mary's Square featured a stainless steel Benny Bufano statue of Sun Yat Sen, activist for the overthrow of the Qing dynasty (1912), "father of modern China," and proponent of democracy. Dr. Sun, born in China and educated in Hawaii, later hid out in exile in San Francisco's Chinatown, relaxed in St. Mary's Square, and fundraised in San José — just down the road from what would become Hau's future home.
Hau knew of East/West art, religious, economic, and political interactions going back over centuries, e.g. Guiseppe Castiglione (Lang Shining), 1688–1766, a Jesuit lay brother from Milan who painted for the emperor for years. At a 2014 event, historian Connie Young Yu elaborated on a famous scroll by Castiglione. The painting is Asian with horses, but combines Western perspective and Chinese stirrup technology; the horses are in games and war is downplayed.
As a participant, scholar, and author (three novels, a history of sociology, a book on Chinese art), Hau has viewed art in Chinese life—contemporary or historical, personal or community, in China or overseas—from ringside. Both Hau and Yu have been tremendous Silicon Valley resources for connecting art with history and exchanges between cultures.

[3] Members of ASACA exhibited at the U.N. Fourth World Women's Conference, China, in 1995. See asaca-art.com/en-us.

Alto artist/educator Nina Ollikainen created a bronze sculpture of Hau and presented it in person for the 2002 inauguration of the Hau-Bei Ren Museum in Kunshan, China, built to honor Hau.

Artist Julie Holding, an electrical engineer retired from Silicon Valley's high-tech industry, is author of *Hau Pei Jen: Bold Horizons in Ink and Color*, with English and Chinese text. In fall 2013, she worked with a film crew from China Central TV, taping in Silicon Valley for a major documentary of Hau's life; then spent a month with the Haus in China for more documentation and new exhibitions. The CCTV documentary *Brilliant Colors—Chinese Art Master Hou Beiren* (unofficial title in English) in their *Great Master* series first aired in April 2014. Holding, current ASACA president, exudes the group's energy, joy, and cross-cultural nature; when she lost her voice before a reception, she gave her presentation as a Charlie Chaplin routine.

Jianhua Shu (left) and Michael Sullivan (middle) at Paul Hau's Los Altos studio on 3/22/2013. Photo: Xinru Xu.

Jianhua Shu, a writer, cultural activist, and entrepreneur, complements Hau's vision of embracing art and community. Shu started the SVAAC in 2004 in a four-story high-tech center on Stevens Creek Boulevard in Santa Clara. A tall man with a big smile, Shu welcomes newcomers to the spacious SVAAC, a hub of exhibition programs that enliven the exchange of art and ideas between the U.S. and China. Shu and colleague Xinru Xu deftly switch languages as needed for congenial hospitality or enhanced communication.

Hau has shared his art, extensive knowledge, and experiences at countless SVAAC events. These events typically stimulate discussion of ideas not familiar to many local audiences, such as honoring the work of late Silicon Valley historian and journalist Iris Chang, or the role of the Bay Area in China's 1911 revolution. Maintaining that "politics is politics, art is art, whether visual or poetry," Hau firmly believes in speaking up to "support what you think is right."

Through SVAAC, Shu advocates "a new wave of art movement" in Silicon Valley with solid financial support. By way of example, Hau and Shu took the leading role in Euphrat Museum of Art's inaugural exhibition and events in 2009 and 2011, working alongside emerging artists and students in order to stimulate dialogue about and support for greater Silicon Valley cultural participation.

In 2013, Hau was featured in *The Moment for Ink* project, covering historical and contemporary ink painting in America. This project, an unprecedented collaboration of the San Francisco State University Fine Arts Gallery, Chinese Culture Center of San Francisco, Asian Art Museum of San Francisco, and SVAAC, generated research, a scholarly publication, exhibitions, and more discussions in Silicon Valley and San Francisco before it traveled to China.[4] Among the scholars participating was renowned British art historian Michael Sullivan, who passed away later that year. Sullivan was a major Western pioneer in the field of modern Chinese art history and head of the Stanford University Department of Oriental Art from 1966 to 1984. His *The Arts of China* is a classic text.

Although years ago Hau experienced painful anti-Chinese prejudice locally, he has continued to use art and poetry to build bridges between cultures and generations and to evoke a transcendent beauty and spirit, all from his home base in Los Altos, once the site of orchards, his "Old Apricot Hall."

A humble man, Hau describes his teaching as being in a "little booth," where students can choose among the apples and oranges and pick up what they need. He says, "Everyone wants success. Don't be impatient. … Every day, pick up your brush and paint what is in your heart."

---

4 Jianhua Shu beams as he speaks about rankings in China: "Paul Hau is the only living artist of the top 38. The Hau-Bei Ren Museum is 19th out of 200." See Silicon Valley Asian Art Center, artshu.com.

Paul Pei-Jen Hau, *Sunset in the Snowy Mountains*, 2009. Ink and color on paper, 36"x71".
"I put all the love of my life in that painting."

Lucy Cain Sargeant: Disregarding Difference

"The guys were mad. Tony was mad. LeRoy was mad. I wouldn't tell [the San José State University art professors] what it meant. 'Why won't you tell us??'"

After retiring as Assistant Art Director, Illustration from *Sunset* magazine[1] in Menlo Park, Lucy Sargeant headed off to San José State University to finish her MFA in painting.

> This was not an easy task for a suburban, "older" mother of two adults, especially a painfully representational artist, in a "concept"-oriented art school.

> The first week I arrived I remember standing in the quad, in my polyester pants and pink shirt, hair teased a little for "loft." All around me, art students and faculty knotted in groups, gesturing, laughing, or striding to the cafeteria across the walkway—all of them wearing a version of jeans and denim shirts, the art uniform of the day. I couldn't help thinking, *"Who's the rugged individualist in this scene, fellas and gals?"*

A few conceptual art seminars later, the former secretary wanted to do "a conceptual piece." Art to think about. An installation. She had Gallery 5 for a week.

So starting on a Friday afternoon in 1998, with two dozen #2 pencils and a ladder, at the top of the room, she snapped light blue carpenters' chalk lines and began to write in Gregg shorthand, dictating aloud to herself from *Independent Spirits: Women Painters of the American West, 1890–1945,* edited by Patricia Trenton. She proceeded to draw from left to right, top to bottom, all around the room. It took her the whole weekend.

When Professor Sam Richardson came into the gallery Monday morning, he didn't see anything because the #2 pencil gave a fine line. He couldn't see till he got close.

> Sam thought the piece was fantastic and promoted it, so that many viewers came. I wouldn't tell them what it said. I said it was sacred. No one could read it. Wasn't that part of the "concept?" But later a secretary from administration came in who could read it. And she wept! Touched that shorthand could be elevated to art.

In shorthand, Sargeant has a "beautiful hand." Her flow and movements are like artful calligraphy, like a dance. A performance piece. A meditative piece. The goal of shorthand was to take dictation from the boss, a fast documentation of speech before computers. But it was also like a secret code, akin to binary, a code I once learned. Except now, few recognize her code.

Early in her working life, as a secretary, Sargeant experienced the common condescension toward women. These indispensable assistants were often referred to as "the girl," rendered invisible and powerless in a subordinate job that was one of the few types of work readily available to women. What a joy to be able to turn low regard into a communication of freedom, beauty, tribute, meaning, respect, and caring.

---

[1] *Sunset* magazine for years epitomized an ideal California lifestyle, yet one not accessible to many. Its former headquarters and gardens along with test kitchens on Willow Road were legendary.

Lucy Cain Sargeant, *David M.*, 1999. Oil on canvas, 48"x36".

With her MFA from SJSU, she went on to teach representational drawing at SJSU for over a decade, and was the instructor de rigueur for those who wanted to grasp the structure of things, faces and bodies, or ideas of space and line quality. She offered a sharp eye and new insights into content and context.

In her art, she created a series of large facial portraits of Bay Area artists. She started with a painting of Sam Richardson, catching his likeness in lively brushwork, charcoal strokes, and drips. Her portraits would also catch an inner essence, reminding me of painter Alice Neel's psychological keenness. She could nail it.

Sargeant and I worked on Euphrat Museum programs, and together we opened up exhibition opportunities. She was the guiding light for our first book, *Staying Visible*, 1981, leading me through the process from concept to execution. All business, we would meet for coffee, and she would say, "I will give you 30 minutes." I asked questions and took notes as fast as I could. We also had many animated discussions about what was missing from the content. She was associate curator of *Staying Visible* and authored one of the articles, traveling to Los Angeles to interview figurative painter Joyce Treiman.

In 1981, Sargeant led as we co-curated *Commercial Artists: Their Art*, featuring 19 leading Bay Area illustrators and designers, with women well represented. "Their art" included their personal art, along with art created for clients. *OnStage Magazine* gave it a full-page review. However, in fine art circles then, commercial art was looked down upon and scarcely recognized.

In our 1983 exhibition *Illustration, Design*, she again spearheaded a commercial art focus, this time highlighting art processes and art—thumbnail sketches on restaurant placemats, finished comps, and camera-ready art—seldom seen in original, unreproduced form, let alone in museums. In our *Illustration, Design* book, we published expository writings from the artists. Graphic designer Sam Smidt wrote on typography. Design professor and illustrator Alice (Bunny) Carter, brand new at SJSU, expounded on concept development—the client-illustrator process in designing a *Star Wars* game cover. Illustrator Glenn Myles wrote about "riding into the cross-cultural community to establish visual identities for persons left out of the mainstream … ." Pulitzer Prize–winning political cartoonist Signe Wilkinson, new at the *San Jose Mercury News,* and feisty even then, commented on client interaction: "I work up several sketches and take them to my editor, where, after some polite discussion that generally stops short of bloodshed, we agree on which best expresses the most salient point."

It's still hard to believe the barriers and narrow definition of art around 1980. Commercial art is now "cutting edge." Sargeant sheds light on the change, "Until the mid 1900s, art for publication wasn't saved. Much of it was done in fugitive inks that faded quickly so had to be covered or tossed. Savvy art collectors and historians retrieved what today are examples hanging in exhibitions and museums."

Her interests have been widespread. Once, she facilitated an installation about Helen Colijn's *Wartime Concert Heard Again*, recreated in 1982 by the Peninsula Women's Chorus of Palo Alto from a concert in Sumatra, where Japan had interned 600 women and children for over three years during World War II. The internees wrote remembered bits of Beethoven, Chopin, and Schubert on precious scraps of paper with carefully hoarded pencil stumps; then arranged the music for four-part choral singing! Thirty women formed the original vocal orchestra, humming vowels, singing syllables. The 1980s recreation was singing for all captives, then and now.

For many years afterwards, Sargeant and I pondered, probed, and poked at an abundance of art, and hashed out ideas on many exhibitions and publications. Currently, she has shifted gears to create a series of watercolors on Sacramento Valley flora and fauna. A dedicated teacher, she translates university-level jargon to everyday language and teaches art to all ages, with love, insight and humor.

Lucy Cain Sargeant, *Greeds*, 1999. Oil on canvas, 36"x48". "Now we have it in full bloom."

Kim Bielejec Sanzo: A Gathering Force

There would be no Euphrat Museum of Art today if it hadn't been for Kim Bielejec Sanzo. In 1980, Proposition 13 eliminated the sole funding for the Helen Euphrat Gallery, as it was then called. Yet I felt rethinking a gallery on a community college campus had potential, so I stepped forward and proposed exhibitions. One day artist Sanzo, fresh with a MFA, walked up to me on campus and said she wanted to work at the Euphrat. I said, "That's nice, but there's no money." She said, "That's OK," in a way that implied we would work something out.

Together we questioned the system and its fundamental assumptions and developed a larger, more inclusive vision for the Euphrat. We scrambled for money and worked with artists, campus, and the community to build a new structure and income stream. We developed a board, programs, fundraisers, and grants—unusual for a community college. Quality of programming was always first on our minds. We offered a professional arts working environment. We created jobs for artists and others, including women, many of whom were homebodies at the time. Sidelined in the workforce, and lacking a professional work ethic and skills, they still had a desire for change.

We did it by keeping things interesting—giving people a title and responsibility, plus opportunities to develop projects or programs. We shared what funds we had, which was very little. To give a sense of the money situation, I was the big earner in 1985 and earned less than $5,000 total, and that included running the Euphrat and my part-time teaching of a museum class and additional art classes. A familiar refrain was, "Do we want to pay ourselves or do a book?" We usually chose the book.

Our first book was the pivotal *Staying Visible, The Importance of Archives*, 1981. In addition to brainstorming and organizing, Sanzo was one of many artists who participated in the project, which included artist interviews and research. We had both been frustrated by the unfair treatment and lack of recognition of women in the arts. Although we decided not to call it an exhibition featuring women, all the artists who were researched for *Staying Visible* were women.

Sanzo chose Beatrice Wood, born in San Francisco in 1895, who spent most of her early life in New York and Europe. Wood collaborated with Marcel Duchamp in the New York Dada movement and was active in the development of the ceramics renaissance that started before 1940. In Sanzo's article Wood spoke of her controversial 1917 drawing of a nude torso with "a piece of soap in a very tactical position," and how it was unacceptable to hardcore art academicians who saw tampering with the perfection of natural beauty of the nude female body as a blasphemous act.

Sanzo collaborated on all early exhibitions, soon becoming an assistant director involved in all programs. On top of exhibitions, events, and lectures, we created more major publications, including *Art, Religion, Spirituality*, 1982; *FACES*, 1984; *Art Collectors In and Around Silicon Valley*, 1985; and *CONTENT: Contemporary Issues*, 1986. These publications were very time-consuming in an age where type was still set and the galley was manually waxed onto boards for printing—a particularly tricky process for last-minute corrections.

Kim Bielejec Sanzo (left) interviewing Beatrice Wood (right), photo taken in Wood's home in Ojai, CA during interview, July 6, 1981, for *Staying Visible*, 1981. Photo: Bill Sanzo.

Inserting a comma meant balancing a speck of paper on the tip of an X-Acto knife. "Hands on" was the mode of the day.

Coming from a large Polish-Irish farm family, Sanzo was used to creative problem solving. For her, collaborations meant being people-friendly in every aspect. She pampered struggling artists, coaxed faculty and staff across disciplines to participate and help out with events, and built bridges with campus departments and community groups. She encouraged civic leaders' arts vision, and engaged students who fed on serious art dialogue, such as Ben Kashkooli, who went on to a life of sculpture and activism.

A sturdy woman with wild blond hair, Sanzo is normally soft spoken, but has a laugh that can wake up the whole room. Her art and community building goes in all directions of life, whether making a commemorative t-shirt for the centenary of the Phoenix Mill Little Falls, N.Y. strike of 1912 or developing art projects for people struggling with life's basics. Over the years, she brought people on board: artists, volunteers, students of all ages, funders, campus and community. It has been almost two decades since Sanzo left for the East Coast, but she is fondly remembered as a person who always knew what needed to be done and did it.

Kim Bielejec Sanzo and artist Joe Sam. at fundraising event at the home of David and Eppie Lam, 1994.

NEW VENTURES

Trudy Myrrh Reagan and YLEM:
The Power of Ideas

In the beginnings of Silicon Valley, artist Trudy Myrrh Reagan in Palo Alto wanted to bring together her loves by connecting "art to the driving forces in our culture: science and technology." Towards that end, she started YLEM in 1981.

In her art, Reagan has loved to explore recurring forms found in nature. She airbrushed crumpled paper into mountainscapes and moon craters. She painted the structure of crystals, spirals of galaxies, glassy cage of a one-celled animal, and the imagining of the human brain. YLEM was "one more aspect of making science vivid in my work."

YLEM (pronounced EYE-lem and capitalized after 2000) is the Greek word for "matter," used by physicist George Gamow's group in 1949 to signify the exploding mass and energy the earth emerged from in the Big Bang. As a nonprofit organization, YLEM's original purpose was to create a community of artists. The organization explored "the humanistic and peaceful uses to which science and technology were being put ... "[1]

> Artists in Ylem use technology for positive purposes, and make abstract science ideas more concrete and approachable. They believe in the power of ideas to take form and spread, like the original matter, ylem, from the Big Bang, into the universe we see today. ... Ylem will explore the impact of new technologies on society. Will art spread like wildfire through new media channels like the web? Only if artists train themselves to use them. ...

YLEM's approach was "deliberately comprehensive," with experimental artists in all forms of digital media participating. Artists who explored scientific ideas in traditional media were also welcome. Because the organization stood outside both academia and commercial art and design, YLEM artists were able to share ideas freely.

YLEM's web history states, "Young people at universities and companies knew for certain that what people were developing there would change the world as we know it." But few artists embraced computers. Computer art wasn't considered real art.

YLEM had help from several sources, including Howard Pearlmutter, whose Homebrew Computer Club at Stanford began Graphics Gatherings, special meetings of computer graphics, often long Saturday afternoons. Stanford professor Robert McKim, author of *Experiments in Visual Thinking*, and graduate student Scott Kim, author of *Inversions*, gave YLEM access to speakers and use of facilities.

YLEM became a membership-supported nonprofit group. Primarily an all-volunteer effort, a half-dozen people kept the organization afloat. Reagan was president of YLEM for seven years, artist Beverly Reiser for 14 years. YLEM would come to have 250 members, a newsletter (later journal), a website, bimonthly forums at the Exploratorium in San Francisco, and an "electronic gallery."

---

1 "A Detailed History of YLEM." ylem.org/Membership/history_detailed.html

Myrrh, *An Essential Mystery: Number Governs Form*, 1994. Acrylic on Plexiglas, incised "crystals." 45" diameter. One of series of *Essential Mystery* paintings: "…amethyst crystals and the flower of a thistle…"

As the website history recounts:

> Stephen Wilson of San Francisco State University regarded art as research and a method of "keeping watch on the cultural frontier." He, Roger Malina of the journal *Leonardo*, ecologist Theodosia Ferguson, Nancy Frank of ArtCom, computer artists Lucia Grossberger Morales and Eleanor Kent, and technology writer Louis M. Brill, associated with Burning Man, helped shape YLEM's programs.[2]

When Reagan and I first worked together around 1980, we both spoke a great deal about the potential and importance of forums and publications as the basis of our budding organizations, YLEM and Euphrat Museum of Art, and we ran with the concept.

Forums, tours, and publications gave a heads-up about technical advances useful to artists that affected society as a whole—starting in 1981 with personal computers, when only a few computer kits and devices were available. From 1982–1984, artist Eleanor Kent organized Silicon Valley computer graphics tours. The inaugural tour included a visit to Ampex with member Glenn Entis, who later headed Dreamworks Interactive in Redwood City. A 1982 forum presented teleconferencing and a demo of 3-D TV. During the 1994–1995 forum series, networked art was discussed and art images could be shown, as the Internet had become generally available to universities, labs and some businesses. YLEM and Leonardo/ International Society for Art, Science, and Technology (ISAST) also joined an international collaboration, Jurgen Claus' Global SolArts Festival, in part hoping solar art would inspire solar energy development.

In 2002, an YLEM forum on *The Secrets of Silicon Valley* presented the first documentary film to note the social impact of high tech: poor health and safety conditions in companies, the need for responsible recycling, and the opportunity for community empowerment. The film chronicles the life of two local activists—Magda Escobar, executive director of Plugged In, and Raj Jayadev, a temporary worker at a Hewlett-Packard plant.[3]

Through YLEM forums, artists, entrepreneurs, designers and architects, writers, digital media organizers, researchers, inventors, and musicians interacted. Astronomers shared their recent discoveries, mathematicians their art. There were presentations of neuropsychology and the geography of the brain, fluid dynamics, computer models of DNA, and art with bioluminescent bacteria. The *YLEM Journal* had interviews with science fiction writers, conceptual artists, and experimental music composers.

The *YLEM Newsletter, Calendar, Journal*, exhibitions, and copiously illustrated *Directory of Artists Using Science and Technology* helped to validate the artists undervalued by the rest of the art world.

---

[2] Ibid.

[3] The film was directed by Alan Snitow and Deborah Kaufman. Magda Escobar, executive director of Plugged In, a community technology center in low-income East Palo Alto, was named one of *Ms. Magazine*'s Women of the Year for 2001. Raj Jayadev, a Manpower, Inc. temporary worker at a Hewlett-Packard plant, encouraged the "temps" there to challenge health and safety conditions. He got fired for this, but found "surprising and funny ways to take the controversy to the Internet, the public and the press," and built Silicon Valley De-Bug, a completely different type of organization. "YLEM Forum: Secrets of Silicon Valley." *YLEM Journal*, no. 10, vol. 22, September–October 2002, p. 2. ylem.org/Journal/2002Iss10vol22.pdf

YLEM exhibitions were curated by Reagan, Reiser, Kent, and Barbara Lee. In 1983, YLEM produced a computer art exhibition in the San Jose Convention Center (a building that later housed the offices of the Tech Museum). The work of 20 artists, mostly YLEM members, included a nonviolent computer game on a Commodore 64.

YLEM members were prominent in conferences. In 1984, YLEM members participated in the first Computers in Art, Design, Research, and Education (CADRE) conference— a national conference with papers and publication—organized by Dr. Marcia Chamberlain, San José State University (SJSU).[4] Kent curated one of the related exhibitions; Grossberger Morales was a panel moderator for the conference, and later an exhibits coordinator for CADRE Institute.[5] She brought a different outlook.

In 1996 she wrote, "The Internet is so white. … When I showed this [CD-ROM] in Bolivia, I was moved by a little girl who said, 'I didn't know you could do that.' She meant she didn't know one could put her culture on the computer." For a March 1996 YLEM newsletter Grossberger Morales described a two-month-long Internet discussion group related to "Art and Community," with comments from activists such as Aida Mancillas of San Diego, who saw the arts as a way to rescue neighborhoods and bring diverse constituencies together.

Reagan recalled in her firsthand history "Ylem Rode the Wave":[6]

> I will never forget being invited to the reception for *Leonardo* [journal] in San Francisco by Roger Malina in 1983. His father, Frank Malina, had just died. The whole magazine was being transferred to where he lived. This magazine was so respected by us! Later, he would tell us, "If YLEM didn't do forums, I would have to." In this way we worked together. For a time he also was a member of our board.

---

[4] See Chamberlain, Marcia. *CADRE '84*, 1983, SJSU Art Department. The conference was held at Mission College and SJSU with 14 Silicon Valley exhibition venues. Chamberlain was the first project director of SJSU's CADRE Laboratory for New Media, an interdisciplinary academic and research program dedicated to the experimental use of information technology and art. In 1988, Joel A. Slayton became director of CADRE Laboratory for New Media. Two dynamic women further championed synergy between art and technology: Andy Cunningham founded ZERO1, the Art and Technology Network in 2000; and six years later, Beau Takahara was a key organizer of the first ZERO1 Biennial, San José's lauded international art and technology festival. Slayton served as ZERO1's executive director from 2008 to 2016.

[5] As an early adopter of technology, Grossberger Morales has hit roadblocks with archiving its past. In 2015, she put together *Huge Pixels*, a magazine describing the *Designer's Toolkit* she coauthored for the Apple II, published by Apple in 1982. Her interactive, storytelling *Sangre Boliviana* (Bolivian Blood) was a mid-1990s installation with CD-ROM, also connected with the Internet, and for years could only run on old Macs. Now "the National Library in France has created a copy that runs on current technology. They are committed to preserving the CD-ROMs." For background information: Grossberger Morales, Lucia. "Sangre Boliviana: Using multimedia to tell personal stories," in Cutting Edge: The Women's Research Group, eds., *Digital Desire: Language, Identity and New Technologies*. I.B. Tauris & Co. Ltd., 2000. pp 184–193. books.google.com/ books?isbn=1860645755 See also luciagrossbergermorales.com, including a downloadable PDF of her book, *Altars/Altares, Computer Interactive Shrines*, 2007. Grossberger Morales is pleased her work has inspired people in Latin America, and to note several Spanish language academic papers about the use of multimedia to express biculturalism over the years.

[6] Reagan, Trudy Myrrh. "Ylem Rode the Wave, 1981–86." Leonardo/OLATS, October 2, 2014. olats.org/ pionniers/memoirs/reagan/ylem.php

Reflecting on YLEM's seminal importance, Grossberger Morales writes:

> Decades-long friendships developed, even across the world. We were a home for isolated people working in unusual media, especially in other parts of the country. Our growth was exponential the first five years, peaking at 250. A decline in membership began in the mid-'90s, settling [around 160]. By then, we were only one of many, many such organizations all over the world.

Reagan's multidimensionality invites questions and expands vision. She did service work with the Quakers in Philadelphia slums in the 1950s, participated in the group political quilt projects in Silicon Valley with Gen Guracar and Connie Young Yu in the 1970s and '80s, helped found the California Crafts Museum, which was housed at the Palo Alto Cultural Center from 1980–1982, worked with refugees in the 1980s and '90s, and chaired a panel on "Women Humanizing Technology" for the 1989 National Women's Caucus for the Arts Conference in San Francisco. In addition to editing and writing for the *YLEM Newsletter* and *Journal* for years, Reagan has written more introspectively in "Can Personal Meaning Be Found from Science?"[7] and a follow-up, "Extracting Wisdom from Science."

> I have endeavored to show people where they are in the universe ... [with] a curiosity about what abides, what is always true. ... Respect for truth is very allied with respect for each person.

7 *Leonardo*, Vol. 47, #1, 2014.

Women's Advocacy in the Arts

The mission of the Women's Caucus for the Arts (WCA)—to create community through art, education, and activism—has goals similar to those of other activists in this book. The WCA started in 1972. Its Silicon Valley chapter, SVWCA [formerly South Bay Area WCA (SBAWCA)], was founded in 1989, with sculptor Marta Thoma as president. Its Peninsula chapter was established in 1991 by sculptor and Stanford graduate Ruth Waters, who also founded the Peninsula Museum of Art in Burlingame.[1]

Marta Thoma recalls the first SBAWCA executive team in 1989: "We worked closely, sharing an ambitious vision. The membership grew to 250 members (three men) and eclipsed all other chapters," with speakers, guest curators, art-and-feminism book groups, critique groups, and publication, program and exhibition groups addressing issues. With 11 subsidiary groups active in 1998, subgroups were "the heart and soul of SBAWCA."

SVWCA terminated at the end of 2016 due to lack of board members. Final board president Susan Kraft cites two factors: increased traffic that diminished the far-flung membership's ability to attend meetings, and the fact that "the Internet has changed everything—including how artists relate to their peers ..."[2]

SVWCA underwrote very large, national-level events as well as smaller local, low-budget ones. Its projects tackled hot subjects, such as the *Control* exhibition, juried by Guerrilla Girls West, a women's activist group promoting the arts. For WCA's 40th anniversary in 2012, Kraft organized the Honoring Women's Rights conference in Salinas, which coincided with a national election and drew much attention.

For many years, SVWCA produced a high-quality publication with a grass-roots foundation entitled *(detail)*. It was founded and edited for five years by Karen Hass.[3] In 1995, Jone Manoogian founded Bay Area Book Arts (BABA) as a subgroup of SBAWCA. BABA, now independent, is very active and retains a strong women's focus.

Eleanor Dickinson, along with artist/publisher Roberta Loach in Los Altos, called attention to the first statistics on women in the arts in the 1970s. She wrote a history of WCA in 2007 and has published updated statistics for women's representation in the arts over the decades.[4]

---

[1] Thoma founded SBAWCA with artists Monroe Hodder and Kathryn Dunlevie. A history of the first 20 years includes the 10-year collaboration with Stanford's Institute for Research on Women and Gender. In the mid-1990s, SBAWCA acted as the umbrella organization for Lifelines, an arts program for cancer patients; formed a group addressing the AIDS crisis; and created dialogue on ethics in the arts with MACLA/Center for Latino Arts. Recent SVWCA history is still available on svwca.org/where-weve-been.html. For older website versions see web.archive.org/web/*/http://www.sbawca.org.

[2] "Facebook SVWCA is very popular; so much that today, we have 119 Facebook members. Compare that to the 33 paid chapter members." Kraft developed the Art 21 Gallery (2002–2007), "the Peninsula's largest gallery," in downtown Palo Alto, across from where Facebook started in 2005.

[3] In 1998, for an issue of *(detail)*, new editors Christine Laffer and Helen Wood dedicated their first issue to "decolonize the mind and imagination." Laffer still laments how "women are shaped by the male dominant culture, how hard it is to get outside of it, shake free." She is currently writing on her own about weaving history and Consuelo Jimenez Underwood.

[4] Dickinson, Eleanor. "Gender Discrimination in the Art Field." eleanordickinson.wordpress.com/gender-statistics/. Dickinson, an extraordinary figurative artist currently living in San José, has been an educator, activist, and mentor to many of us.

A fact from Guerrilla Girls: Less than 4% of the artists in the Modern Art section of New York's Metropolitan Museum of Art are women, but 76% of the nudes are female.[5]

Briones biographer Jeanne Farr McDonnell started the Women's Heritage Museum (WHM) in Palo Alto in 1985 and was its executive director for 10 years. Her vision for the organization was to cover the study and preservation of women's history in California. The WHM later moved to San Francisco to reach a wider audience. It changed to an international focus, becoming the International Museum of Women (IMOW) in 1997; then merging to become the Global Fund for Women (2014). Its larger mission, however, left a vacuum for dedicated promotion, documentation, and discussion of regional women's heritage. The Asian American Women Artists Association in San Francisco remains strong in its support and presentation of Asian American women in art. Silicon Valley residents participate enthusiastically in national- and international-level endeavors. But there are still few hubs of opportunity here for those interested in promoting and developing expertise in the broad, deep history of women—including locals—in art.

Marta Thoma, *Earth Tear*, 1993. Welded steel and 250 recycled bottles, 8'x5'x5'. Created during an artist residency at Sanitary Fill Company in South San Francisco, "the dump" for much of the Bay Area. In 1990, artist Jo Hanson founded the groundbreaking Sanitary Fill Residency, now at Recology San Francisco; the artist residency program continues to nurture artists concerned about the environment.

In 1996, artists Jo Hanson (San Francisco), Susan Leibovitz Steinman (East Bay) and Estelle Akamine (SJSU graduate, formerly Citadel artist who cofounded Open Studios) created WEAD, Women Environmental Artists Directory, later to become Women Eco Arts Dialog (weadartists.org), to promote women's unique perspective in ecological and social justice art. They first presented their ideas and networking goals in March 1996 to the Northern California WCA.

5 See also "Advocate: Get the Facts." *National Museum of Women in the Arts*, 2014, nmwa.org/advocate/get-facts.

José Antonio and Cecilia Preciado Burciaga: Mentoring Cultura

José Antonio Burciaga (1940–1996), artist, poet, and writer, and Cecilia Preciado Burciaga (1945–2013), former high-ranking administrator at Stanford University and at California State University Monterey Bay (CSUMB), were Euphrat Museum board members in the early 1990s. Our intense dinner table discussions about art, education, and exhibitions were a joy, as they brought in new ideas, coupled with a zing of humor and a lot of love. Both lived on the Stanford campus, serving as Resident Fellows in the Chican@/Latin@ themed dorm, Casa Zapata (1985–1994)—a who'd-have-guessed springboard for premier shapers of Silicon Valley cultural development. They created a family-oriented community.

The Burciagas at Stanford University, 1984. Photo: Jesús Manuel Mena Garza.

Cecilia Burciaga, Challenging Academia

Described by the *Los Angeles Times* as "one of the first high-ranking Latina administrators at a top American private university,"[1] Cecilia Burciaga went way beyond the extra mile,

---

1 Trounson, Rebecca. "Cecilia Preciado Burciaga dies at 67; longtime Stanford administrator." *Los Angeles Times*. (March 27, 2013) articles.latimes.com/2013/mar/27/local/la-me-cecilia-preciado-burciaga-20130328.

inspiring and mentoring hundreds of students and faculty. To me, as a museum director at a community college struggling with academic systems often repressive to diversity, she also brought new ways to work with academic bureaucracy. She courageously sought to make academia more open to diversity and to meeting diverse students' needs.

Professor emerita Amalia Mesa-Bains, former head of visual and public arts at CSUMB, said in a *Monterey Herald* obituary, "If things were unjust, unfair, not right, Cecilia would take up the cause and she wouldn't back down until the problem was fixed. I would consider her one of the people who most embodied the movement toward justice."[2]

Stanford's student-run Chican@/Latin@ magazine *El Aguila* has been intertwined with the Burciagas' legacy, starting from the early days when Tony Burciaga inspired its creation and helped teach layout. In the spirit of the Burciagas' work, the independent quarterly has covered current cultural, economic, political and social issues affecting the Chican@/Latin@ community on a campus-wide, local, and national level, and shared the artistic expression of the *comunidad* with the greater Stanford community.[3]

In a 2013 issue, student Alicia Hamar[4] described how Cecilia Burciaga's compassion and wisdom helped those having trouble adjusting to Stanford's rigors. Julia Gonzalez Luna ('94, M.A. '95) recalled seeing Burciaga during her freshman year when she was considering dropping out of college due to not fitting in. "She looked straight into my eyes and said, 'For everyone that makes it into Stanford, there are a thousand who don't make it, so then you are responsible for the thousand.'" Burciaga's words and influence helped Luna graduate.

Hamar also wrote about Burciaga's firing from Stanford in 1994, allegedly due to budget cuts, which led to the Hunger Strike of 1994.

> This resulted in a multiple day hunger strike, where students camped out in the main quad, devastated by the University's decision. Eva Silva ('94, M.A. '95), now a program coordinator at CSU Monterey Bay, was involved in the hunger strike. ... [She] remembered Burciaga telling the protestors that she did not want them to carry out the hunger strike for her sake. "[Do the

---

2 Taylor, Dennis. "Latina activist, CSUMB administrator Cecilia Burciaga dies." *Monterey Herald* (March 26, 2013) www.montereyherald.com/obituaries/20130326/latina-activist-csumb-administrator-cecilia-burciaga-dies.

3 Gutierrez, Stephanie. "Taking Flight Through Words: *El Aguila*." Posted as a stand-alone article on the former El Aguila website stanfordelaguila.com/taking-flight-through-word s-el-aguila/. (April 26, 2015) Now posted on stephaniemgutierrez.wix.com/portfolio#!blank/mdlhl. Gutierrez wrote for *El Aguila* about how the magazine started around Fall 1987 after she interviewed one of the original founders, Chris Gonzalez Clarke. Other early participants included Gina Hernandez, now Clarke's wife and Director of Arts in Undergraduate Education at Stanford, and Marcos Pizarro, now a professor at San José State University. Gonzalez Clarke said Chican@ students in the 1980s were inspired by El Centro Chicano's publication *Estos Tiempos*, which focused on arts and culture, but wanted to create a publication with a student focus and political bent. At the time Tony Burciaga helped teach needed layout skills. The magazine had ups and downs until 1990–1991, when, student activist Eva Silva recalled, Burciaga urged students to reignite the publication. While *El Aguila* went silent in the late 1990s, coinciding with a reduction in campus activism, it was revived again in 2011–2012. Although offline and quiet at the moment, in recent years the magazine has reflected and recounted the Burciagas' lasting legacy.

4 Hamar, Alicia. "Cecilia Burciaga, Chican@ advocate, mentor, dies at 67." *El Aguila*, Spring 2013, p. 5. See issuu.com/hizosu/docs/el_aguila_spring13.

hunger strike] to gain things for the students here and if you can, use this to give you more strength, but don't do the hunger strike for my position."

Stephanie Gutierrez[5] later elaborated on what the hunger strikers specified.

> They demanded [that] the university stop serving grapes in dorms and the Faculty Club, set up a Chicano Studies major, and establish a community center in East Palo Alto. For three days, Tamara Alvarado, Julia Gonzalez Luna, Elvira Prieto, and Eva Silva camped in the Quad and consumed only water until their demands were met. Approximately 200 students and faculty showed support for the four Chicanas at a rally on the Stanford Quad on Cinco de Mayo, Thursday May 5, 1994. …

> On May 6, 1994, the Hunger Strike ended when Stanford President Gerhard Casper, Provost Condoleezza Rice, and MEChA signed the negotiations agreement and promised to address the issues brought up during the strike. … The fall 1996 Issue of *El Aguila* … highlighted an achievement of the Hunger Strike: the establishment of a Chicano Studies major within the Comparative Studies in Race and Ethnicity (CSRE) Program.

> …This is Silva's favorite issue of *El Aguila* … "It reminds me of when she [Rice] was supposed to be signing the agreement and she didn't want to sign and everybody started saying 'Sign it! Sign it! Sign it!' Then, with the pressure, she finally signed.

Hamar described what happened after Cecilia Burciaga left Stanford and became a founding administrator at CSUMB:

> …she continued her work helping the Latino community at the newly established university. According to Silva, many students from the Monterey County area were first generation … Burciaga served as their mentor and advocate.

> In 2002, Burciaga played an important part in a lawsuit that was settled with the CSU Monterey Bay administration over issues regarding policy and diversity. "She demanded that they have a scholarship for low-income students, and that's something to show the heart that she had, and how well she knew the community that she was working with,"…

> The lawsuit was settled and a scholarship fund of $1.5 million dollars was established to aid the low-income students from the area.

Gina Hernandez-Clarke, Director of Arts in Undergraduate Education at Stanford, once a leading student activist at Stanford, recalls:

> Cecilia stood her ground. Tony brought in artists, created his own museum, and wrote essays. I didn't live in Casa Zapata, so I wasn't a part of the immediate family, but I still feel its impact. The family is wide. They sustained nurturing of cultural workers and impacted creators year in, year out—in a quiet, family-nurturing way.

> Just to follow one path of the Burciagas' legacy: Tamara Alvarado is the executive director of the now four-year-old School of Arts and Culture at the Mexican Heritage Plaza. Julia Gonzalez Luna teaches in Salinas. Elvira Prieto is Assistant Dean for Student Affairs and Associate Director of El Centro Chicano at Stanford, which advises *El Aguila*. Eva Silva is a program coordinator at CSU Monterey Bay.

---

5 Gutierrez, op. cit.

Tamara Alvarado reflects in more detail:

> In the ivory towers of academia and privilege, at one of the best universities in the country, and with Cecilia as part of the president's cabinet, they negotiated their presence with critical analyses, different perspectives, and art as a platform. Both led. Systems are not going away. She showed how to navigate. He smashed on the system by using a different voice.
>
> I honored grapes [the boycott]. My family never ate them. "We have to do something. They're serving grapes!!" I was angry. "It's 1991!!" Tony, paintbrush in hand, quietly said, "Let's talk about it." And we spoke about organizing, taking action, involving staff, artists, supporters. How do we engage with broader society? Diversity, what does it mean?
>
> [We took on] the Hunger Strike. Ralph Armbruster-Sandoval, UC Santa Barbara, has written a book about hunger strikes as a quest for dignity.[6] The intellectuality of arts and administration holding space at Stanford was powerful. [There's] a direct lineage to the Mexican Heritage Plaza. *We* can determine.

The Burciagas' legacy goes beyond advocacy and mentoring. They challenged academia in multiple ways, called attention to systemic deficiencies, and spoke up for change—all unusual, stressful, and hard to do, requiring courage and imagination. Cecilia Burciaga's legacy lives on at both universities, in cultural institutions large and small, and in the hearts of those she mentored and those who have understood and participated in the struggles.[7]

Tony Burciaga: Fearless Audacity

Tony Burciaga grew up in Texas, then served abroad in the U.S. Air Force. He first participated in the Chicano movement in Washington D.C. There he met Cecilia and they married in 1972. I knew him as an artist, activist, educator, and writer, although he had talents across the board, such as taking part in the comedy troupe Culture Clash[8] he helped found. Caring, sensitive, and keenly observant, he was unafraid to speak up. He balanced his heavy seriousness with a good dose of humor and playfulness. He died of cancer at the premature age of 56, two years after the contested layoff.

---

6 Armbruster-Sandoval, Ralph. *Starving for Justice: Hunger Strikes, Spectacular Speech, and the Struggle for Dignity.* Unpublished book manuscript (under review).

7 A few select writings about the Burciagas' legacy:
Dominguez, Daniel. "Casa Zapata Resident Fellows reflect on years of service." *El Aguila,* Spring 2013, pp. 14–15. Gina Hernandez-Clarke and Chris Gonzales Clarke were Casa Zapata resident fellows for six years. In part, Hernandez-Clarke wanted to invigorate the artistic spirit of the dorm, including walls covered by murals, most commissioned or painted by Tony Burciaga. Hernandez-Clarke was a leader of the spring 1989 takeover of the President's Office; her student activism has been immortalized in the Casa Zapata mural *The Spirit of Hoover.* Chris Gonzalez Clarke is Director, Enhancing Diversity in Graduate Education (EDGE) Doctoral Fellowship Program at Stanford; he served as the first Associate Director of El Centro Chicano from 1993–2005.
Noriega, Chon A. "Cecilia Preciado Burciaga, Presente!" (April 1, 2013; updated June 1, 2013) *The Huffington Post blog* huffingtonpost.com/chon-a-noriega/post_4547_b_2975846.html. Noriega, Director of the UCLA Chicano Studies Research Center, blogged an informative and emotional tribute to Burciaga, who died March 25, 2013, after battling cancer for seven months, in which he proclaims, "Presente!"—she is still with us.

8 He co-founded Culture Clash at the Galería de la Raza in San Francisco's Mission District along with Marga Gómez, Monica Palacios, Richard Montoya, Ric Salinas, and Herbert Sigüenza. Burciaga performed with the group until 1988.

As a Resident Fellow at Stanford, José Antonio Burciaga—known as Tony or Toño—painted, wrote, and worked with students. His ideas and presence were a handful for Stanford, along with his controversial murals, ever present in Casa Zapata. He encouraged students' questions, their cultural expressions, and their taking action when necessary through print, like *El Aguila*, and other forums. He strategized with activists in the greater Bay Area. He energized the Euphrat and Movimiento de Arte y Cultura Latino Americana (MACLA) boards in the 1990s. He spoke at social justice events in the Bay Area, including East Palo Alto, Redwood City, and San José. Burciaga supported actions that opposed anti-immigration movements such as California Proposition 187 and other English-only policies.

Last Supper of Chicano Heroes, central panel of *The Mythology and History of Maiz*, 1985–1987. Detail with Frida Kahlo, Luis Valdez, Dolores Huerta, and Cesar Chavez seated together. Mural for inside wall of Casa Zapata dining room, Stern Hall, Stanford University.

Whether in academia, the community, or the art world, he was not afraid to stick his neck out for the sake of critical discussion or for what was right. I repeatedly witnessed this firsthand. In 1990, he wrote an article on the impact of artist Francisco Zúñiga. The piece began innocently and then began to probe deeper. He queried Cecilia and two outspoken activist women well known in the art world, Juana Alicia and Yolanda Lopez: [9]

9 Rindfleisch, Jan with Albers, Patricia, eds. *Drawing from Experience, Artists Over Fifty*, 1990, in conjunction with the Euphrat Gallery exhibition.

When we deal with [Zúñiga's] drawings or sculpture, the intrigue is with his women, forever waiting, reclining, resting, squatting, or walking. He clothes and covers them in shawls and dresses that never hide the massive human proportions, the gestures, the slouches, comfortably accommodating them to the earth, one with the earth. ...

And so I ask Cecilia, my wife. "What do you think of Zúñiga?" She answers. "They're lovely but they lack something, they lack individual personality."

I ask muralist Juana Alicia, a Chicana, and she answers. "Beauty and sensuality. But his crux, his axis is from another generation, another perspective, which I respect. There is a woman-ness, but they are icons ... There is no struggle *y la mujer Mexicana tiene que luchar*. There is no pain. This idealized *indigena*, does it really exist? Just posing, resting. We can't do that anymore." ...

And I ask artist Yolanda Lopez, another Chicana, who herself has captured the essence of womanhood in drawings of her mother, grandmother, and *tias*.

Yolanda admits, "Zúñiga's women are very beautiful on the surface but do not touch or move me ... I admire his technical craft but there is no emotional or spiritual content. ... And there is a salability to these comfortable non-threatening images of women, barefoot and indolent. It is the romanticization of native women which is very much in vogue throughout the Southwest and the Santa Fe motif galleries. This is a leftover from the mid-nineteenth century intellectual and esthetic concept of the peasant and the Indian as romantic figures. Once they were conquered, the artists nostalgically recaptured them as they wanted them to be."

And I have to agree with these three women. Although not wanting to be descriptive or political, Zúñiga asserts a political description of native women. There has to be individuality, not just generic forms. ... In spite of his technical mastery, Zúñiga's refusal to be "descriptive, political, illustrative or archaeological" does have political repercussions.

Burciaga initiated heated discussion with his own art, too. His essay, "Birth and Death of a Mural,"[10] describes the life cycle of the 22'x150' *Danzas Mexicanas* mural he painted around 1977 with Mexican maestro Gilberto Romero Rodriguez in Redwood City. Given the lack of cooperation from arts administrators, late and minimal payment, topped off with a dedication invitation that credited the sponsors and didn't mention the artists, the two decided to protest at the dedication ceremony. In front of 500 people including the mayor and supervisors, Burciaga courageously spoke about the exploitive situations artists often faced. Then both artists flung bottles of paint at areas of the mural away from the dancing figures. At first stunned, the audience response transitioned to more cheers than jeers. The protest remained part of the mural, "an inevitable part of the artistic process."

Burciaga's *The Last Supper of Chicano Heroes* mural again provoked impassioned discussion about the politics behind the decisions on the participants. Burciaga had decided to go with a student vote rather than put his own choices forward.[11] The breadth

---

10 Essay in Burciaga, José Antonio. *Spilling the Beans*, 1995. Joshua Odell Editions.

11 The "Last Supper" mural, located in the dining hall, is part of a larger mural entitled *The Mythology and History of Maiz*. Many of his murals were painted with students. José B. Cuéllar discusses the mural in "*Chicanismo/Xicanism@*" for *The Oxford Encyclopedia of Mesoamerican Cultures*; see user www.sfsu.edu/ josecuel/chicanismo.htm.

of choices of a 200-person student and activist survey included nun and poet Sor Juana Inés de la Cruz, civil rights leader Martin Luther King, Jr., activist artists, freedom fighters, and numerous members of the dining hall staff. The front row includes activists with local roots—Cesar Chavez and Dolores Huerta, co-founders of the United Farm Workers, and playwright Luis Valdez, founder of El Teatro Campesino, a bilingual theater company based in Mission San Juan Bautista south of San José. Through his process, Burciaga brought up many questions, including where/how responsibility is situated in education. What stands out for me are words painted large on the tablecloth, running across the bottom of *The Last Supper of Chicano Heroes* mural: "…and to all those who died, scrubbed floors, wept and fought for us."

Burciaga taught us how to *Drink Cultura*, in essays first published in 1979, later compiled in the 1993 book, *Drink Cultura: Chicanismo*. José B. Cuellar, professor of Chicano Studies at San Francisco State University, aka saxophone player "Dr. Loco," elaborates:[12]

> Burciaga's *Drink Cultura* contains twenty-six stories and commentaries, starting with the symbolic significance of *c/s (con/safos)* as a perennial Chicano graffiti sign-off and closing with a cheeky proposal for a national magazine for *los muertos*/the dead. Between these two we also learn about the joy of a jalapeño pepper-induced gastronomic ecstasy and the significance of *Cinco de Mayo*/Fifth of May.

T-shirt accompanying *Drink Cultura*, 1992.

Bilingual Love Poem, Poema de amor bilingüe, 1992, plays with his love of two languages and reflects his fascination with Spanish and English words that look alike but mean something entirely different.[13] In *Dreams and Flowers for Margarita*, Burciaga grappled

---

12 Burciaga, José Antonio. *Drink Cultura: Chicanismo*, 1992. Joshua Odell Editions. First published in 1979 in San José by Lorna Dee Cervantes' Mango Press. See also userwww.sfsu.edu/josecuel/chicanismo.htm.

13 Burciaga thoughts in baylor.edu/lariatarchives/news.php?action=story&story=8596.

with cancer and life.[14] His outline for integrating art, education, and life was originally published in spring 1992—it's also a subtle lesson on how to make and judge fine art:[15]

> It was in a hot desert alley behind our El Paso home that I found scattered small pieces of broken wood. I wasn't more than six years young when I picked up these fascinating pieces of jagged wood. One of them looked like the head of an axe and another like the handle. I put the pieces together, found a piece of wire, and tied my axe together. With care, this axe would last for a game or two. I was so excited …

> We have all been there, when as children we created a mountain from sand, a house from a box, a boat from half a nut shell, a tent from our bed covers, or the fastest vehicle on earth from a skate and a board. Once, we were pilots on World War II flying fortresses made of wooden fruit boxes, and, though we never left the ground, we flew to the farthest reaches of our imagination. We constructed a world and a heaven of our own, fragile as our imagination.

> … As for my little wooden axe: My mother kept it for forty-some years, and when she passed away it was returned to me. I never played with it, but I now have it inside a little glass case as one of my first, and perhaps finest, works of art. It can be categorized as found object art or assemblage art. I look at it, and my imagination takes me back to a hot desert alley where perhaps a crucial seed was planted.

Burciaga's writings include poetry, novel, essays, and books. His 1992 poetry book, *Undocumented Love/Amor Indocumentado*, won the American Book Award. In 1995, while in temporary remission from cancer, Burciaga won the Hispanic Heritage Award for Literature.

---

14 Burciaga, José Antonio. *Undocumented Love/Amor Indocumentado, A Personal Anthology of Poetry*, 1992, Chusma House Publications. Also *Spilling the Beans: Loteria Chicana*, 1995. Ibid.

15 Rindfleisch, Jan and Albers, Patricia, eds. *The Fourth R: Art and the Needs of Children and Youth*, (Spring 1992), in conjunction with the Euphrat Museum exhibition. Later included in Burciaga, José Antonio. *Drink Cultura: Chicanismo*, 1992: Joshua Odell Editions.

From Sal Si Puedes to Mayfair and Mexican Heritage Plaza

Many Spanish-speaking people settled in East San José; mostly Puerto Rican in the 1920s, then mostly Mexican and Mexican-American in the late 1930s. The neighborhood's unpaved streets, poverty, crime, and police violence earned its nickname, Sal Si Puedes (Get Out if You Can). Cesar Chavez first settled there as a youth in 1939 while following field work with his family throughout California. After serving for two years in the U.S. Navy, Chavez met Helen Fabela while working the fields and vineyards near Delano. The couple married and started their family in Delano before moving back to the East San José barrio.

Nuestra Señora de Guadalupe, a glass mosaic mural created by Katherine Oppenheimer, Marie Hutton and Lois Cronemiller c. 1967, is featured prominently on the side of OLG Church in East San José. The mural depicts key images of the area's history, from an early encounter with the Ohlone to the rise of the United Farm Workers movement. Image courtesy of History San José.

Our Lady of Guadalupe (OLG) Catholic parish was born from the 1950 request by the people of the area for a church with Masses in Spanish, and neighborhood residents have continued their activism ever since. The story goes that St. Martin's Church in San José's Burbank neighborhood donated a building to Father Donald McDonnell for a church in East San José. Chavez and other church members sawed it in half and brought it to land donated by the Mayfair Packing Company—today the site of the Mayfair Community Center. In the mid-1960s, parishioners constructed a new, larger church building with their own hands. The original chapel, named McDonnell Hall, is on historic city tours and under consideration for National Historic Landmark status.

McDonnell introduced Chavez to Fred Ross, an organizer for the Community Service Organization (CSO), who recruited Chavez to the organization in 1952. Six years later, Chavez became CSO's national director. In 1962, Chavez co-founded the National Farm Workers Association (NFWA) with Dolores Huerta. When Filipino-American farm workers initiated the Delano grape strike in 1965, Chavez supported them. Later, the NFWA was called United Farm Workers after merging with the Filipino-based Agricultural Workers Organizing Committee, headed by longtime activist and Army veteran Larry Itliong.

Murals and other visual arts were integral to Eastside life. In addition, music, theater, and dance gave expression to social issues, built unity, and lifted spirits. Groups with Eastside origins have included Los Tigres del Norte, El Centro Cultural, Teatro de la Gente, Teatro Visión, Teatro Familia Aztlan, and Los Lupeños de San José. Today, the nonprofit Somos Mayfair creates community by training residents to be neighborhood *promotores*, helping parents to form neighborhood reading circles to promote early-childhood literacy, and encouraging exercise and a healthy diet.

The Mexican Heritage Plaza (MHP) was founded by Eastside revitalization visionary Blanca Alvarado, the first Latina to serve on the San José City Council and Santa Clara County Board of Supervisors. Artist Carlos Pérez created a 3' mosaic plaque depicting its history, activist roots, and an inspirational poem written by the artist's son, former Santa Clara County Poet Laureate David Pérez. Executive Director Tamara Alvarado places the plaza in its context:

> The plaza site is rooted in great cultural meaning, historical meaning, and social activism. It is ¼ to ½ mile from where Cesar Chavez lived. The Mayfair area was a hothouse [for activism]. The plaza is situated at the [former site of] Safeway, where one of the first boycotts of grapes was held. Story and King was a historic thoroughfare in the 1950s, 1960s. At this intersection, marches and demonstrations starting on King turned to head downtown. [The MHP demonstrates the community's] connection at a philosophical level, a historical level. [East San José is] a place where people are creating community, taking on blight, [demanding better] lighting, through efforts like Somos Mayfair.

Eastside Art & History, a project of the City of San José Public Art Program and History San José (HSJ), introduces East San José history, culture, and legacy, bringing together photos and public artwork at MHP, OLG and four other locations.[1]

Local Latino culture was also chronicled in *El Excentrico*, a bimonthly magazine published from 1949 until 1981. In the 1970s, poet Lorna Dee Cervantes (SJCC 1976, SJSU B.A. 1984) wrote about the destruction of the San José's downtown barrio by Interstate 280; she also founded her own Mango Publications. Today the El Excentrico Magazine Project[2] increases understanding about the Latino community's role in the development of San José and the region; El Excentrico Project collaborators include SJSU Cesar E. Chavez Community Action Center and the SJSU Mexican American Studies Department.

---

1 See koolturamarketing.com/corridor/ and eastsideartandhistory.com/ on HSJ website historysanjose.org, and see the Somos Mayfair website somosmayfair.org.

2 See the El Excentrico Magazine Project website excentrico.org.

Doing that Latino Art Thing: The Story of MACLA and the San José Center for Latino Arts

Gathering All the Memories

The story of MACLA and the San José Center for Latino Arts is first and foremost a story about arts advocacy and steadfast determination. In the wake of intense economic and social change in San José in the mid-1960s, who would have thought that a new Latino arts center could emerge and flourish? The only other successfully institutionalized Latino art centers in the nation were at least 20 years old. In a perhaps ironic way, from its inception, MACLA has sometimes been backhandedly complimented as "too ambitious" and too "political." But it has been those qualities exactly, and an unqualified dedication to excellence and planning on the part of its founders, that have made possible today what most people deemed impossible only six years ago.

Consider this scenario: in the mid-1980s, San José was undergoing an unprecedented transformation. A redevelopment program for the urban downtown core had been set in motion and many in the Latino community had been directly affected by the changes. Public debates about the identity and future of our city and the fair distribution of resources in a new era of "multicultural" explosion had been simmering across many areas of social life: housing, employment, education, public services.

In a new national climate where investments in public services and community cultural life had severely diminished, San José's Latino community found itself in a peculiar dilemma: on the one hand, there was a rich and vibrant cultural heritage and presence nurtured by Chicano artists and cultural workers; on the other hand, the survival of cultural organizations was precarious.

Resources for the stabilization of any ethnic-based cultural institution in San José were absent. Only a few years earlier, the Centro Cultural de la Gente, a cultural arts center in the tradition of the Chicano centers that emerged in the United States in the 1960s, had closed its doors and its leadership had disbanded. Artistically, Chicano/Latino arts in San José remained alive and growing, but institutionally there was no anchor, no visible markers in the "new" downtown core, no established professional venues for Latino visual and literary innovation, no gathering site for sustained Latino cultural expression and criticism. It is out of this tradition of cultural activism, firmly planted in the contested politics of San José's urban transformation, that MACLA was born.

Poetry and Rhythm in the "New" Downtown

In 1968, poets Margarita Luna Robles and Juan Felipe Herrera began to cook up a poetry storm in unlikely places throughout downtown: Marsugi's, Upstairs Eulipia, the State building auditorium, San José State University, wherever they could perform. With the help of Alan Soldofsky and the San José Poetry Center, they would bring their ensemble of poetry and percussion and talk to people about the need for a Latino cultural center in downtown. Two of the three official incorporators of MACLA as a nonprofit corporation—

Rick Sajor and Maribel Alvarez—were part of the ensemble which Robles called Media Mix. The third incorporator—Eva Terrazas—would join the efforts at a later time.

By the end of 1986, Sajor and Robles had convened a Latino arts advocacy group called The Arts Lobby. The first item on the agenda of this group was to increase Latino representation in the city's Art Commission. Sajor coordinated an intense advocacy effort to promote Latino "candidates" to two open seats on the commission. The Arts Lobby was successful. An active member of the group, Mary Jane Solis-Robledo, was appointed art commissioner. The Arts Lobby was a loose organization with no officers or long-term plans. However, the meetings, almost always held in Robles' kitchen or Solis-Robledo's living room, were always action-driven. The group's interests were diverse; the main purpose was to monitor policies in the arts locally and regionally.

Advised that they would have problems in obtaining nonprofit status from the IRS by having the word "lobby" in the name, the organizers decided to continue working under another name: Movimiento Artistico Latino Americano, for short, MALA. The group went through great lengthy discussions to choose a name that reflected the vision of the new organization. It was decided to choose a name in Spanish that included the word "movimiento" (movement) to reflect the history and grounding of the Chicano political mobilization and to indicate constant action, evolution, and grassroots participation, and that at the same time was inclusive of other Latin American experiences and identities. However, the acronym MALA (meaning "bad," as in reference to a female) was not well received in the community. Finally, in April 1988, MACLA (Movimiento de Arte y Cultura Latino Americana) was adopted as the official name of the organization.

On July 19, 1987, a retreat was convened at Sanborn Park, Saratoga, to discuss and plan the "revival" of a Latino cultural center in downtown San José. The community response was enthusiastic. A number of key cultural activists attended the retreat and pledged to work to make this dream a reality. Among them were Elisa and Jorge Gonzalez, Cruz Mendoza, Vicky Robledo, Esteban Cervantes, Lupe Lujan, Adrian Vargas, Gil VIllagran, Eva Terrazas, and the core organizers Sajor, Alvarez, Solis-Robledo, Robles and Herrera. At the same time, it became clear that the task ahead was daunting.

The "action-list" from the retreat included: acquiring a building, staff, access to political channels, artistic programs to establish a "track record," legal incorporation, a board, committees, policies, mission statement, multicultural advocacy and alliances, a mailing list, etc., etc., etc., and on top of it all, money. Nonetheless, the retreat set off a very exciting period for the group. MACLA sponsored a dance at Marsugi's attended by over 200 people. At the dance, an impassioned plea to invite people to join the efforts for a cultural center was made. Many responded, but the more that the group set about organizing its goals and purposes, the more evident it became that the effort would be prolonged, intense, difficult, and would require more time and energy than most people simply had available. By early 1988, Robles and Herrera had left San José and it was very difficult to sustain a high level of energy in the group. Instead of playing congas and reading poetry, the meetings of MACLA became complex and tiring strategy sessions at Solis-Robledo's house to figure out just exactly how in the world one goes about building a new alternative cultural institution.

Taking Off: Response and Mobilization

At the same time that these planning discussions for the cultural center were taking place, MACLA was becoming fully engaged in two equally intense tasks: one, developing Latino artistic/cultural programs in collaboration with other art groups and institutions; and two, leading the efforts for multicultural advocacy at the Art Commission and the City Council. By early 1988, MACLA was spearheading a protest against a proposed city policy to grant exclusive access to the Montgomery Theater to two mainstream art organizations. As a result of the organized mobilization of Latino and other ethnic-based art groups, the city withdrew its plans for the Montgomery and the Arts Commission called for the formation of a "Multicultural Arts Committee" (MAC) made up of commissioners as well as community representatives.

The advocacy efforts consumed most of the energy of the members of MACLA. MACLA members began a series of meetings with then Councilmember Susan Hammer, Council liaison to the Arts Commission, to ask for increased support for multicultural arts. In October 1988, MACLA made a presentation to the Arts 2020 Task Force public hearings and recommended that a position for multicultural, community arts development coordinator be created in the Arts Commission office. In 1989, MACLA was instrumental in convening a large group of multicultural art organizations into a coalition for advocacy. This coalition, called MAAG, Multicultural Arts Action Group, was initially led by two MACLA board members: Rick Sajor and Sonia Gray. By March 1989, MACLA was actively involved in advocating for an increase in the city's Transient Occupancy Tax (TOT) and for a new allocation policy that would allow increased funding opportunities for multicultural arts. Working closely with Mary Jane Solis-Robledo and with Deputy City Manager Dan MacFadden, MACLA helped develop the proposal for an NEA-funded Multicultural Arts Incubation Project. Finally, working persistently behind the scenes with Solis-Robledo and other art commissioners, MACLA was a key player in the dramatic overhaul of the city's funding policies for multicultural art groups.

While these advocacy efforts were taking place, MACLA also attempted to maintain an artistic presence in the community. An exhibition entitled *Lo del Corazon* was co-sponsored with the San José Museum of Art. A memorable exhibition and performance for Day of the Dead were co-produced by MACLA with Los Lupenos and WORKS Gallery. A Gala Reception for Teatro Vision's play *No Se Paga* was organized by MACLA. A special outreach night for Latinos was organized by MACLA and the San José Symphony. In addition, for two years MACLA participated in the Living History Days exhibits at the San José Historical Museum.

Those first three years, from 1986 to 1989, were a time of intense activity and also of profound learning. Along the way, mistakes were made and lessons learned. MACLA was being pulled in many directions, and although it was accomplishing successfully what it had set out to do, the sheer intensity and controversial nature of the political decisions made along the way were taking a toll on the cohesion and vision of the group. By the time 1990 came around, MACLA was suffering, as an organization as well as through its individual members, of severe exhaustion and confusion. Nonetheless, the community kept asking: what about the cultural center you said you would establish? While MACLA had slowly gained the respect of many in the community who had witnessed the great amount of energy and time that the art advocacy work required, others grew impatient and frustrated. Finally, in August 1989, MACLA had its first organizational retreat to revisit its vision and purpose, as well as to consider organizational development strategies.

Mapping a Plan of Action

The retreat, facilitated by Cecilia Arroyo, made clear to the group that if it was really serious about establishing an art center in downtown San José, it would have to work very hard to create an "organizational infrastructure" that could actually sustain such a huge undertaking. If up to that point MACLA had worked hard in advocacy activities, from now on, in order to reach the dream of a cultural center with ongoing programs and resources, it would have to work especially hard to develop resources and organizational skills of a different nature.

Learning step by step how to build that organizational infrastructure was both the most rewarding and the most difficult thing that MACLA has ever accomplished. It was one thing to say that San José *should* have a Latino art center in the downtown, but without any money whatsoever, no staff, no programmatic structure, and no sponsoring organization behind MACLA (such as the city, the Redevelopment Agency, or significant private patrons of the arts), the question in everyone's mind was: how do we do it? The board of directors at that time—composed of Rick Sajor, Eva Terrazas, Maribel Alvarez, Sonia Gray, Milita Samaniego, Liz Marcos, Elisa Gonzalez, and Vicky Robledo—made several important decisions: MACLA would withdraw from its leading role in the advocacy efforts and would focus instead on organizational development, planning, and in producing its own, but very carefully selected, cultural programs. At that time, it also became evident that to make the center a reality, MACLA would need the financial assistance of the city, but that it would first have to "prove" to both city officials and the community at large that the investment would be worthwhile and that MACLA could do something very special for Latino arts in San José. The challenge was how to build a center from ground zero that was responsive to community needs while at the same time not claiming to be everything for everyone.

These changes in strategy coincided with a very critical internal change in MACLA's leadership. Alvarez, who up that point had been board president, shifted her focus to programming and fund-development, and Terrazas, who had been primarily involved with advocacy, became board president. The impact of this internal shift cannot be underestimated. Terrazas, masterfully skillful at organizational development, led MACLA through an unprecedented process of organizational "infrastructure" building, which cemented the first real leap forward towards the establishment of the center. Alvarez turned her attention to fundraising and cultural programming, setting in motion an effort that would increase MACLA's budget from $1,000 to over $100,000 in less than three years.

Under Terrazas' leadership, two significant processes got underway. First, a large and careful effort for board recruitment and board development expanded MACLA's base of support. The new board members who joined in 1990 gave MACLA a completely different sense of purpose and direction. Their collective contributions lead MACLA through a path of careful planning and rapid growth and without their dedication, the center would not be a reality today. The new members were: Dennis Gaxiola, Erin Goodwin-Guerrero, Fred

Spratt, Fred Yepiz, Monica Gallardo, Paul Niedermeyer, Jeff Steinhardt, and Ron Arroyo. From the old guard, there remained Alvarez, Terrazas, Gray, Robledo, and Elisa Gonzalez. Secondly, Terrazas instituted a systematic process of strategic planning. In January 1990, MACLA submitted its first grant request ever: it was a request for $1,500 to the Arts Council of Santa Clara County to develop a strategic plan. The grant was matched one-to-one by IBM.

The strategic planning process spanned a period of two years. The board conducted a community needs assessment to determine what artistic programs the community would envision for the center. Today, the center's two primary artistic and programmatic objectives—visual arts and literature—are the same ones that surfaced as community priorities for a downtown cultural center back in 1990.

As with any strategic planning effort, the board participated in an intense process where strengths and weaknesses were identified, as well as threats and opportunities. It took a tremendous amount of work, but finally, MACLA's vision and "plan of action" was taking shape. Internally, Terrazas made sure that board committees were fully operational and that policies were spelled out clearly. With the support and leadership of Paul Niedermeyer and Telemundo-Channel 48, MACLA began to establish bookkeeping records and more systematic management structures. Additional support was provided by the Nonprofit Development Center.

On the artistic front, many exciting things began to happen. Under Alvarez's leadership, a collaboration for a Day of the Dead exhibition was established with the San José Institute of Contemporary Art. The exhibition, entitled *Altares: Contemporary Interpretations*, was curated by Kathryn Funk, and served as a prototype of the kind of work that MACLA hoped to bring to its own center one day. The opening night was attended by hundreds of people, who were beginning to see what a "Latino art center" could possibly offer. In 1990, with the support of Jim Reber, MACLA produced its first 100% independent cultural program: the visit and performance of the Voladores de Papantla, from Veracruz, Mexico. Over 10,000 people saw the Voladores perform their spectacular dance-ritual in downtown San José.

Pressing On

While definite steps towards growth were being taken, much remained to be done. The next three years, 1991–1993, were the most accelerated period of growth that MACLA, or almost any other cultural organization, has ever seen. This period of growth, characterized by tenacity and perseverance, was not always easy to endure. Artistically, MACLA began to develop, for the first time, a fledgling programmatic structure. The anchor of this programmatic emphasis was a commitment to developing young artists. The "talleres de arte" for high school Latino artists, the brainchild of Ron Arroyo, was the first program that MACLA submitted to the Arts Commission for funding under the new funding guidelines that MACLA had helped change. The first year the Talleres were offered, under the coordination of Erin Goodwin-Guerrero and Dennis Gaxiola, the success was so large that MACLA had to keep a waiting list for the following year. The program was also very important because for the first time MACLA was able to hire local visual artists.

Internally, MACLA kept getting stronger, with board committees fully operational and a board standing unified in its purpose. However, it soon became evident that the work involved in this huge undertaking required the assistance of a staff person. While the board continued to be engaged in serious strategic planning for the center, fund development, and program planning, the volunteer management resources were being gradually drained. Hiring an executive director who could work with the board to make the center a reality was the most critical turning point for MACLA. With the support of Mayor Susan Hammer, who believed in MACLA at a critical crossroad of development, MACLA was able to secure funds to hire its first staff person. Marcos Sanchez-Tranquilino, a noted Chicano scholar and curator, became MACLA's first executive director in 1992. In his short tenure with MACLA, Sanchez-Tranquilino made a significant impact. He wrote the strategic plan document that culminated a two-year process of board planning, and added his own unique contribution by setting up a thematic matrix for program planning for the first five years of the center's operations. Sanchez-Tranquilino also shared with MACLA the "unique" experience of first occupying the present facility of the Center for Latino Arts at a time when it was nothing more than a messy, run-down, inoperable warehouse.

At this time, the board went through yet another significant change. Several of the key leaders in the critical period of strategic planning—Steinhardt, Terrazas, Spratt, Goodwin-Guerrero, Arroyo—had to leave the board for professional or personal reasons. New board members were recruited to see MACLA through its most difficult period: the transition from an all-volunteer organization to institutionalization. Over the next two years, new board members Elisa Goti, Bea Espinoza, Connie Yepiz, José Antonio Burciaga, Fred Hernandez, Louis Lopez, Alicia Mendeke, Bob Ruiz, Roma Dawson and the architect David Zamora (who made the renovation of the San José Center for Latino Arts his "labor of love" every day for over three years) worked alongside the "older" board members to solidify the vision of the center.

Artistically, MACLA continued to be active and risk-taking. In 1991, the board commissioned renowned Chicana muralist Juana Alicia to paint the mural *Regeneración*— the first professional mural ever "authorized" by the City of San José in the downtown core. The mural was very significant for MACLA. Not only did it break through the previous official anti-mural stance of city policies, but it also told the story of San José's Latino/indigenous community in a bold and unique manner, right in the core of the "new" downtown. In addition, in the summer of 1992, MACLA brought the Voladores de Papantla back to San José for a second time. Other programs, such as the San José premiere of the film *Danzón*, a literary event with 12 Chicano/Latino poets organized by Lucha Corpi, and an evening of music with Nueva Trova singers from Mexico and Nicaragua, Gabino Palomares and Enrique Mejia Godoy, generated a new level of enthusiasm for MACLA's programming.

Of all the exciting possibilities surfacing for MACLA, none was more dramatic, and at the same time challenging, than the opportunity to finally have a facility for a center. In the spring of 1992, Alvarez and Terrazas went to lunch one day with José Jimenez of Dura Enterprises and Hermelinda Sapien, Executive Director of Center for Employment Training (CET). After a very long discussion about San José, the arts, the cultural struggle of the Latino community, and many other topics, Jimenez and Sapien agreed to consider

The mural, REGENERACION/ REGENERATION, inspired by MACLA, deserves to be permanently installed somewhere in Silicon Valley. Problems arose during the making of it—the panels were not permanently installed, and later were put in storage. In retrospect, this project was a bold undertaking for a young MACLA during a difficult growth period. Activist lawyer and art collector Karen Rudolph of Los Altos has assisted continuing efforts to find the right wall.*

Juana Alicia's public art gives a face to local activists—the strong visage of tribal leader Rosemary Cambra in From the Ground Up / Desde las Raices (with Tirso Araiza, Project Director), 2014, a student mural project at Berkeley City College;

SJSU student athletes John Carlos and Tommie Smith, raising their fists in the Black Power salute at the 1968 Olympics in Mexico City, in The Spiral Word: El Codex Estánfor, 2012, named by Juan Felipe Herrera. It was commissioned to replace a mural Juana Alicia created with the Yo Puedo program in the mid-'80s that had been inadvertently destroyed during renovation.

This latter suite of murals for Stanford's El Centro Chicano is a compact, narrative-dense work transforming, as Juana Alicia states, "an institutional-feeling entryway into a sanctuary for some of our collective narratives ... a gift of ideas and images to the past, present and future generations of Latin@/Chican@/Indigenous and

Juana Alicia, *REGENERACION/ REGENERATION*, ©1991 World Rights Reserved. Acrylic mural on panels, 12' x 24', commissioned by MACLA at 1st and San Carlos streets, downtown San José. Local imagery included the legendary Tiburcio Vásquez's gravestone on the SCU campus (see upper right-hand corner).

multiracial students ... open to everyone to enjoy." Again, the muralist collaborated with Stanford students to research and create the work. An analysis of *The Spiral Word: El Codex Estánfor* is included in SJSU student Allison Connor's thesis "Juana Alicia: A Case Study of the Artist as Critical Muralist."

Juana Alicia has had ongoing collaborations in Silicon Valley. Starting in the mid-1980s, Juana Alicia and I worked together on multiple exhibitions, publications, and events related to public art and issues—one on greater Bay Area interdisciplinary arts programs for youth, *Youth Art/Changing Lives*, 1995. In *Maestrapeace Art Works*, 2000, we exhibited the work of its seven muralists,

including Juana Alicia; these fearless women designed and painted the internationally acclaimed, monumental mural *Maestrapeace* on the San Francisco Women's Building.

* For more information about Juana Alicia, see www.juanaalicia.com. Rudolph, who assisted with the biographical documentary of her husband Jimi Dexter Simmons (Muckleshoot/Rogue River) in the 2008 film *Making the River*, directed by Sarah Del Seronde (Navajo), values the mural's deeply felt art and history connections. She shares Juana Alicia's deep concern for indigenous rights and recognition.

MACLA's request: the use of one of CET/Dura's vacant buildings downtown. But Alvarez and Terrazas waited until the end of the conversation to mention one small detail: MACLA did not have any money for rent. Jimenez and Sapien said: Well, first let's see what you can do; then let's talk about money. And so it was—MACLA had to "prove" itself.

The Board received the news of Alvarez and Terrazas' feat with mixed feelings. On the one hand, it was the best news MACLA had ever had; on the other hand, it was too soon, at least three years earlier than what the strategic plan called for. The board did not have the resources it needed to renovate or operate a facility that needed a lot of work. The first visit to the facility at 510 South First Street did nothing to relieve the fear that perhaps MACLA was "biting off more than it could chew." Intense, heartfelt board discussions debated the pros and cons of assuming such a big responsibility without resources. Paul Niedermeyer, board treasurer at the time, insisted that MACLA would not engage in deficit spending; to do so would contradict everything MACLA had been learning for the last three years. Finally, the board reached a consensus: they would put their own labor and as much donated resources as possible into a preliminary clean-up/renovation to bring the center to a basic level of operation. Maybe if the community actually "saw" the center in operation, resources could be harnessed to continue the development.

The process was extremely difficult, but the facility began to slowly change its looks and most importantly, grassroots partnership with other Latino/Chicano cultural organizations began to develop for the use of the center. The first "users" of the new facility were Teatro Vision, for rehearsals, and Adrian Vargas and Teatro Familia Aztlan, who produced a series of plays. However, it was the relationship with Academia Aztlan and Javier Salazar that ultimately grounded MACLA in a partnership that made possible the incredible transformation of the center for its first shows and performances. Without the work and support of the members of Academia Aztlan, it is almost certain that MACLA could not have passed the "test" that it had set for itself.

We Are Only Just Beginning

The renovation work at the facility that today houses the San José Center for Latino Art occurred in several stages. At the beginning everything was improvised and temporary. Finally, by June 1993, the board, Academia Aztlan, and a dozen or so volunteers, without any capital funds whatsoever, finished the first stage of renovation that allowed the center to open its door for year-round programming during 1993–94. The center's first exhibition featured the works of young Latino artists who had participated in MACLA's second-year Talleres de Arte. The exhibition entitled *Raices y Alas* (Roots and Wings) was symbolic of MACLA's own identity: rooted in a story of community struggle and positioned towards the future as an anchor of Latino culture in the heart of the City's center.

Other very important exhibitions and performances followed: Yolanda Lopez' installation *Cactus Hearts/Barbed Wire Dreams*, Guillermo Gomez-Pena's performance of *New World (B) Order*, poetry readings, and a community altar for Day of the Dead 1993. As MACLA finally reached a level of growth and development to make that dream of a cultural center a reality, new leadership and sources of support also emerged. It seemed as if MACLA had reached a point in its development when it was ready to re-establish its own presence and identity in the community, rooted in the vision of its founders but different in its own time and space. It seemed as if MACLA was ready to forge new partnerships, incorporate new ideas and new energy and begin to walk a new path of growth and development, ultimately, a new path of cultural leadership in San José.

After Marcos Sanchez' departure, the board of directors chose Jaime Alvarado to take the helm and lead MACLA to this new moment of growth and consolidation. Alvarado's love for San José and for the arts and his integrity and commitment as an actor, a labor activist, and a writer have been great assets in this, yet another moment of transition. This last— but not final—stretch of growth for MACLA was also to a large degree made possible by a number of large grants from funding sources which really saw MACLA as a "community investment" at a time in which that help was absolutely critical. Although *all* grants and contributions, whether small or large, are always community investments and MACLA is deeply grateful to each and every one of our supporters, the "big push," so to speak, came at a critical time. Among these most valuable "investment partners" are The Irvine Foundation, The Knight Foundation, and the City of San José's Redevelopment Agency.[1]

In the mid-1990s, Maribel Alvarez wrote this slightly edited history, titled after what was then an unpublished poem/performance by Juan Felipe Herrera.

---

1 Maribel Alvarez, Ph.D., served as executive director of MACLA from 1996–2003. Alvarez is an anthropologist, folklorist, curator, and community arts expert. She holds a dual appointment as associate research professor in the School of Anthropology and associate research social scientist at the Southwest Center, University of Arizona. Through an executive-on-loan arrangement with the university, she currently serves as executive program director of the Southwest Folklife Alliance.
For information regarding programs and artist resources, see MACLA's website. maclaarte.org

MACLA: Multicultural Arts on the Move

Anjee Helstrup-Diaz, MACLA's Executive Director, sees the organization's establishment as the result of a broad community mobilization in the City of San José and throughout the country on behalf of multicultural arts. As its website states:

> MACLA has retained since its inception an alternative vision of arts programming as a vehicle for civic dialogue. Rather than perpetuate a static view of culture and ethnicity, MACLA's programs seek to challenge preconceived notions and contribute to deeper thinking and social representation for the city's largest ethnic group.

MACLA today produces programming in visual arts, performance and literary arts, youth arts education, and community development through the arts. It provides a strong foundation in the humanities that engenders a culture of critical thinking. It values literary development of youth—drawing in low-income youth—and always focuses on the creation and presentation of contemporary work.

Pilar Agüero-Esparza, *Sisters (Hawk & Little Big Sister)*, 1999. Charcoal on paper, wax, nests, 96"x72"x10". An installation about home, relationships, and life processes. Agüero-Esparza, artist, educator, and arts administrator, served as director of visual arts at MACLA, and was featured in MACLA's publication *Poetic Paradox: Ten Years of Innovation in Latino Arts*, 2001.

MACLA has grown with the community, city, and SJSU, and attracted a range of help from a wide circle. The following two artists highlighted here had divergent ways of working for the arts community. One approach involved funding and insider or committee politics; the other involved an artist landing the project or the funding. Both greatly influenced MACLA's development.

Tejano Joe Bastida Rodriguez was fortunate to be able to study in Florence, work for the NEA, and collaborate with muralist Judith Baca at Social and Public Art Resource Center (SPARC) in Los Angeles. He developed and ran programs in Texas, Washington D.C. and California, and did his art on the side. These experiences aided him in administering the Multicultural Arts Program at the City of San José's Office of Cultural Affairs, critically important to MACLA and other small to mid-size groups that participated in the Multicultural Arts Incubation Program. Rodriguez's guidance of this city program, plus its subsidies and office space, helped many arts organizations get to the next level. Nearly all of the groups are still alive and thriving, including Teatro Visión, Kaisahan of San Jose, Abhinaya Dance Company of San José, San Jose Taiko, Multicultural Artists Guild, South Bay Guitar Society, Arte Flamenco, and San Jose Jazz Society.

Brochure for Incubation Project (detail) produced by Carlos Pérez and Ann Sherman in 2000.

Carlos Pérez, born in Jalisco, Mexico, came to Stockton as a child. He excelled in art and made his way to SJSU. He worked with Regis McKenna, drew the Apple logo, and ultimately developed his own art and design business, ArtOrigin. His art ranges from graphic design to fine art and public art, such as installations in Evergreen Valley High School's library and the Norman Y. Mineta San José International Airport. His painting imagery has honored the inspiration of labor leader Dolores Huerta and activist artists Frida Kahlo and Yolanda Lopez. He has quietly helped nonprofits and mentored art leaders: Jaime Alvarado at MACLA, George Rivera at the Triton Museum. Another little known fact: around 2007, he and Analisa Escobedo Pérez, his wife, started a group that met in their home to brainstorm ways to promote local arts and artists; it later morphed into 1stACT Silicon Valley. Most recently, he has mentored young entrepreneurs in marketing and communications as part of San José Small Business Ignite.

The Anatomy of an 'Un-Organization': Explaining #DebugScience

I was in San Antonio the week the Spurs won the 2014 NBA championship. The fans' rallying cry, "Built Not Bought," was a comment on their competitors, the Miami Heat, which had famously acquired some of the NBA's best players with the goal of winning multiple championships.

Yet, despite what some saw as a talent discrepancy between the two teams, the Spurs won. Convincingly. The lesson: A set of seemingly disparate players committed to a shared philosophy can achieve greatness.

As the coordinator of Silicon Valley De-Bug, a community-based organization in Northern California that works with young adults and families, I often poke my head up to look at other fields—in this case, sports, but I also look at the business, faith, politics and pop culture sectors—to see what I can draw from them.

Why do I look around?

Because in the field of movement making, personal transformation and community building, we are developing the language of our work as we go. The search for naming, or understanding, the science of today's community organization is an open-ended one.

Once the offspring of political ideologies, community organizing no longer follows a party line and there is no rule book to reference—which is what makes organizing in today's America exciting.

Interestingly, metaphors are often the only expressions we have to describe the mechanics of our community work, which is instinctual, exploratory and sometimes, uncomfortably vague.

So, yes, I like the Spurs' "built not bought" metaphor and believe it is applicable to decision making in today's community organizations.

At De-Bug, we strive for the same ethic and believe our collective can achieve tremendous feats through the deliberate "slow-building" of the organization.

For example, though our organization has existed for more than a decade, the staff did not come about as the result of job postings, applications and an interview process. Instead, our staff is made up of those who walked through our doors and committed to us, as we committed to them.

Our lack of a traditional hiring process is also to prove a point—that greatness can be found in anyone if the organization is willing to see it.

Our art director came to us as an undocumented teen graffiti writer; our lead organizer, as a mother whose son was facing a prison sentence; and our youth director as a condition of probation.

We are not weaker for being inclusive; in fact, everything good our organization has done has come out of a spirit of inclusion.

We, too, were built rather than bought, and though we don't have an NBA championship, we have witnessed how the building-on-trust approach can transform lives, hold powerful institutions accountable and change the trajectory of an entire community.

At De-Bug, we have seen dreams literally come true—people becoming professionals in occupations they once felt were out of their reach, loved ones coming home from wrongful convictions, institutions improbably bending to demands of justice by marginalized communities—and more.

The Un-Organization

In a conventional organization, the individual often yields to the will, history and direction of the group. In a business, team or nonprofit organization, the entering individual also often gives up his or her personal agenda for the good of the group.

That approach, presumably, allows for more coherence and harmony for the organization. At De-Bug, we have done the opposite.

Jean Melesaine of Silicon Valley De-Bug made this image of Daniel Zapien. He arrived at De-Bug as a requirement of court-ordered community service. He is now De-Bug's youth organizer and a videographer for the group.

We say to the person entering our space—bring all of your audacious dreams as well as all of your personal baggage, and you lead us. We will follow and support your direction, and you will expand us in the process.

In this way, everyone is an architect of our institution, rather than merely a caretaker of something others have constructed. This allows for a stronger sense of ownership.

That is why De-Bug makes much more sense from the inside looking out than it does looking in from the outside.

The poster on our window lists all the things we currently are: media hub, criminal justice court organizing model, silk-screening shop, meditation circle and photography darkroom. And that's just what made it onto the poster.

In 2010, Chris Melesaine, then a teenager with De-Bug, attended a rally held at San José City Hall to denounce racial profiling. A police official had called community members "thugs." So, De-Bug supporters made shirts and flipped the meaning of the word, transforming it into something new. Nuns and elected officials showed up in support. Photo by Charisse Domingo of Silicon Valley De-Bug.

We started by publishing a magazine featuring the unheard voices of Silicon Valley manufacturing workers. But people are complex and multidimensional. We found we couldn't ask people to write only about their work.

They had fuller lives they wanted to discuss, including their families, their streets, their cultures, interests and larger beliefs. So our magazine expanded, because in order to respect people's total personhood, we had to honor all aspects of who they were and couldn't place people in "issue" boxes.

An assembly worker may also be a meditation expert, a formerly incarcerated person may also be an artist, a recent immigrant may be an emcee.

Eventually, as we became more intimate as an organization, the question evolved from "What do you want to write about?" to "What do you want to do?"

Every one of our enterprises, whether a political campaign or an entrepreneurial endeavor, came from an individual who came to us with a hope, dream, idea.

The De-Bug community followed that individual's lead.

What's Important? The Process Trumps the Product

The common theme of all our activities is the process, not the product. Indeed, what has sustained our work has been focusing on the integrity and relationships of the group rather than on the projects.

Before we had an office, a budget or a tax ID code, we had each other. We met and talked at a Vietnamese café once a week. We often say that if all the elements that dress us up as an organization were stripped from us, we would simply return to sit-downs at the café.

Relationships are still our most important focus.

Our approach allows for new creations based on the synergy of the different projects. For example, on weekends, we had families coming to De-Bug to strategize on how to advocate for loved ones facing the criminal court system. What they wanted above all was for the judges deciding the fate of their family members to know them beyond the police report.

During the week, youth videographers were honing their storytelling skills. We introduced the two groups. The result was something we call "social biography videos"—short videos that illuminate the lives of those facing prison, deportation or even execution in ways court documents cannot.

Those videos, which show how potential incarceration or deportation would affect the lives of families and the community, have prevented prison sentences and immigrant detentions and even overturned life sentences.

The Sangha

One of the frameworks we work within at De-Bug is a belief from Buddha. He said to achieve liberation, one needs the eyes to see the path, the legs to walk it, and a "sangha"—that is, a community of practitioners.

As community builders, we interpret "having eyes to see the path" as having an organizational theory, and interpret "legs to walk it" as employing the theory through practice. But what is particularly powerful and unique is the sangha.

The word "sangha" comes from Pali, a long-extinct language from the time of Buddha in India. Though the De-Bug community came about a couple thousand years after the origin of the word, we see De-Bug as a modern-day sangha—a community of practitioners who are all seeking their own liberation.

That does not mean that every person at De-Bug is aiming for the same end—liberation can mean different things to different people.

Some are trying to free their loved ones from incarceration, some are trying to start a business, some are trying to challenge economic inequality in Silicon Valley, some are trying to get over an addiction.

The point is that the journey to liberation need not be a solitary one and, in fact, liberation may become more possible when couched in the support of a community.

Democracy After the Romance

I am not saying that our approach does not have its drawbacks, losses and failures. The hardest part of trying to create the "world you wish to live in" is that it has to interface with the actual world.

For example, an inclusive and non-hierarchical decision-making process is not only difficult to put into operation but also likely to collapse because of the power dynamics we have all been taught since childhood.

We were taught to look up to authority not across our own horizon. Students are trained to look to teachers, employees to employers and so on. Add the lenses of race, class and gender, and one can see implicit hierarchies being built, even in spaces like community organizations.

Ramon Vasquez, whose family came to De-Bug when he was falsely arrested on suspicion of murder, is seen last year in front of the jail that once housed him. De-Bug members helped win his freedom, including a "factual finding of innocence" from the court. That is a rarely-used legal term when the court declares that an incarceration was undeserved. Vasquez now helps other families at De-Bug. Photo by Charisse Domingo of Silicon Valley De-Bug.

To combat those implicit hierarchies, De-Bug rotates facilitators in its meetings so that people get used to seeing each other at the front of the table. It's why we are mindful of who is being heard in discussions and who is not and why.

The process may be longer, but efficiency is not the goal of democracy.

The value of that hyper-vigilance is that people may carry the values and decision-making culture at De-Bug into aspects of their lives beyond the organization, whether that's their school, their workplace or their neighborhood.

That is, in many ways, the opportunity of larger impact—for the organization's values to be so embedded that it advances in aspects of people's lives beyond the office parameters.

But to move in the world in this way—to make decisions collectively, to challenge what is unfair or unjust, to strive toward what others have said is unreachable—is a risk in the real world.

As such, the organization can provide something invaluable, well beyond a campaign victory or a career opportunity—a point of reference in a lived experience of when collective action allowed for something that otherwise would not have been achieved.

It is why we have also drawn upon a lesson from another philosopher, Krishnamurti, who once said, "You can't get wet talking about water."

We take this to mean that some things need to be experienced in order to be truly understood. Democratic decision making, inclusive community building—these need to be practiced, rather then taught, to be real and sustaining.

When our decision-making process matters most is when the group must make a key fork-in-the-road decision or an urgent one.

For example, this could mean making the decision as to which court cases we will take and which we will not, or whether we will publicly criticize an elected official with whom we disagree or hold a private meeting with that official to find areas on which we can agree.

In those moments, organizational decision-making is like a martial art. You practice the motions over and over each day so that when you are suddenly in a position in which you need to act, non-hierarchical decision-making comes quickly and naturally.

Your values become your practice, and your practice becomes your instincts, and hopefully, when it matters the most, your instincts become your actions.

(De-Bug uses the hashtag #debugscience when we see or experience moments that describe the approach. Check it out on Instagram and Twitter.)

Raj Jayadev wrote the foregoing piece for the September 11, 2014 edition of Equal Voice News *about Silicon Valley De-Bug's approach and philosophy.*[1]

---

[1] See caseygrants.org/equal-voice-news. As coordinator of De-Bug, Raj Jayadev works with artists who share his keen understanding of community. He also coordinates the Albert Cobarrubias Justice Project, an organizing model for families and communities to impact their local court systems. He is an Ashoka Fellow. Silicon Valley De-Bug offers media production and training, organizes grassroots social justice campaigns, and incubates small businesses started by its members, showing how the arts can be part of solutions. In 2014, Silicon Valley De-Bug won a Santa Clara County Office of Humans Relations Award for justice work and contributing to our community fabric.
In terms of art, De-Bug has grown with exceptional artists, such as Jean Melesaine, producing museum-quality work. Charisse Domingo's striking photography graced Euphrat Museum's *Looking Back, Looking Ahead* exhibition coordinated with the California Studies Conference, "Debugging the Silicon Dream: Real Life in a Virtual World." In conjunction with the exhibition *Learn to Play*, De-Bug member Fernando J. Perez created a fascinating video of Suzanne Ruiz, co-founder of Take Action Games, loaded with lively commentary about game design and game play. For a more complete picture of the organization's contributions, check out the De-Bug website www.siliconvalleydebug.org/ and Jayadev, Raj and Melesaine, Jean, eds. *De-Bug: Voices from the Underside of Silicon Valley.* Heyday Books, 2016.

Epilogue

Art can give visibility to the invisible, voice to the voiceless. It is not just static on the wall, but an embrace of expression that ripples out, touching us. It's a matter of heart. The artists/activists in this book open us up to the art of daily life and to the artist within each of us. They get us to examine ourselves, to question our lives, and to think freely. They inspire us to dream and imagine and effectuate change—to build connections and enliven our communities.

Face-to-face conversations and stories are the starting point for harvesting the ideas and experiences of artists/activists who have contributed to the creative blossoming of Silicon Valley. We have introduced some of these contributors, presented a context of community building, and raised questions, as well as suggested areas for research, documentation, teaching, discussion, and collaboration. Communities can transform public dialogue and practices. Here are some recent efforts to build enlightened cultural policy in Silicon Valley.

The City of San José itself has been participating regionally and nationally with other large cities to share best practices for promoting a thriving arts community. John Kreidler, former executive director of Cultural Initiative Silicon Valley (CISV) and former San José Mayor Susan Hammer polled and encouraged community input from the bottom up. Hammer inspired Silicon Valley's 10-year cultural plan. Between 1996 and 2006, CISV implemented its key features, with the community's choice of art education in the schools as the plan's #1 priority. The organization published research on immigration and participatory arts, and offered a computer game as a tool to consider Silicon Valley's cultural future.[1] CISV supported the celebration and examination of art and technology, and spread the word that cultural policy could impact quality of life.[2]

The mantle for the regional approach to support for the arts has been carried by a succession of organizations, each with a different focus. Arts Council Silicon Valley had the longest term, from 1982 until 2011, when 1st ACT (Arts, Creativity, Technology) Silicon Valley took over. The two groups merged in 2013 to form the current nonprofit regional arts advocate Silicon Valley Creates.

---

[1] One of Kreidler's main interests during his term as executive director of CISV (2000–2006) and since has been cultural policy. As he put it, with "… Silicon Valley's prowess …why not produce a computer game that provided a platform for thinking about the region's cultural future?" "Medici's Lever," a CISV gift to the field of cultural policy, contains three modules: two games for educating cultural policy students, including "SJ Renaissance," which employs Silicon Valley plot lines; and an online laboratory that allows policy makers to simulate conditions in a real or imagined region.
In 2014, Kreidler wrote generally about achieving a healthy regional cultural ecology in the British journal *Cultural Trends*, and made a case "that demand-side policies may offer a more democratic way forward for both arts and sports policies." See: Kreidler, John. "Modeling the future of US arts policy: Beyond supply-side pump-priming." *Cultural Trends*, 2013, 22:3-4, 145-155. http://dx.doi.org/10.1080/09548963.2013.817643

[2] Results included upgraded arts education programs in 75% of the region's elementary schools through funding, teacher training and curriculum development. CISV's arts education staff transferred to the Santa Clara County Office of Education, along with transitional funding. All of the research generated by CISV, including two books on the region written by cultural anthropologists, was previously available at the organization's website, which no longer exists.

Independent, grassroots arts-and-idea people also have expanded definitions and impact. Through the Art Box Project founded by Tina Morrill, artists now paint drab utility boxes with color and imagination in far-flung, quotidian corners of the South Bay. The San Jose Multicultural Artists Guild, a coalition of professional performing arts groups, offers theatre productions, arts education, and a community arts program that includes a month of marigold-strewn Día de los Muertos arts activities throughout the South Bay. At SCU, lecturer Renee Billingslea (Art) and professor Laura Ellingson (Communications) work with community across disciplines on a project exploring "the photovoice" of cancer survivors. The films and public art installations of former SCU communications lecturer Jonathan Fung,[3] now teaching at the Art Institute of California–San Francisco, expose human trafficking. "Environmental sculptors" persevere to carve out open space, so that we might breathe and enjoy natural beauty. Thanks to the 1962 bequest of a former dairy farm to the City of San José from city native Emma Prusch, we now have Veggielution, which artfully "connects people through food and farming" at Emma Prusch Park, located at Story and King roads.

Visions for the future and planning always confront changing conditions and times. On September 2, 2015, for an Imagine SJ Showcase, a collaboration between FutureArtsNow! and Kooltura Marketing, Demone Carter led discussion on the future of visual arts in San José. Artists included Sam Rodriguez and Sean Boyles, who spoke about challenges of exhibiting and urgency of creating multifunctional art spaces like Cukui in Japantown and the Arsenal, originally on The Alameda, now on North Fifth Street in Japantown.[4] Cherri Lakey, who along with Brian Eder launched Anno Domini in the SoFA district and Phantom Galleries for vacant spaces, had a list of requests for action, starting with allowing live-work spaces for artists. Silicon Valley De-Bug recorded the wide-ranging event.[5]

Activism in education and leadership is challenging the region and affecting policy and plans. In traditional academia, a habitual focus on the biggest names drowns out the motivated but lesser-known people who have opened vistas and made exceptional contributions. Women's contributions and those of early activists may get sidelined and

---

[3] Instructor Jonathan Fung, also a filmmaker and installation artist, produced and directed *The Soul Show*, a live, weekly arts-themed talk show to inspire urban youth. He has raised social consciousness and exposed human trafficking through his films *Down the Rabbit Hole* and *Hark*. Fung's public art installation *Peep* was installed in downtown San José in February 2016 for Super Bowl 50, because a spike in sex trafficking often occurs during major sporting events. *Coolie*, an installation for 2016's *Gold Rush* exhibition at Santa Clara University's de Saisset Museum, examined forced labor during the mid-1800s. When not using art as a tool for positive change, Fung coaches middle school basketball in San José.

[4] Sam Rodriguez came out of street culture and graffiti. He went on to create public art, design bikes, and with friend and tattoo artist Orly Locquiao develop Cukui. "Rooted from a melting pot of Chicanos, South Pacific Islanders, tattoo artists, and graffiti heads," the hip streetwear boutique and art gallery is driven by limited-edition designs and exclusive releases. The inaugural Cukui Music Festival was held at California's Great America in Santa Clara September 3, 2016.
Sean Boyles and partner painter Roan Victor started the Arsenal, because "if University Arts didn't have it, there was nowhere else to buy art supplies." He teaches at SCU. She is a SJSU graduate. He feels "everyone should open an art gallery. It's hard to show here, live here. They don't equate."

[5] On a more encompassing scale, the Knight Cities Challenge has elicited multiple ideas from the South Bay creative community and offered grants to innovative projects [that are] "attracting and keeping talent, expanding economic opportunity, and creating a culture of civic engagement."

relegated to social history.[6] Recent Silicon Valley publications and projects, such as those by Guracar and Yu, Fukuda and Pearce, and Guinn and the California History Center put contributions in context. They cite specific artists/activists who inspire and push the envelope by calling attention to idea generation, to challenges to the establishment, and to the larger process of change.

Furthering the integration of broad-based cultural concepts into specialized fields yields benefits beyond a well-rounded education. The community gains when its leaders can see beyond the immediate or specific to understand the big picture. Examples of this are when majors in political science, economics, urban studies and community development consider the impact of sports as well as the ever-evolving arts and cultural scene; or when police science curricula teaches not only community policing but also creative options for addressing problems of the troubled and mentally ill. Silicon Valley De-Bug, which partners with the SCU journalism department, speaks to community and educators about community organizing and advocacy; social justice and the rights of youth, workers, and immigrants; how to engage and affect change in the criminal court system; and the role of arts and culture. It has received numerous prestigious awards, including one for "giving voice to the voiceless."

PJ and Roy Hirabayashi, the founding members of San Jose Taiko previously profiled, continue to be actively involved as individuals and in organizations, such as the American Leadership Forum Silicon Valley (ALFSV), where both are senior fellows. Based on years of experience, they offer ideas on how to work through rough spots or avoid leaving people behind:

> To look to the future, we start from what we know and find others thinking the same way, at the same time stepping outside the box and exploring other viewpoints—ideally stepping into someone's shoes for awhile, and vice versa, creating an empathy exchange, a culture of compassion.

> ALFSV is now in its 30th year. [We're] creating models of coexistence leaders [can] tap into, [where] everyone has a voice.

Throughout Santa Clara County, other leaders demonstrate how open-minded, open-hearted activism, education, and leadership create a circular feedback loop and work in synergy.

Gina Hernandez-Clarke, a former student activist, is now Director of Arts in Undergraduate Education at Stanford. She served as executive director of Stanford's Institute for Diversity

---

6 Tricia Creason-Valencia's film *Changing Boundaries: The History of San Jose*, covering the city's history in 70 minutes, is a star example of the difficulties women face in challenging the status quo. Given a list of white male historians to work with (still happens in this day and age!), she began, as she says, her own "representative" list. This decision is noteworthy, yet the choice process is full of pitfalls worthy of serious discussion, from the pressure and intrusion of political choices to what gets lost in the quest to "tell the story." Moreover, the establishment may sidetrack (or sub-track) the results as "social and/or political history" as opposed to (real) "history." *Changing Boundaries* was funded with wide community support and participation of nonprofits CreaTV San Jose and History San José. It can be viewed on the CreaTV San Jose website creatvsj.org/watch/changing-boundaries/.

in the Arts from 2001–2011. Concurrently, from 2007–2013, she and her husband were resident fellows in the Casa Zapata dorm:

> We wanted to create a home for transitory students and invigorate its artistic spirit, following in the footsteps of Cecilia and Tony Burciaga. Now, among my roles, I continue the Burciagas' tradition of helping first-in-the-family university students through the system, where these students often feel like a fish out of water.[7]

Tamara Alvarado, a former student from the Burciaga fold, has also become a major cultural leader.[8] When the Mexican Heritage Plaza (MHP) in the Mayfair area faced challenges, she helped reinvent the facility with the community's vision, and the School of Arts and Culture was created. She recalls, "Many people helped lift it up!" Since 2011, Alvarado has been its executive director.[9]

> When I was Director of Multicultural Leadership at 1st ACT Silicon Valley, I helped develop the Multicultural Arts Leadership Initiative (MALI). A program of the school at MHP, MALI, now the Multicultural Arts Leadership Institute, is a hotbed of creative collaborations and advocacy initiatives, and a strong contributor to downtown San José's growth as a creative urban center.

Ruth Tunstall Grant sums up the relationship between education, activism and leadership, and reconfigures the challenge:

> Through education, you learn you DO have a voice. The leaders we admire are constantly changing, working on themselves so they can be good leaders. Established groups like American Leadership Forum Silicon Valley are quietly changing, taking a chance. More walls are coming down. Yet there continues to be a Silicon Valley power elite, in the arts, sports, everything. We chip away at it to include more players.

This book is a letter of gratitude to those who have paved the way, like Ruth Tunstall Grant, and a note of encouragement to new leaders, many of whom are learning and changing the system as they go. If we can increase awareness across all sectors—government, academic, and business—we can make a difference. This is just the beginning. More key artists, organizations and community members who have opened new doors are deserving of recognition and proper context. Let us build upon shared experiences to create a truly vibrant arts culture, wherever we may live.

---

[7] Hernandez-Clarke knows that the community-oriented and activist experiences of faculty, students, and staff at Stanford can inspire more community action. She cites the late Dr. Susan Cashion, who in 1969 was a co-founder of Los Lupeños de San José, one of the earliest Mexican folk dance companies in California. Similarly, the Stanford magazine *El Aguila* was an early training ground for current U.S. Poet Laureate Juan Felipe Herrera.

[8] Alvarado went from program director for Washington United Youth Center, 1999–2003, to executive director of MACLA, 2003–2008, then to Director of Multicultural Leadership at 1stACT Silicon Valley.

[9] See schoolofartsandculture.org

Appendix

This appendix gives a selected timeline of arts activism and cultural development in Silicon Valley. To give additional context for arts and community building, it focuses on key individuals who moved beyond the mainstream and worked communally to expand the conversation and breadth of opportunity for those sidelined. A few examples of the destruction of culturally significant places, structures or artworks are also included for context. The timeline is not comprehensive, and any amplification, refinement, and dialogue about it are welcome.

The early local contemporary art scene was anchored by the academic/exhibiting centers of SCU, Stanford University, and SJSU. It was augmented by the new community colleges, and by city arts commissions, other organizations, art associations, centers, leagues, guilds, societies, estates, and clubs of a regional nature or related to a specific arts medium. A partial listing online gives an expanded view of the Silicon Valley art scene as it developed. For more information: janrindfleisch.com/History.html#Appendix.

c.1100
Kuksu ceremonial pendants made of red and black abalone shells are found in archaeological sites in downtown San José and CA-ALA-329 in Coyote Hills, Fremont. Jewelry is one example of the long history of Ohlone art.

1844
Juana Briones purchases the 4,400-acre Rancho la Purísima Concepción in the Palo Alto foothills from two Mission Santa Clara (Clareño) Ohlone men and brings her vision to the land: a hilltop home for her family with an architecturally rare construction. A humanitarian and initiator of creative spaces, she builds community, models freedom and courage, and advances opportunities for women.

1873
Purchase of three marble sculptures created by artist Edmonia Lewis, who identifies as African American and Ojibway/ Chippewa and works out of Rome in a neoclassical vein. The Friends of San José Library purchases *Bust of Lincoln*. San José leader and suffragist Sarah Knox Goodrich purchases *Awake and Asleep*. Lewis is the first internationally known artist to come exhibit in San José.

1875–1876
Art Association is formed in San José. The first Art Association exhibition is held at the Normal School, now San José State University (SJSU).

1887
Arson demolishes San José's Market Street Chinatown (one of five in the city). Within weeks, the site is voted for San José's new City Hall.

1891
Stanford Museum of Art is established (revival in 1963).

1917
Hakone Estate and Gardens, designed and built by Isabel and Oliver Stine, is established. Inspired by the 1915 Pan-Pacific Exhibition, Isabel Stine travels to Japan. Upon seeing Fuji-Hakone National Park, she retains architect Tsunematsu Shintani and landscape gardener Naoharu Aihara to build her own Hakone Gardens in Saratoga.

1921
Pacific Art League is founded in Palo Alto (founded as Palo Alto Art Club; name would be changed in 1984).

Late 1920s
Artist/actress Marjorie Eaton initiates a family-like arts colony in Palo Alto built around the stage Juana Briones set at her home on the hill. The colony flourishes for most of the century, encouraging women in the arts and crossing racial barriers during decades of de facto segregation in Palo Alto. (Eaton and her colony would be featured in a local documentary video in the 1970s and in a local publication in the early '80s.)

1930

Muwekma Ohlone language songs sung by Muwekma Elder Jose Guzman, the great-grandfather of Muwekma Tribal Councilwoman and Language Committee Co-Chair Sheila Guzman-Schmidt, are recorded in Niles. Linguist John P. Harrington records 27 songs from Guzman, which are currently housed at the Smithsonian Institution's Bureau of American Ethnology.

1938

San Jose Art League established.

1939

Montalvo Arts Center, Saratoga is established, including the third artist residency program of its type in the United States. (Now known as the Sally and Don Lucas Artist Residency Program, it continues to support new contemporary work.)

1948

YWCA of the Mid-Peninsula opens as a recreation center for businesswomen. It expands to provide recreational and social services for women that meet the organization's mission of "empowering women and eliminating racism," and exhibits local artists, including self-taught painter Huellar Banks from East Palo Alto. (The organization would be based in Palo Alto until its closing in 2003.)

1955

The de Saisset Museum is established at Santa Clara University (SCU), covering art and history; includes Santa Clara Mission art from the Galtes Museum, formerly housed in the basement of O'Connor Hall. (The de Saisset would develop a focus on exhibitions exploring social justice issues.)

1950s and subsequent decades

SJSU art professor John De Vincenzi, WWII veteran, is a key arts and community organizer, from the San Jose Art League to the Italian American Heritage Foundation of San José. He keeps substantial archives. Atlanta-born artist/educator Mary Parks Washington works with De Vincenzi in expanding the South Bay's arts vision beyond cultural barriers.

1965

John De Vincenzi becomes chair of the Gallery Advisory Committee to the San José Fine Arts Commission. The advisory committee carries out the planning process for the proposed conversion of a San José public library building into a city art gallery.

Triton Museum of Art, Santa Clara, is founded as first non-university art museum in the county.

1965–1968

Spurred by his volunteer activities in Mississippi during 1964's Freedom Summer, Frank Cieciorka, graphic artist, former SJSU student and activist, develops the iconic clenched-fist image of the New Left.

1968

Artist/educator Cozetta Gray Guinn and her physicist husband Isaac "Ike" Guinn establish Nbari Art, a shop and museum-quality gallery in Los Altos, featuring imported African art and African American art.

1969

With a grant from Signetics, artist Talala Mshuja starts the Nairobi Cultural Center in East Palo Alto, which includes classes for children.

1971

San Jose Civic Gallery (now known as San José Museum of Art) opens.

1973

Artist Mary Jane Solis and activist Adrian Vargas (founder/director of San José's Teatro de la Gente, 1967–1977) co-found El Centro Cultural de la Gente, the South Bay's first Chicano/Latino cultural center, in downtown San José. El Centro features exhibitions; art programs; Lorna Dee Cervantes and her Mango Press; performance by Teatro de la Gente; and Luis Valdez, the father of Chicano theater. [Solis would serve as gallery curator (1973–1976) and mural program manager (1978–1981). El Centro's first staff member Elisa Marina Alvarado would later go on to co-found Teatro Visión, where she continues as artistic director to this day.]

Painter Paul Pei-Jen Hau and Mary Hau open the Chinese Fine Arts Gallery in Los Altos.

Emphasizing performing arts, PJ and Roy Hirabayashi found San Jose Taiko and collaborate to revitalize San José's Japantown, one of only three Japantowns left in the country.

1974

Artist Gen Guracar, Mountain View, organizes dozens of women for the valley's first large-scale quilt project, *The People's Bicentennial Quilt.*

1975

Visual Dialog, a quarterly magazine with essays, dialogs, reviews, and columns, edited by artist Roberta Loach, Los Altos, first appears. The publication challenges discrimination against women.

1976

Historian Connie Young Yu writes *The People's Bicentennial Quilt: A Patchwork History*, a book telling the story behind each quilt square. [First edition, UP PRESS, East Palo Alto, 1976; revised edition, Saratoga Historical Foundation, 2010.]

Mid- and Late 1970s

SJSU faculty member Jessica Jacobs leads artists in developing city exhibition space with broader representation and more freedom than the now "established" SJMA. Jacobs and a number of her students pioneer the first modern art galleries in San José, starting with Merz Gallery (later to be replaced by Wordworks).

On the Peninsula, First Generation—Deanna Bartels (now Tisone), Betty Estersohn and Joan Valdes—use new video technology to explore and document Bay Area art, including that of artists Marjorie Eaton and Bea Wax.

Consuelo Santos Killins directs Pacific Peoples Theater and begins three decades of activism—with the San José Fine Arts Commission, California Arts Council, Santa Clara County Arts Council, SJSU's Institute for Arts and Letters, Santa Clara County Mental Health Association, and Friends of Guadalupe River Park. She pushes for substantive school and community arts programs and more diverse participation across the board.

Artist Anthony Quartuccio paints a mural above the altar of Holy Cross Church (1906) in an early Italian immigrant area of San José. (It would be lost in a fire in 2015.)

1977

San Jose Museum of Quilts & Textiles opens in Los Altos, the first U.S. museum to focus exclusively on quilts and textiles as an art form. (It would be essentially a collaborative, volunteer organization for its first two decades.)

Professor Diane Middlebrook becomes director of Stanford's Center for Research on Women (CROW, founded 1972). [In 1979 Professor Dr. Carl Djerassi would found the Djerassi Resident Artists Program. Initially administered through the art exhibition program of CROW, he and Middlebrook would establish an independent, comprehensive program by 1982. CROW would later become the Institute for Research on Women and Gender (1983), with exhibitions at Serra House, and still later, Clayman Institute for Gender Research (2004).]

1978

Nairobi Cultural Center moves north to San Mateo County.

Photographer Mary Andrade creates a vehicle for art as co-founder, co-publisher of the bilingual *La Oferta*, the oldest continuous Hispanic publication in San José.

1979

With Paul Pei-Jen Hau as its guiding spirit, artists and friends found the American Society for the Advancement of Chinese Arts (ASACA).

Euphrat Art Gallery (1971), De Anza College, is resurrected after funding loss from Proposition 13, differentiated by an unusual vision of collaboration across cultures and disciplines. Jan Rindfleisch, director, develops a unique college/community

partnership that produces innovative, vibrant museum programming for over three decades. (Gallery becomes the Euphrat Museum of Art in 1992.)

Early 1980s

Poets Juan Felipe Herrera and Margarita Luna Robles organize poetry readings in downtown and East San José, and at the Euphrat Gallery.

Artist Ruth Tunstall Grant directs and expands the children's art school at the San José Museum of Art, initiating art classes in underserved city schools.

San José State University professor José Colchado creates murals, working with youth in the East Side Union High School District and Janie Perez, director of the Barrio Leadership Training Program (later known as East Side Youth Center).

Activist artist Julia Iltis creates artwork for political posters. *Stop the Repression!* (1982) commemorates the final speech made by Monsignor Oscar Romero, Archbishop of San Salvador, the day before his 1980 assassination. *Guilty of the Gospel* promotes a 1984 presentation in honor of four U.S. women missionaries martyred in El Salvador in 1980. (Both would be added to the Oakland Museum of California's All of Us or None Archive in 2010.)

1980

Mythili Kumar founds Abhinaya Dance Company, teaching and performing Bharatanatyam, a South Indian classical dance.

1981

In Palo Alto, artist Trudy Myrrh Reagan starts YLEM: Artists Using Science and Technology to exchange ideas, explore the intersection of the arts and the sciences, and consider the impact of science and technology on society.

Jan Rindfleisch, Lucy Cain Sargeant and Kim Bielejec Sanzo create the Euphrat exhibition and publication *Staying Visible: The Importance of Archives*; foreword by Paul J. Karlstrom, West Coast director, Archives of American Art, Smithsonian Institution. The pivotal project focuses on women in the arts, featuring multiple interviewers and authors.

1982
Arts Council of Santa Clara County is established.

1984
SJSU art professor Marcia Chamberlain organizes the first Computers in Art, Design, Research, and Education (CADRE) conference and publication, and becomes the first director of SJSU's CADRE Laboratory for New Media, an interdisciplinary academic and research program dedicated to the experimental use of information technology and art.

1985
Cecilia and José Antonio Burciaga become Resident Fellows living at Stanford's Casa Zapata—she as a top university administrator, he as resident artist, both working closely with student and community needs. [For the next nine years, José (aka Tony, Toño) would create murals at Casa Zapata, use comedy to attack racism and narrow divisive thinking, and publish poetry and writings.]

Jeanne Farr McDonnell starts the Women's Heritage Museum, with a focus on California history and culture. (To create a larger organization, in 1997 it would become the International Museum of Women.)

The Dr. Martin Luther King, Jr. Association of Santa Clara Valley inaugurates the Freedom Train on Martin Luther King, Jr. Day. The train travels the 54 mile–Caltrain route from San José to San Francisco to approximate the distance of the historic 1965 civil rights march from Selma to Montgomery, Ala. led by Dr. King to spur passage of the Voting Rights Act. (The group will organize the annual event for the next 30 years.)

1986
While serving on the Arts Council of Santa Clara County, Ruth Tunstall Grant initiates Hands on the Arts as an Arts Council project. (The all-day children's art festival would become a joint venture of the Arts Council and the City of Sunnyvale the following year, and beginning in 1988, an annual city event.)

Activist Connie Young Yu, longtime promoter of the art of marginalized Chinese and Chinese Americans, highlights renowned painter Hau Bei Ren (Paul Pei-Jen Hau) in her book *Profiles in Excellence: Peninsula Chinese Americans*, published by the Stanford Chinese Club.

Rick Sajor and Margarita Luna Robles convene "The Arts Lobby" to increase Latino representation on the San José Art Commission and to monitor policies in the arts locally and regionally.

1987
Consuelo Jimenez Underwood (Huichol, mestiza), Cupertino, begins teaching at SJSU. (She would develop and head the textile department for over 20 years, simultaneously illuminating indigenous and hybrid cultures and border issues.)

Salwa Mikdadi Nashashibi, Lafayette, founder and director of International Council for Women in the Arts, participates in a Euphrat Museum exhibition and publication on refugees. (She would later co-author *Forces of Change: Artists in the Arab World*, the catalog for an unusual 1994 traveling exhibition of artwork by contemporary Arab women sponsored by Nashashibi's organization.)

San Jose Multicultural Artists Guild is formed from Maiko Women's Poetry and Drum Ensemble, Tabia African American Theater Ensemble, and Teatro Familia Aztlán, with executive director Arlene Sagun. (Venues would include social service agencies, battered women's shelters, juvenile detention facilities, Juneteenth and Kwanzaa celebrations, plus academic and community sites for *Dia de los Muertos* arts exhibitions. Mary Jane Solis would curate their Day of the Dead exhibitions from 1986–2013.)

Dr. Jerry Hiura chairs San José Arts Commission (SJAC) and appoints Mary Jane Solis chair for Multicultural Arts Development (1987–1995). Almost 92% of grant allocations in the mid-1980s goes to six large-budget institutions, such as the San Jose Symphony, San Jose Cleveland Ballet, and SJMA.

1988
Joel A. Slayton is named director of CADRE Laboratory for New Media.

1989
Artists Betty Kano of Berkeley and Flo Oy Wong of Sunnyvale found the Asian American Women Artists Association (AAWAA) in the Bay Area to

"promote the visibility of Asian American women artists," who lack recognition even in their own traditional culture. Local artists Terry Acebo Davis and Dawn Nakanishi participate.

Maribel Alvarez, Mary Jane Solis, Rick Sajor and Eva Terrazas envision arts programming as a vehicle for civic dialogue and social equity and found Movimiento de Arte y Cultura Latino Americana (MACLA) in downtown San José.

Multicultural Arts Action Group (MAAG), led by two MACLA board members, Rick Sajor and Sonia Gray, with representatives from existing multicultural arts groups, is established to encourage more civic support for small organizations meeting different cultural needs.

After the Northern California Chapter hosts the 1989 Women's Caucus for Art (WCA) National Conference, artists Ruth Waters and Marta Thoma develop Peninsula and South Bay chapters. [The South Bay Chapter would become Silicon Valley Women's Caucus for Art (SVWCA) in 2014.]

1990
Under Mayor Janet Gray Hayes, the City of San José establishes the Office of Cultural Affairs (OCA) to work with the San José Art Commission. Yankee Johnson becomes its Director (1990–1999).

1991
SJMA opens a new wing.

Mayor Susan Hammer (1991–1999) appoints the Mayor's Task Force on Multicultural Arts Development and issues the "Vision 2000 Report" to address immediate needs of the growing

diverse multicultural community and its artists.

Mexican Heritage Corporation is founded, the first and only multicultural arts organization to be considered a "major institution" by the City of San José. In its first year, MHC establishes the Mariachi Festival in San José.

1992
The Multicultural Arts Incubation Pilot (MAIP) becomes a national model for supporting the development and stabilization of multicultural arts programming. Artist Joe B. Rodriguez, arts program manager (1990–2011) for the OCA, implements the program. (Between 1992–2004, the city would invest and secure federal, state, and foundation grants totaling over $1 million for Arts Incubation initiatives. Thirty MAIP graduates would generate $3.2 million of new revenues by the end of their third year, creating arts-related jobs and enhancing local economic potential.)

Ruth Tunstall Grant founds Genesis / A Sanctuary for the Arts in San José with exhibitions, presentations, performing arts, and artist studios, bringing together different cultures at three locations—Ryland Street, 40 North First Street, and The Alameda—with Claude Ferguson as artistic director. (At the Alameda site, she would renovate and build studios in a warehouse that is now The Alameda Artworks studios. Tunstall Grant also would develop the art program for foster youth at the Santa Clara County Children's Shelter.)

The Association for Viet Arts is founded by Hoa Trinh Glassey and Man Bui to foster excellence in Vietnamese-American

performing, visual, and literary arts. AVA is the first nonprofit Vietnamese arts organization in the Bay Area.

Chike Nwoffiah starts Oriki Theatre, Mountain View, to provide a shared experience of authentic African culture, from recreating an African village to school programs and seasonal productions.

In East Palo Alto, Bart Decrem founds Plugged In, one of the nation's first digital-divide programs.

The Muwekma Ohlone Tribe reclaims the arts of naming and installation. Tamien Station, an intermodal passenger transportation station in San José, is named after the valley and tribal region which the Spanish priests recorded as Thámien when they founded the first site of Mission Santa Clara de Thamien in 1777. Tamien Station is named to honor the ancestors of the Muwekma Ohlone after its construction uncovered a major ancestral heritage archaeological site containing around 172 ancestors. (A planned permanent exhibition of artifacts found on the site has not yet been constructed.)

1995
The Arts Council, under new director Bruce Davis, convenes a forward-looking countywide event to applaud the "arts as an intervention for social ills," connecting arts with government, schools, youth, veterans, social services, and prisons. Director Davis (1994–2011), working with Diem Jones, Lissa Jones, and Audrey Wong, expands the Arts Council's community importance and increases seed funding to small and mid-sized organizations.

Working with Muwekma, Amah-Mutsun and Esselen Nation Costanoan/Ohlone tribal communities, artist Jean LaMarr creates a mural (restored in 2013) *The Ohlone Journey*, located in Ohlone Park in Berkeley, which celebrates Ohlone life and culture on four walls. The local Muwekma Ohlone Tribe, led by chairwoman Rosemary Cambra, uses performance art, academic research, language revitalization, and public art to build community.

1996
Cultural Initiatives Silicon Valley (1996–2006) is inspired by Mayor Susan Hammer, a leader in regional cultural planning. The initiative advances cultural policy and art education. [Executive Director John Kreidler (2000–2006) would implement a 10-year cultural plan for Silicon Valley, and produce two major publications on participatory arts with Pia Moriarty (2004) and Maribel Alvarez (2005). Arts Council of Santa Clara County would later be renamed Arts Council Silicon Valley.]

1997
David Yohn (Ojibway), executive director, and Diane Way (Lakota/Cheyenne), artistic director, start ABLEZA: Native American Arts and Media Institute in San José. Exhibitions are held at the American Indian Center, part of the Indian Health Center off The Alameda, a long-standing community gathering point. (ABLEZA programming would include a 1999 virtual art exhibit entitled *Honor and Pain*, juxtaposing computer-rendered photos of traditional powwow dancers with sports mascots and images on commercial products.)

Mary Jane Solis initiates an extended period highlighting arts programming in conjunction with her work in community and public relations at the Office of Human Relations, Santa Clara County.

1999
Mexican Heritage Plaza, a cultural center built with San José Redevelopment Agency funds, opens in San José.

2000
ZERO1, the Art and Technology Network is founded by Andy Cunningham. (Joel A. Slayton would serve as director, 2008–2016.)

2001
Silicon Valley De-Bug, a media, community organizing, and entrepreneurial collective coordinated by Raj Jayadev, is established in San José. Part of SV De-Bug's core group, community artists Adrian Avila, Charisse Domingo, and Jean Melesaine, would tackle projects with photo-essays and videos.

Diane Way becomes the first Native American artist to win the Literary Fellowship in Playwriting from Arts Council of Silicon Valley. In addition to her visual art, Way taught script writing and oral tradition at SJSU and Stanford.

2003
MACLA is recognized in 2003 by Cultural Initiatives Silicon Valley as Santa Clara County's "most practiced and mature site of cultural-citizenship-building through participatory arts."

2004
Jianhua Hsu establishes the Silicon Valley Asian Arts Center in Santa Clara, offering exhibitions of local and Chinese art, seminars, music recitals, publications, art education and community fundraising events.

Mid-2000s
Self-taught muralist Frank Torres makes positive impact on gang infestation through community collaborations: murals at Pop's Mini-Mart, Payless Shoes store, the visitors' room at the Santa Clara County Hall of Justice, and the Elmwood Correctional Facility (Elmwood's history).

2008
Empire Seven Studios and Gallery is founded by Juan Carlos Araujo and Jennifer Ahn in San José's Japantown, as "a beacon to underground art culture in the South Bay."

Content Magazine, The Innovative and Creative Culture of Silicon Valley, is started by Daniel Garcia, Cultivator.

2011
Activist Tina Morrill starts Art Box San José, a community-driven project depicting art on utility boxes.

The Juana Briones House, a key link to a woman who was a California change-agent in multiple fields, is torn down. A careful deconstruction occurs, both to salvage materials and to preserve a section of wall that shows its unusual construction.

2013
Juan Carlos Araujo and Jennifer Ahn establish the E7S Mural Project in San José to promote community murals.

2014

Raj Jayadev writes an essay about De-Bug's approach and philosophy: "The Anatomy of an 'Un-Organization': Explaining #DebugScience."

2015

Exhibition District is a nonprofit established to paint 40,000 sq. ft. of blank space in downtown San José. Organized by local muralist Erin Salazar, the plan is a follow-up to work done by muralists like Paul J. Gonzales and Phuong-Mai Bui-Quang. (ED murals completed to date include *Labor of Love*, a tribute to the working men and women who built the valley on the side of the Workingman's Emporium on N. First Street, and *Life Abundant in the Face of Imminent Death*, on the Hotel De Anza.)

Artists Robin Lasser, Trena Noval, and Genevieve Hastings create *Our Lives in This Place* at the request of the city. The project is part of Envision San José 2040 planning for "urban villages" such as East Santa Clara Street from Seventh to 17th Street. Community members are brought together and voice ideas to make the neighborhood more interesting. "Imagine" postcards featuring these ideas are created and circulated via a kiosk that travels the neighborhood.

2016

Bay Area Society for Art & Activism develops a timeline for the Bay Area's history of art and media activism: http://artandactivism.org/timeline/.

2017

For the Women's March in downtown San José, about 30,000 people marched for civil rights, many wearing handmade pink "pussyhats," in diverse, intergenerational groups. As part of a global awakening and rededication, they spoke up through words, music, attire, and artful signs about concerns, values, and hope.

For additional information pertaining to the greater San Francisco Bay Area:

See the digital archive/wiki FoundSF.org; docspopuli. org, a digital archive of protest and advocacy artwork of the 20th century; and Women Eco Arts Dialog (weadartists.org), promoting ecological and social justice art.

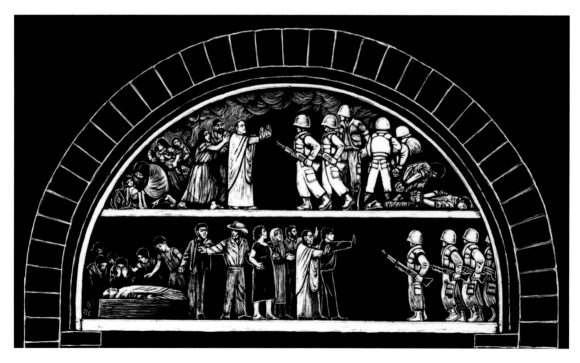

Julia Iltis, *Stop the Repression!*, c. 1982. Offset lithograph on paper, 22.5"x19". Detail of Iltis drawing. Poster, with 1980 quotation from Archbishop Oscar Romero, created for Refugee Project for Central America, Catholic Social Services, San José. Poster image courtesy of Lincoln Cushing / Docs Populi.

Angela Buenning Filo, *Biotechnology Company Headquarters, Mountain View*, March 2001. Chromogenic print.

Acknowledgments

Roots and Offshoots is a collaborative effort. The following contributors questioned and challenged the project, offering very different perspectives and overviews that elucidated the narrative.

Besides being exceptional editors, Nancy Hom and Ann Sherman have long lived and breathed arts, activism, and community. They brought insights and perspective, giving alternative frames of reference with understanding and discernment. Their input was invaluable for idea development as we probed and analyzed each chapter.

The *Roots and Offshoots* essay and investigation were buoyed by discussions, insight, and impetus from Ruth Tunstall Grant, Judy Goddess, Laurel Bossen, Lucy Cain Sargeant, PJ Hirabayashi, Mary Jane Solis, Sal Breiter (De Anza College), Gen Pilgrim Guracar, and Connie Young Yu. Maribel Alvarez and Raj Jayadev provided two thought-provoking essays on their organizations, MACLA and Silicon Valley De-Bug, as well as on the community and the times.

I was inspired and challenged by Consuelo Jimenez Underwood, Mary Parks Washington, Juana Alicia, Bruce Davis, John Kreidler, Michael Bell, Thomas Rindfleisch, Janet Burdick, Samson Wong, Stephanie Gutierrez, and the many artists, activists, and scholars with whom I spoke, both mentioned and not mentioned in this book. Kent Manske, Nanette Wylde, and Marta Thoma Hall provided context and support at critical junctures.

The project involved collaboration with the California History Center (CHC). The CHC published the original "Roots and Offshoots" essay. Tom Izu and Lisa Christiansen were helpful in the project's early development and later in discussing and reviewing book sections.

The historical "Spiral" bridge essay and a related 2015 online article, "Ohlone Art and Community Building," would not have been possible without additional discussions and insight from Alan Leventhal (SJSU) and the Muwekma Ohlone Tribe, Jean LaMarr, Albert Camarillo (Stanford), Lee Panich (SCU), Jeanne Farr McDonnell, Clark Akatiff and Palo Alto Stanford Heritage, Susan Kirk, Deanna Bartels Tisone, Tom Hunt, and many others.

Samson Wong's web and book design supported a blend of overt and layered meaning, and of factual and emotional content. Hom added her distinctive design sensibilities, and Kent Manske, Bob Hsiang, Scott Miller, and Anna Koster provided advice and assistance.

The process of writing this book has been a long and fruitful journey, with many different and rare personifications of dedication, scholarly perspective, community understanding, courage, fortitude, and humor. The contributors all shared a love of art, design, and words; plus a longstanding commitment to community engagement and inclusion. To them I express my deepest gratitude.

Kathy Aoki, *The Lawyer*, 2000. Multiple plate linocut, c. 9"x11".

Aoki, associate professor and chair of the Santa Clara University art and art history department, has used cartoon styles to activate an urban world populated with women challenging gender-related expectations. One series is about women superheroes, such as the urban lawyer, who are just really good at their jobs.